CHEVY & GMC 4-WHEEL DRIVE
1967-1982
TUNE-UP · MAINTENANCE

By
MIKE BISHOP

ERIC JORGENSEN
Editor

JEFF ROBINSON
Publisher

CLYMER PUBLICATIONS

World's largest publisher of books
devoted exclusively to automobiles and motorcycles

12860 MUSCATINE STREET · P.O. BOX 20 · ARLETA, CALIFORNIA 91331

FIRST EDITION
First Printing February, 1976
Second Printing February, 1977

SECOND EDITION
Revised to include 1976-1977 models
First Printing May, 1977
Second Printing February, 1978
Third Printing August, 1978

THIRD EDITION
Revised by Mike Bishop to include 1978-1979 models
First Printing May, 1979
Second Printing July, 1980
Third Printing May, 1981

FOURTH EDITION
Revised by Kalton C. Lahue to include 1980-1982 models
First Printing May, 1982

Printed in U.S.A.

ISBN: 0-89287-159-8

*Thanks to Tom Cepek, Dick Cepek, Inc., for his assistance in
the preparation of the* Off-road Preparation *chapter.*
•
COVER:
*Photographed by Mike Bishop at Mono Lake, California.
Vehicle courtesy of Dick Cepek, Inc., Southgate, California.*

CONTENTS

CHAPTER TWELVE

CHEVY & GMC 4-WHEEL DRIVE

1967-1982
TUNE-UP · MAINTENANCE

CHAPTER ONE

GENERAL INFORMATION

This manual provides lubrication, general maintenance, and tune-up information for the Chevrolet/GMC 4-wheel drive light utility and sport vehicles. Specific models covered are:

K10 and K20 Series Chevrolet 4 x 4 pickups and Suburbans—1967 through 1982.
K105 Chevrolet Blazer—1969 through 1982.
K1500 and K2500 Series GMC pickups and Suburbans—1967 through 1982.
GMC Jimmy—1970 through 1982.

If you have a 1976 or later model, be sure to check the Supplement at the rear of this book for the latest information.

Procedures for major mechanical work, such as rebuilding of the engine, transmission, differentials, etc., are not covered. Extensive experience and many special tools are required for major work and in these cases required service and repair should be entrusted to a dealer or automotive specialist.

SERVICE HINTS

The procedures used in this manual avoid special tools and test equipment whenever possible. When necessary, special tools and test equipment are illustrated, either in actual use or alone. Most special tools are available through dealers or can be purchased through professional suppliers such as Snap-On. In many cases, a well-equipped hobbyist mechanic may find he can substitute similar tools or make his own to fulfill a requirement.

Recommendations are occasionally made to refer service or maintenance to a Chevrolet or GMC dealer or a specialist in a particular field. In these cases, work will probably be done more quickly and economically than if you performed the work yourself.

When you order parts from a Chevrolet/GMC dealer or a parts distributor always order by vehicle identification number (VIN). See **Figure 1**. Minor mechanical changes are occasionally made during a model year rather than at the beginning of the next model year and they could involve a replacement part. Write down the VIN of your vehicle and carry it in your wallet. The VIN plate is located on the inside panel of the glove compartment door.

Pertinent vehicle data codes are explained in **Table 1**. Non-essential codes such as color and trim are omitted.

Throughout this manual, keep the following conventions in mind: "front" refers to the front of the vehicle and the front of the engine; "left" and "right" refer to the sides of the vehicle as

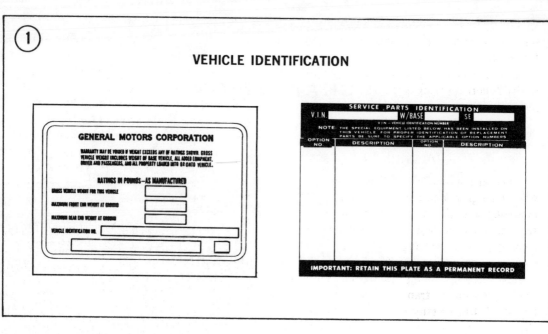

(1)

VEHICLE IDENTIFICATION

Table 1   VEHICLE DATA CODE

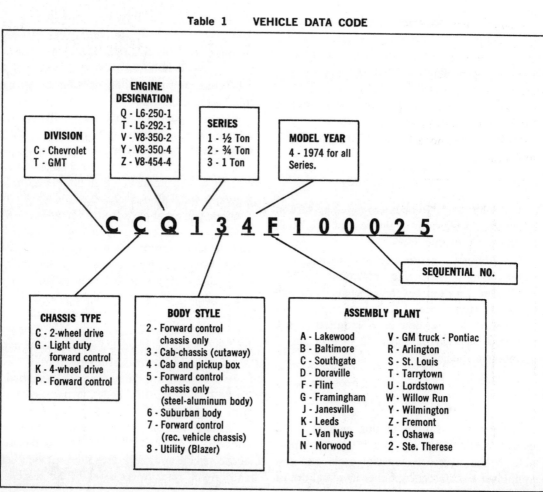

viewed by a person sitting in the vehicle facing forward; cylinders are numbered as shown in **Figure 2**.

All dimensions and capacities are expressed in the American (English) system (inches, feet, pints, quarts, etc.).

JACKING AND SUPPORTING THE VEHICLE

When lifting one wheel of the vehicle, such as when changing a tire or dismantling a hub or removing a brake drum for bearing or brake service, make certain the vehicle is sitting as level as possible and firmly block the wheels— front and rear— at the opposite end of the vehicle. Set the parking brake firmly and select PARK (automatic transmission) or REVERSE (standard transmission). Position the jack as close as possible to the wheel being raised, making sure the jack is positioned vertically. Raise the jack slowly until it just begins to support the axle. Then, loosen all of the wheel lug nuts about ¼ turn. Continue to raise the jack slowly until the wheel just clears the ground and will rotate freely. Unscrew the lug nuts and remove the wheel. When installing the wheel, tighten the lug nuts snugly in a criss-cross pattern, lower the jack and remove it, and tighten all of the nuts firmly.

When lifting the entire front of the vehicle, block the rear wheels, set the handbrake firmly, and select PARK (automatic transmission) or REVERSE (standard transmission). Apply the head of the jack to the front axle differential (**Figure 3**), or to the center of the front frame crossmember if the weight is to be taken off the suspension. Make certain the jack head does not lift against sheet metal, suspension or steering components, or the bottom radiator tank, and check to see that it does not contact electrical leads or hydraulic or oil lines.

When lifting the entire rear of the vehicle, block the front wheels and apply the head of the jack to the differential. After the vehicle has been

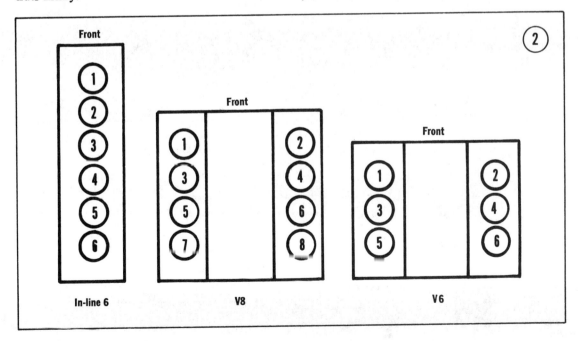

lifted with a jack, support it on frame stands located beneath the frame rails or the front or rear axle (**Figure 4**).

WARNING
Never work beneath the vehicle when it is supported only with a jack.

When raising the vehicle on a service station hoist, position the front hoist arms or lifting pads so they contact the axle as near the wheels as possible, making sure they do not contact the steering linkage. The rear hoist arms or pads should be positioned beneath the rear axle housing or the spring mounting pads (**Figure 5**), but they should not contact the shock absorber mounting brackets.

TOWING

If the front and rear axles are not damaged, the vehicle may be towed for short distances at low speed (less than 20 mph) with both drive shafts connected. In this case, shift the transmission to neutral. With conventional 4-wheel drive, set the transfer case selector at TWO-WHEEL HIGH, and if the hubs are equipped with lockouts, set these at the FREE position. With Full-Time 4-wheel drive, set the transfer case selector at HIGH.

If one of the axles is damaged, it must be raised so its wheels do not contact the road. If both axles are damaged, the vehicle must be towed with the aid of a dolly.

If the vehicle is to be towed for long distances at highway speeds, the drive shafts must be disconnected at the axles and tied up and out of the way of the differentials (Chapter Nine). If the vehicle is equipped with conventional 4-wheel drive and fitted with lockout hubs, make sure the hubs are set in the FREE or unlocked position (**Figure 6**).

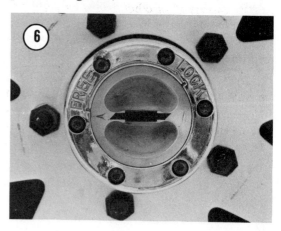

Connect a towbar to the vehicle in accordance with the towbar manufacturer's instructions, and refer to Chapter Six and connect the vehicle's lights to the towing vehicles lighting system.

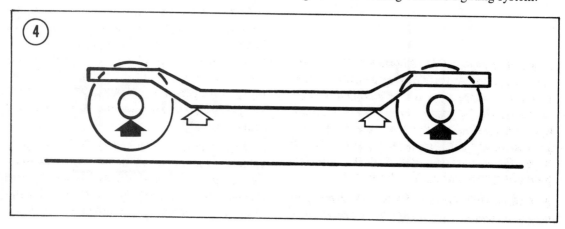

TOOLS

To correctly service your vehicle, you will need an assortment of ordinary hand tools. As a minimum, these include.

1. Combination wrenches
2. Socket wrenches
3. Plastic mallet
4. Ball peen hammer
5. Snap ring pliers
6. Phillips screwdrivers
7. Slot screwdrivers
8. Impact driver
9. Allen wrenches
10. Pliers
11. Feeler gauges
12. Spark plug gauge
13. Spark plug wrench
14. Dial indicator
15. Drift

Special tools that are required are shown in the chapter covering the particular service in which they are used.

Electrical system servicing requires a voltmeter, ohmmeter, or other device for determining continuity, and a hydrometer.

Engine tune-up and troubleshooting procedures require a few more tools.

1. *Hydrometer* (**Figure 7**). This instrument measures the state of charge of the battery and tells much about battery condition. Hydrometers are available at auto parts stores and through most large mail order outlets. A satisfactory one costs less than $3.

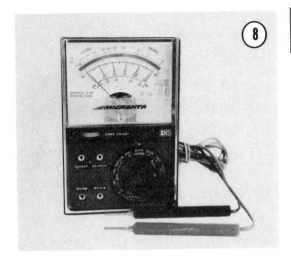

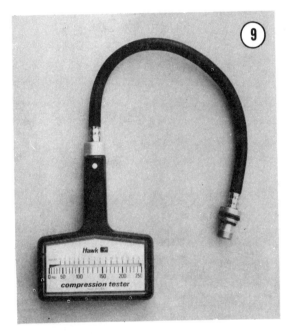

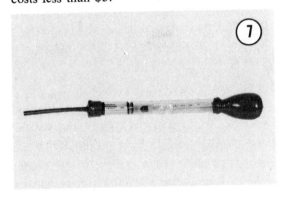

2. *Multimeter or VOM* (**Figure 8**). This instrument is invaluable for electrical system troubleshooting and service. A few of its functions may be duplicated by locally fabricated substitutes, but for the serious hobbyist, it is a must. Its uses are described in the applicable sections of this book. Prices start at about $10 at electronics hobbyist stores and mail order outlets.

3. *Compression Gauge* (**Figure 9**). An engine with low compression cannot be correctly tuned and will not develop full power. A compression gauge measures cylinder compression (pressure). The one shown has a flexible stem which enables it to reach cylinders where there is little clearance between the cylinder head and the frame. Inexpensive compression gauges start at around $3, available at auto accessory stores and mail order outlets.

4. *Impact Driver* (**Figure 10**). This tool is invaluable for loosening tight screws without damaging screw slots as well as tightening screws that are prone to backing out. Good ones run about $12 at auto accessory and hardware stores.

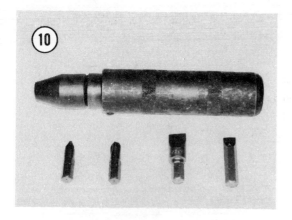

5. *Ignition Gauge* (**Figure 11**). This tool is designed expressly for measuring point gap and spark plug electrode gap.

EXPENDABLE SUPPLIES

Certain expendable supplies are also required to correctly service your vehicle. These include grease, oil, gasket cement, shop rags, cleaning solvent, and distilled water. Ask your dealer or auto parts specialist for special fastener locking compounds and silicone lubricants which make maintenance simpler and easier. Solvent is available at most service stations and distilled water for the battery is available at most supermarkets.

SAFETY HINTS

A professional mechanic can work for years without sustaining a serious injury. If you observe a few rules of common sense and safety, you can enjoy many hours safely servicing your own vehicle. You can also hurt yourself or damage your vehicle if you ignore these rules.

1. Never use gasoline as a cleaning solvent.

2. Never smoke or use a torch around flammable liquids, such as cleaning solvent.

3. Never smoke or use a torch in areas where batteries are being charged. Highly explosive hydrogen gas is formed during the charging process. And never arc the terminals of a battery to see if it is charged; the sparks can ignite the explosive hydrogen as easily as an open flame.

4. If welding or brazing is required on the vehicle, make sure that it is not in the area of the fuel tank or lines. In such case, the work should be entrusted to a specialist.

5. Always use the correct size wrench for turning nuts and bolts, and when a nut is tight, think for a moment what would happen to your hand if the wrench were to slip.

6. Keep your work area clean and uncluttered.

7. Wear safety goggles in all operations involving drilling, grinding, the use of a chisel, or an air hose.

8. Do not use worn tools.

9. Keep a fire extinguisher handy. Be sure it is rated for gasoline and electrical fires.

10. When drying bearings or other rotating parts with compressed air, never allow the air jet to rotate the bearing or part; the jet is capable of rotating them at speeds far in excess of those for which they were designed. The likelihood of a bearing or rotating part disintegrating and causing serious injury and damage is very great.

MAINTENANCE AND LUBRICATION SCHEDULES

Suggested maintenance schedules are presented in **Table 2** (1974 and earlier) and **Table 3** (1975). Lubrication schedules are presented in Chapter Four. Pay particular attention to footnotes when using the schedules; vehicle use can affect the required maintenance intervals.

Some of the points presented in the tables are not covered in this handbook; in most cases these points involve emission control-related work that should be entrusted to a dealer or a certified automotive emission specialist. The points have been included in the tables to provide a complete and detailed picture of total vehicle maintenance, both owner- and dealer-performed.

Table 2   VEHICLE MAINTENANCE SCHEDULE — 1974 AND EARLIER

Interval	Service
Every 4 months or 6,000 miles	Chassis lubrication Fluid levels ① ② Engine oil ① Air conditioning system
Every 6,000 miles	Tire rotation
At 1st oil change—then every 2nd	Engine oil filter ①
Every 12,000 miles	Rear axle
Every 12 months or 12,000 miles	Cooling system ①
Every 24,000 miles	Wheel bearings Automatic transmission ①
Every 36,000 miles	Manual steering gear
Every 4 months or 6,000 miles	Owner safety checks Tires and wheels Exhaust system Drive belts ① Suspension and steering Brakes and power steering
Every 6,000 miles	Disc brakes
Every 12 months or 12,000 miles	Drum brakes and parking brake Throttle linkage Headlights Underbody
At 1st 4 months or 6,000 miles—then at 12-month/12,000-mile intervals	Thermostatically controlled air cleaner Carburetor choke Timing, dwell, carburetor idle, distributor and coil Manifold heat valve
At 1st 4 months or 6,000 miles	Carburetor mounting
Every 6,000 miles	Spark plugs (vehicles using leaded fuels)
Every 12 months or 12,000 miles	EGR system (vehicles using leaded fuels) Carburetor fuel inlet filter Thermal vacuum switch and hoses Vacuum advance solenoid and hoses Transmission control switch Idle stop solenoid PCV system
Every 24 months or 24,000 miles	Engine compression ECS system Fuel cap, tank, and lines AIR system
Every 24,000 miles	Air cleaner element
At 1st 24/24—then every 12/12	Spark plug and ignition coil wires

① Also an emission control service   ② Also a safety service

Table 3   VEHICLE MAINTENANCE SCHEDULE — 1975

Interval	Service
Every 6 months or 7,500 miles	Chassis lubrication ②
	Fluid levels check ① ②
	Engine oil change ②
At 1st oil change—then every 2nd	Oil filter change ②
See explantion ③	Tire rotation (steel belted radial)
	Rear axle lube change
Every 12 months	Air conditioning check
Every 12 months or 15,000 miles	Cooling system check ②
	Coolant change and hose replacement
Every 30,000 miles	Wheel bearing repack
	Automatic transmission fluid and filer change ②
	Manual steering gear check
	Clutch cross shaft lubrication
Every 6 months or 7,500 miles	Owner safety checks
	Tire and wheel inspection
	Exhaust system check ②
	Drive belt check ②
	Belt replacement ②
	Suspension and steering check
	Brake and power steering check
Every 12 months or 15,000 miles	Drum brake and parking brake check
	Throttle linkage check
	Underbody flush and check
	Bumper check
At first 6 months or 7,500 miles—then at 18-month/ 22,500-mile intervals	Thermostatically controlled air cleaner check
	Carburetor choke check
	Engine idle speed adjustment
	EFE valve check
	Carburetor mounting torque
Every 12 months or 15,000 miles	Fuel filter replacement
	Vacuum advance system and hoses check
	PCV system check
	PCV valve and filter replacement
Every 18 months or 22,500 miles	Idle stop solenoid check
	Spark plug wires check
Every 22,500 miles	Spark plug replacement
	Engine timing adjustment and distributor check
Every 24 months or 30,000 miles	ECS system check and filter replacement
	Fuel cap, tank, and lines check
Every 30,000 miles	Air cleaner element replacement

① Also a safety service
② Also an emission control service

③ Steel-belted radials should be rotated (front/rear on same side only) at 7,500 and then 15,000-mile intervals. Bias-belted tires should be rotated every 7,500 miles.

CHAPTER TWO

TROUBLESHOOTING

Troubleshooting can be relatively simple if done logically. The first step is to define symptoms as closely as possible. Subsequent steps involve testing and analyzing areas which could cause the symptoms.

The procedures in this chapter are not the only ones possible. There may be several approaches to solving a problem, but all methods must have one thing in common—a logical, systematic approach.

TROUBLESHOOTING EQUIPMENT

The following equipment is necessary to accurately troubleshoot the engine and its components.

1. Voltmeter, ammeter, and ohmmeter (see Chapter One)
2. Hydrometer (see Chapter One)
3. Compression tester (see Chapter One)
4. Vacuum gauge
5. Tachometer
6. Dwell meter
7. Timing light
8. Exhaust gas analyzer

Items 1 through 7 are essential. Item 8 is necessary for exhaust emission control compli-

ance. The following is a brief description of the function of each instrument.

Voltmeter, Ammeter, and Ohmmeter

For testing the ignition and electrical systems, a good voltmeter is required. The range of the meter should cover from 0 to 20 volts, and have an accuracy of ±½ volt.

The ohmmeter measures electrical resistance and is required to check continuity (open- and short-circuits), and to test fuses and lights.

The ammeter measures electrical current. One for automotive use should cover 0-10 amperes and 0-100 amperes. An ammeter is useful for checking battery charging and starting current. The starter and generator procedures use an ammeter to check for shorted windings.

Hydrometer

A hydrometer gives an indication of battery condition and charge by measuring the specific gravity of the electrolyte in each cell.

Compression Tester

The compression tester measures pressure buildup in each cylinder. The results, when properly interpreted, can indicate general cylinder and valve condition. To perform the compression check, proceed as follows:

1. Run the engine until normal operating temperature is reached.

2. Block the choke and throttle in the wide-open position.

3. Remove all spark plugs.

4. Connect the compression tester to one cylinder, following manufacturer's instructions.

5. Have an assistant crank the engine for at least 4 compression strokes of the cylinder being tested.

6. Remove the tester and record the reading.

7 Repeat the above steps for each cylinder.

If the lowest compression reading is within 75 percent of the highest, the rings and valves are in good condition (see **Table 1**). The important point is the difference between the readings.

> NOTE: *If the highest cylinder and lowest cylinder are not within a maximum/minimum range, valve or ring trouble is indicated.*

Compression Defects

Low Compression in One Cylinder. If a low reading (see Table 1) is obtained on one cylinder, this indicates valve or ring trouble. To determine which, pour about a tablespoon of engine oil through the spark plug hole onto the top of the piston. Turn the engine over once to clear some of the excess oil, then take another compression test and record the reading. If the compression rises markedly, the valves are good but the rings are defective on that cylinder. If compression does not increase, the valves are sticking or not seating correctly.

Low Compression in 2 Adjacent Cylinders. This may indicate that the head gasket has blown between the cylinders and that gases are leaking from one cylinder to the other.

To isolate the trouble more closely, compare the compression readings with vacuum gauge readings as described below.

Vacuum Gauge

The vacuum gauge is easy to use but difficult for an inexperienced mechanic to interpret. The results, when considered with other findings, can

Table 1   COMPRESSION LIMITS

Maximum PSI	Minimum PSI	Maximum PSI	Minimum PSI
134	101	192	144
136	102	194	145
138	104	196	147
140	105	198	148
142	107	200	150
144	108	202	151
146	110	204	153
148	111	206	154
150	113	208	166
152	114	210	157
154	115	212	158
156	117	214	160
158	118	216	162
160	120	218	163
162	121	220	165
164	123	222	166
166	124	224	168
168	126	226	169
170	127	228	171
172	129	230	172
174	131	232	174
176	132	234	175
178	133	236	177
180	135	238	178
182	136	240	180
184	138	242	181
186	140	244	183
188	141	246	184
190	142	248	186
		250	187

Example:

Cylinder No.	1	2	3	4	5	6	7	8
Compression Reading	134	128	140	127	122	135	100	129

Note: If the highest cylinder and lowest cylinder are not within a Maximum/Minimum range, valve or ring trouble is indicated.

provide valuable clues to possible trouble. Manifold vacuum is affected by many factors, including valve timing, clearance, and condition; cylinder condition; carburetor adjustment; ignition timing; manifold, carburetor, and head gasket leakage; and the condition of the PCV system or device.

Because some abnormal gauge readings may indicate several possible causes, it is important that corrective work be thorough, beginning with the simplest correction and continuing on until the problem has been remedied. Once again, it is important that vacuum gauge readings be interpreted in light of compression readings, valve adjustment, carburetor adjustment, and ignition timing.

1. Run the engine until normal operating temperature is reached.

2. Connect vacuum gauge with a T-connector in the hose from the intake manifold to the vacuum advance on the distributor.

3. Connect a tachometer (see below), start the engine, and set the idle as described in Chapter Five.

4. Check the reading on the gauge and compare it to **Figure 1**.

> NOTE: *Subtract one inch from the reading for every 1,000 feet of altitude. Also, on engines equipped with dual-diaphragm distributors, the vacuum at idle will read about one inch less than indicated in Figure 1.*

If the reading is abnormal and corresponds to numbers 2, 4, 12, or 14 in Figure 1, refer to the appropriate checks and adjustments in Chapter Five. If an abnormal reading corresponds to number 15 in Figure 1, check for possible cause.

Problems indicated by the remaining readings shown in Figure 1 are not covered in this manual and should be entrusted to a dealer or appropriate automotive specialist.

Fuel Pressure Gauge

This instrument is vital for evaluating fuel pump performance. Often a vacuum gauge and fuel pressure gauge are combined into one instrument.

Tachometer

A tachometer is essential for tuning engines with exhaust emission control systems. Ignition timing and carburetor adjustments must be performed at specified idle speeds. The best instrument for this purpose is one with a range of 0-1,000 or 0-2,000 rpm. Extended range (0-6,000) instruments lack accuracy at low speeds. The instrument should be capable of detecting changes of 25 rpm.

Dwell Meter

A dwell meter measures the distance in degrees of cam rotation that the distributor breaker points remain closed while the engine is running. Since this angle is determined by breaker point gap, dwell angle is an accurate indication of point gap. Many tachometers incorporate a dwell meter as well. Follow the instrument manufacturer's instructions to measure dwell.

Stroboscopic Timing Light

This instrument permits accurate engine timing. By flashing a light at the precise instant that cylinder No. 1 fires, the position of the crankshaft pulley at that instant can be seen. Marks on the pulley are lined up with the crankcase pointer to time the engine.

Suitable lights are neon bulb and xenon strobe types. Neon bulb timing lights are difficult to see and must be used in dimly lit areas. Xenon strobe timing lights can be used in bright sunlight. Use the light according to the manufacturer's instructions.

Exhaust Analyzer

Of all instruments, this is the least likely to be owned by an amateur mechanic. The most common type samples exhaust gases from the tailpipe and measures thermal conductivity. Since different gases conduct heat at varying rates, thermal conductivity is a good indication of gases present.

STARTER TROUBLESHOOTING

Starter system troubles are relatively easy to isolate. The following are common symptoms.

Engine Cranks Very Slowly or Not At All

Turn on the headlights; if the lights are very dim, the battery or connecting wires most likely are at fault. Check the battery with a hydrometer. Check wiring for breaks, shorts, and dirty connections. If the battery and wires are all right, turn the headlights on and crank the engine. If the lights dim drastically, the starter is probably shorted to ground.

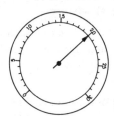  

1. NORMAL READING
18-22″ at idle.

2. LATE IGNITION TIMING
14-17″ at idle. Normal cam.

3. LATE VALVE TIMING
8-15″ at idle.

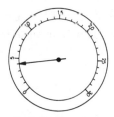 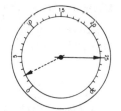  

4. INTAKE LEAK
Low steady reading.

5. NORMAL READING
Drops to 2, then rises to 25 when accelerator is rapidly depressed and released.

6. WORN RINGS, DILUTED OIL
Drops to 0, then rises to 22 when accelerator is rapidly depressed and released.

7. STICKING VALVE(S)
Normally steady. Intermittently flicks downward about 4″.

 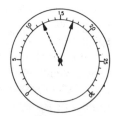 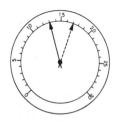 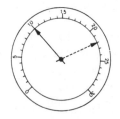

8. LEAKY VALVE
Regular drop about 2″.

9. BURNED OR WARPED VALVE
Regular, evenly spaced down-scale flick about 4″.

10. WORN VALVE GUIDES
Oscillates about 4″.

11. WEAK VALVE SPRINGS
Violent oscillation (about 10″) as rpm increases. Often steady at idle.

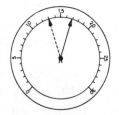   

12. IMPROPER IDLE MIXTURE
Floats slowly between 13-17″.

13. SMALL SPARK GAP or DEFECTIVE POINTS
Slight float between 14-16″.

14. HEAD GASKET LEAK
Floats between 5-19″.

15. RESTRICTED EXHAUST SYSTEM
Normal when first started. Drops to 0 as rpm increases. May eventually rise to about 16.

If the lights remain bright or dim slightly when cranking, the trouble may be in the starter, solenoid, or wiring. To isolate the trouble, short the 2 large solenoid terminals together (not to ground); if the starter cranks normally, check the solenoid and wiring to the ignition switch. If the starter still fails to crank correctly, refer the problem to a dealer or automotive electrical specialist.

Starter Turns, But Does Not Engage With Engine

Usually caused by defective pinion or solenoid shifting fork. The teeth on the pinion, flywheel ring gear, or both may be worn too far to engage properly. Refer the problem to a dealer or automotive specialist.

Starter Engages, But Will Not Disengage When Ignition Switch Is Released

Usually caused by sticking solenoid, but occasionally the pinion may jam on the flywheel. The pinion can be temporarily freed by rocking the vehicle in high gear.

Loud Grinding Noises When Starter Runs

The teeth on the pinion and/or flywheel are not meshing properly or the overrunning clutch mechanism is broken. Refer the problem to a dealer or automotive specialist.

CHARGING SYSTEM TROUBLESHOOTING

Charging system troubles may be in the generator (alternator), voltage regulator, or drive belt. The following symptoms are typical.

Dashboard Indicator or Ammeter Shows Continuous Discharge

This usually means that battery charging is not taking place. Check the drive belt tension. Check battery condition with hydrometer and electrical connections in the charging system. Finally, have the alternator and/or voltage regulator checked.

Dashboard Indicator Shows Intermittent Discharge

Check drive belt tension and electrical connection. Trouble may be traced to worn alternator brushes or bad slip rings.

Battery Requires Frequent Addition of Water or Lamps Require Frequent Replacement

Alternator may be overcharging the battery or the voltage regulator is faulty.

Excessive Noise From the Alternator

Check for loose mountings and/or worn bearings (see Chapter Six).

ENGINE TROUBLESHOOTING

These procedures assume the starter cranks the engine over normally. If not, refer to the *Starter* section of this chapter.

Engine Won't Start

Could be caused by the ignition system or fuel system. First, determine if high voltage to spark plugs occurs. To do this, disconnect one of the spark plug wires. Hold the exposed wire terminal about ¼ to ½ in. from ground (any metal in the engine compartment) with an insulated screwdriver. Crank the engine. If sparks don't jump to ground or the sparks are very weak, the trouble may be in the ignition system. If sparks occur properly, the trouble may be in the fuel system.

Engine Misses Steadily

Remove one spark plug wire at a time and ground the wire. If engine miss increases, that cylinder is working properly. Reconnect the wire and check the other. When a wire is disconnected and engine miss remains the same, that cylinder is not firing. Check spark as described above. If no spark occurs for one cylinder only, check distributor cap, wire, and spark plug. If spark occurs properly, check compression and intake manifold vacuum.

Engine Misses Erratically at All Speeds

Intermittent trouble can be difficult to find. It could be in the ignition system, exhaust system, or fuel system. Follow troubleshooting procedures for these systems to isolate the trouble.

Engine Misses at Idle Only

Trouble could be in ignition or carburetor idle adjustment. Have the idle mixture adjustment checked and check for restrictions in the idle circuit (see Chapter Five).

Engine Misses at High Speed Only

Trouble is in the fuel system or ignition system. Check accelerator pump operation, fuel pump delivery, fuel line, etc. Check spark plugs and wires (see Chapter Five).

Low Performance at All Speeds, Poor Acceleration

Trouble usually exists in ignition or fuel system (see Chapter Five).

Excessive Fuel Consumption

Could be caused by a number of seemingly unrelated factors. Check for clutch slippage (Chapter Eight), brake drag (Chapter Eight), defective wheel bearings (Chapter Nine), poor front-end alignment (Chapter Nine), faulty ignition (Chapter Five), leaky gas tank or lines, and carburetor condition.

Low Oil Pressure Indicated by Oil Pressure Gauge

If the oil pressure gauge shows low oil pressure (less than 5 psi) with the engine running, stop the engine immediately. Coast to a stop with clutch disengaged. The trouble may be caused by low oil level, blockage in an oil line, defective oil pump, overheated engine, or defective pressure sending switch. Check the oil level and drive belt tension. Check for a shorted oil pressure sender with an ohmmeter. Do not re-start the engine until you know why the low indication was given and are sure the problem has been corrected.

Engine Overheats

Usually caused by trouble in the cooling system. Check the level of coolant in the radiator, condition of the drive belt, and water hoses for leaks and loose connections. Check the operation of the cooling fan (see Chapter Seven). Can also be caused by late ignition or valve timing.

Engine Stalls As It Warms Up

The choke valve may be stuck closed, the manifold heat control valve may be stuck, the engine idling speed may be set too low, or the emission control (PCV) valve may be faulty.

Engine Stalls After Idling or Slow-speed Driving

Can be caused by defective fuel pump, overheated engine, high carburetor float level, incorrect idle adjustment, or defective emission control valve.

Engine Stalls After High-speed Driving

Vapor lock within the fuel lines caused by an overheated engine is the usual cause of this trouble. Inspect and service the cooling system (see Chapter Seven). If the trouble persists, changing to a different fuel or shielding the fuel line from engine heat may prove helpful.

Engine Backfires

Several causes can be suspected: ignition timing, overheating, excessive carbon, wrong heat range spark plugs, hot or sticking valves, and/or cracked distributor cap.

Smoky Exhaust

Blue smoke indicates excessive oil consumption usually caused by worn rings. Black smoke indicates an excessively rich fuel mixture.

Excessive Oil Consumption

Can be caused by external leaks through broken seals or gaskets, or by burning oil in the combustion chamber. Check the oil pan and the front and rear of the engine for oil leaks. If the oil is not leaking externally, valve stem clearances may be excessive, piston rings may be worn, and/or cylinder walls may be scored. Excessive oil consumption can also be caused by a clogged vent valve (**Figure 2**). Unplug the

vent valve from the rocker cover and check to see that the plunger moves freely up and down. If it does not and if the valve is excessively clogged, it should be replaced.

Engine Is Noisy

Regular Clicking Sound—Valves and/or tappets out of adjustment.

> NOTE: *On engines equipped with hydraulic lifters, oil will run down out of the lifters when the engine remains shut off for an extended period of time, such as overnight. Upon start up, the lifters may clatter for several seconds until the oil pressure has built up. This is a normal condition and is not harmful.*

Ping or Chatter On Load or Acceleration—Spark knock due to low octane fuel, carbon buildup, overly advanced ignition timing, and causes mentioned under engine backfire.

Light Knock or Pound With Engine Not Under Load—Worn connecting rod bearings, worn crank pin, and/or lack of engine oil.

Light Metallic Double Knock, Usually Heard During Idle—Worn or loose piston pin or bushing and/or lack of oil.

Chattering or Rattling During Acceleration—Worn rings, cylinder walls, low ring tension, and/or broken rings.

Hollow, Bell-like Muffled Sound When Engine Is Cold—Piston slap due to worn pistons, cylinder walls, collapsed piston skirts, excessive clearances, misaligned connecting rods, and/or lack of oil.

Dull, Heavy Metallic Knock Under Load or Acceleration, Especially When Cold—Regular noise: worn main bearings; irregular noise: worn thrust bearings.

IGNITION SYSTEM TROUBLESHOOTING

The following procedures assume the battery is in good enough condition to crank the engine at a normal rate. Ignition checks, specifications, and adjustments are presented in Chapter Five.

No Spark to One Plug

The only causes are defective distributor cap or spark plug wire. Examine the distributor cap for moisture, dirt, carbon tracking caused by flashover, and cracks. Check spark plug wire for breaks or loose connections.

No Spark To Any Plug

This could indicate trouble in the primary or secondary ignition circuits. First remove the coil wire from the center post of the distributor. Hold the wire end about ¼ in. from ground with an insulated screwdriver. Crank the engine. If sparks are produced, the trouble is in the rotor or distributor cap. Remove the cap and check for burns, moisture, dirt, carbon tracking, cracks, etc. Check rotor for excessive burning, pitting, and cracks.

If the coil does not produce any spark, check the secondary wire for a break. If the wire is good, turn the engine over so the breaker points are open. Examine them for excessive gap, burning, pitting, or loose connections. With the points open, check voltage from the coil to ground with a voltmeter or test lamp. If voltage is present, the coil is probably defective. Have it checked or substitute a coil known to be good.

If voltage is not present, check wire connections to coil and distributor. Disconnect the wire leading from the coil to the distributor and measure from the coil terminal to ground. If voltage is present, the distributor is shorted. Examine breaker points and connecting wires carefully. If voltage is still not present, measure the other coil terminal. Voltage on the other terminal indicates a defective coil. No voltage indicates a broken wire between coil and battery.

Weak Spark

If the spark is so small it cannot jump from the wire to ground, check the battery. Other causes are bad breaker points, condenser, incorrect point gap, dirty or loose connection in the primary circuit, or dirty or burned rotor or distributor cap. Check for worn cam lobes in the distributor.

Missing

This is usually caused by fouled or damaged plugs, plugs of the wrong heat range, or incorrect plug gap.

FUEL SYSTEM TROUBLESHOOTING

Fuel system troubles must be isolated to the carburetor, fuel pump, or fuel lines. The following procedures assume the ignition system has been checked and is in proper working order. Carburetor checks and adjustments are covered in Chapter Five.

Engine Will Not Start

First, determine that fuel is being delivered to the carburetor. If fuel is delivered to the carburetor, check the carburetor and choke system for dirt and/or defects.

Engine Runs at Fast Idle

Misadjustment of fast idle screw or defective carburetor.

EXHAUST EMISSION CONTROL TROUBLESHOOTING

Failure of the emission control system to maintain exhaust output within acceptable limits is usually caused by a defective carburetor, poor general engine condition, or defective exhaust control valves.

CLUTCH TROUBLESHOOTING

Several clutch troubles may be experienced. Usually the trouble is quite obvious and will fall into one of the following categories:
1. Slipping, chattering, or grabbing when engaging.
2. Spinning or dragging when disengaged.
3. Clutch noises, clutch pedal pulsations, and rapid clutch disc facing wear.

Clutch adjustment is covered in Chapter Eight.

Clutch Slips While Engaged

Improper adjustment of clutch linkage, weak or broken pressure springs, worn friction disc facings, and grease or oil on clutch disc.

Clutch Chatters or Grabs When Engaging

Usually caused by misadjustment of clutch linkage, dirt or grease on the friction disc facings, or broken and/or worn clutch parts.

Clutch Spins or Drags When Disengaged

The clutch friction disc normally spins briefly after disengagement and takes a moment to come to rest. This sound should not be confused with drag. Drag is caused by the friction disc not being fully released from the flywheel or pressure plate as the clutch pedal is depressed. The trouble can be caused by clutch linkage misadjustment or defective or worn clutch parts.

Clutch Noises

Clutch noises are usually most noticeable when the engine is idling. First, note whether the noise is heard when the clutch is engaged or disengaged. Clutch noises when engaged could be due to a loose friction disc hub, loose friction disc springs, and misalignment or looseness of engine or transmission mounts. When disengaged, noises can be due to a worn release bearing, defective pilot bearing, or misaligned release lever.

2

Clutch Pedal Pulsates

Usually noticed when slight pressure is applied to the clutch pedal with the engine running. As pedal pressure is increased, the pulsation ceases. Possible causes include misalignment of engine and transmission, bent crankshaft flange, distortion or shifting of the clutch housing, release lever misalignment, warped friction disc, and damaged pressure plate.

Rapid Friction Disc-Facing Wear

This trouble is caused by any condition that permits slippage between facings and the flywheel or pressure plate. Probable causes are "riding" the clutch, slow releasing of the clutch after disengagement, weak or broken pressure springs, clutch pedal linkage misadjustment, and warped clutch disc or pressure plate.

TRANSMISSION TROUBLESHOOTING

With the exception of transmission troubles that are related to clutch adjustment, repair and adjustment should be referred to a dealer or a transmission specialist.

Hard Shifting Into Gear

Common causes are the clutch not releasing, misadjustment of linkage, linkage needing lubrication, detent ball stuck, or gears tight on shaft splines.

Transmission Slips Out of First or Reverse Gear

Causes are gearshift linkage out of adjustment, gear loose on main shaft, gear teeth worn, excessive play, insufficient shift lever spring tension, or worn bearings.

Transmission Slips Out of Second, Third, or Fourth Gear

Gearshift linkage is out of adjustment, misalignment between engine and transmission, excessive main shaft end-play, worn gear teeth, insufficient shift-lever spring tension, worn bearings, or defective synchronizer. Gear may be loose on main shaft.

No Power Through Transmission

May be caused by clutch slipping, stripped gear teeth, damaged shifter fork linkage, broken gear or shaft, and stripped drive key.

Transmission Noisy in Neutral

Transmission misaligned, bearings worn or dry, worn gears, worn or bent countershaft, and excessive countershaft end-play.

Transmission Noisy in Gear

Defective clutch disc, worn bearings, loose gears, worn gear teeth, and faults listed above.

Gears Clash During Shifting

Caused by the clutch not releasing, defective synchronizer, or gears sticking on main shaft.

Oil Leaks

Most common causes are foaming due to wrong lubricant, lubricant level too high, broken gaskets, damaged oil seals, loose drain plug, and cracked transmission case.

DIFFERENTIAL TROUBLESHOOTING

Checks and service of the differentials and the drive shafts are covered in Chapter Nine.

Usually, it is noise that draws attention to trouble in the differentials. It is not always easy to diagnose the trouble by determining the source of noise and the operating conditions that produce the noise. Defective conditions in the universal joints, wheel bearings, muffler, or tires may be wrongly diagnosed as trouble in the differentials or axles.

Some clue as to the cause of trouble may be gained by noting whether the noise is a hum, growl, or knock; whether it is produced when the vehicle is accelerating under load or coasting; and whether it is heard when the vehicle is going straight or making a turn.

Noise during acceleration—May be caused by shortage of lubricant, incorrect tooth contact between drive gear and drive pinion, damaged or misadjusted bearings in axles or side bearings, or damaged gears.

Noise during coasting—May be caused by incorrect backlash between drive gear and drive pinion gear or incorrect adjustment of drive pinion bearing.

Noise during turn—This noise is usually caused by loose or worn axle shaft bearing, pinion gears too tight on shafts, side gear jammed in differential case, or worn side gear thrust washer and pinion thrust washer.

Broken differential parts—Breaking of differential parts can be caused by insufficient lubricant, improper use of clutch, excessive loading, misadjusted bearings and gears, excessive backlash, damage to case, or loose bolts.

A humming noise in a differential is often caused by improper drive pinion or ring gear adjustment which prevents normal tooth contact between gears. If ignored, rapid tooth wear will take place and the noise will become more like a growl. Repair as soon as the humming is heard so that new gears will not be required. Tire noise will vary considerably, depending on the type of road surface and type and tread pattern. Differential noises will be the same regardless of road surface. If noises are heard, listen carefully to the noise over different road surfaces to help isolate the problem.

BRAKE SYSTEM TROUBLESHOOTING

Checks, adjustments, and service of the brake system are covered in Chapter Eight.

Brake Pedal Goes to Floor

Worn linings or pads, air in the hydraulic system, leaky brake lines, leaky wheel cylinders, or leaky or worn master cylinder may be the cause. Check for leaks and worn brake linings or pads. Bleed and adjust the brakes. Rebuild wheel cylinders and/or master cylinder.

Spongy Pedal

Usually caused by air in the brake system. Bleed and adjust brakes.

Brakes Pull

Check brake adjustment and wear on linings. Check for contaminated linings, leaky wheel cylinders, loose lines, or hoses. Check front-end alignment and suspension damage such as broken front or rear springs and shock absorbers. Tires also affect braking; check tire pressures and tire condition.

Brakes Squeal or Chatter

Check brake lining thickness and brake drum condition. Ensure that shoes are not loose. Clean away all dirt on shoes and drums.

Brakes Drag

Check brake adjustment, including handbrake. Check for broken or weak shoe return springs, swollen rubber parts due to improper brake fluid or contamination. Check for defective master cylinder.

Hard Pedal

Check brake linings for contamination. Check for brake line restrictions.

High Speed Fade

Check for distorted or out-of-round drums and contaminated linings.

Pulsating Pedal

Check for distorted or out-of-round brake drums.

COOLING SYSTEM TROUBLESHOOTING

Checks, tests, and service of the cooling system are covered in Chapter Seven.

Engine Overheats

May be caused by insufficient coolant, loose or defective drive belt, defective thermostat, defective water pump, clogged water lines, incorrect ignition timing, and/or defective or loose hoses. Inspect radiator and all parts for leaks.

Engine Does Not Warm Up

Usually caused by defective thermostat or extremely cold weather.

Loss of Coolant

Radiator leaks, loose or defective hoses, defective water pump, leaks in cylinder head gasket, cracked cylinder head or engine block, or defective radiator cap may be the cause.

Noisy Cooling System

Usually caused by defective water pump bearings, loose or bent fan blades, or defective drive belt.

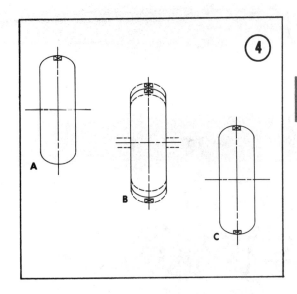

STEERING AND SUSPENSION TROUBLESHOOTING

Steering and suspension system checks, adjustments, and service are covered in Chapter Nine.

Trouble in the suspension or steering is evident when any of the following occur:

1. Hard steering
2. Vehicle pulls to one side
3. Vehicle wanders or front wheels wobble
4. Excessive play in steering
5. Abnormal tire wear.

Unusual steering, pulling, or wandering is usually caused by bent or misaligned suspension parts. If the trouble seems to be excessive play, check wheel bearing adjustment first. Next, check steering free-play and kingpins and balljoints. Finally, check tie rod ends by shaking each wheel.

Tire Wear Analysis

Abnormal tire wear should always be analyzed to determine the cause. The most common are incorrect tire pressure, improper driving, overloading, and incorrect wheel alignment. **Figure 3** identifies wear patterns and their most probable causes.

Wheel Balancing

All 4 wheels and tires must be in balance along 2 axes. To be in static balance (**Figure 4**),

weight must be evenly distributed around the axis or rotation. (A) shows a statically unbalanced wheel. (B) shows the result—wheel tramp or hopping. (C) shows proper static balance.

To be in dynamic balance (**Figure 5**), the centerline of weight must coincide with the centerline of the wheel. (A) shows a dynamically unbalanced wheel. (B) shows the result—wheel wobble or shimmy. (C) shows the proper dynamic balance.

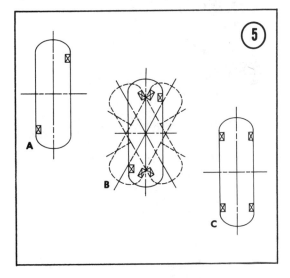

If wheel imbalance is indicated immediately after the vehicle has been subjected to hard, off-road use, check both sides of each wheel for missing wheel balance weights and have them replaced where they have been thrown off.

(3)

Underinflation—Worn more on sides than in center.

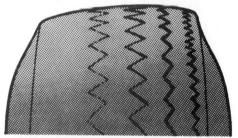

Wheel Alignment—Worn more on one side than the other. Edges of tread feathered.

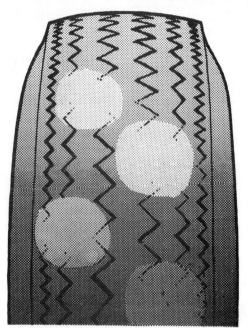

Wheel Balance — Scalloped edges indicate wheel wobble or tramp due to wheel unbalance.

Road Abrasion—Rough wear on entire tire or in patches.

Overinflation—Worn more in center than on sides.

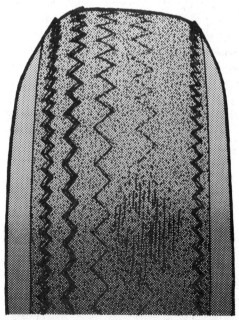

Combination—Most tires exhibit a combination of the above. This tire was overinflated (center worn) and the toe-in was incorrect (feathering). The driver cornered hard at high speed (feathering, rounded shoulders) and braked rapidly (worn spots). The scaly roughness indicates a rough road surface.

CHAPTER THREE

PERIODIC CHECKS AND MAINTENANCE

To ensure good performance, dependability, and safety, regular preventive maintenance is essential. This chapter outlines periodic maintenance for a Chevrolet/GMC 4 x 4 vehicle subjected to average use (a combination of urban and highway driving and light-duty off-road use). A vehicle that is driven extensively off-road or used primarily in stop-and-go traffic may require more frequent attention; but even without use, rust, dirt, and corrosion cause unnecessary damage if the vehicle is neglected. Whether maintenance is performed by the owner or a dealer, regular routine attention helps avoid expensive repairs.

NOTE: *This chapter covers 1967-1975 models. If you have a 1976 or later model, be sure to check the Supplement at the rear of this book for the latest information.*

The recommended checks and inspections in this chapter include routine checks which are easily performed at each fuel stop, or daily if the vehicle is operated under adverse road and weather conditions. By no means do they represent a complete inspection and maintenance schedule (see Chapter One). However, they are points which if neglected are most likely to cause trouble.

ROUTINE CHECKS

The following simple checks should be performed at each fuel stop.

1. Check the engine oil level. The oil should be checked with the engine warm and the vehicle on level ground. The level should be between the 2 marks on the dipstick (**Figure 1**)—never below and never above. If necessary, add oil to bring the level above the lower mark.

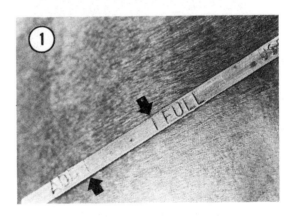

Oil being added should be the same viscosity grade as the oil that is in the engine.

2. Check the battery electrolyte level. It should be even with the top of the vertical separators in the case (above the plates). Top up any cells that are low with distilled water; never add electrolyte to a battery that is in service.

3. Check the radiator coolant level. If the vehicle is fitted with a coolant recovery tank, the level should be at the half-full mark or somewhere between the full and low marks (**Figure 2**). On systems without a recovery tank, loosen the radiator cap to the first notch, using a shop rag folded in several thicknesses to protect your hand. Wait until you are certain the pressure in the system has been relieved then unscrew the cap. The coolant level should be above the tubes in the top radiator tank. If the level is low, add water (or coolant if the vehicle is being operated in sustained low temperatures).

4. Check the windshield washer fluid level and top it up if necessary (**Figure 3**). If the vehicle is being operated in sustained low temperatures, add a windshield washer fluid compounded to resist freezing. Don't add cooling system antifreeze. It can damage painted surfaces.

5. Check the tire pressures. Refer to **Table 1**.

> NOTE: *Tire pressures should be checked when the tires are cold (before the vehicle has been run). For this reason, it is a good idea to keep a tire pressure gauge in the glove compartment. If the tire pressure is checked when the tires are warm, it will be about 3 psi higher following a low-speed drive and about 7 psi higher following a high-speed drive.*

In addition to pressure, the condition of the tire tread and sidewalls should be checked for damage, cracking, and wear. Wear patterns are a good indicator of chassis and suspension alignment (see Chapter Two). If detected early, alignment can be corrected before the tires have worn severely. Checking tire condition is particularly important following hard off-road usage. Pay particular attention to signs of severe rock damage usually evidenced by fractures and cuts in the tread and sidewalls. This type of damage presents an extreme driving hazard when the vehicle is operated at highway speeds. A damaged tire should be replaced as soon as it is detected.

PERIODIC CHECKS AND INSPECTIONS

The following checks and inspections should be made at least monthly or at the intervals indicated. In addition, it is a good idea to perform these checks after the vehicle has been used off-road for an extended period of time.

Brake Fluid Level

Brake fluid level should be checked monthly as well as any time the pedal can be pushed

Table 1 MINIMUM TIRE INFLATION PRESSURE AT GROSS VEHICLE WEIGHT RATING

		K 105 Blazer						K10, 15 Pickup						K10, 15 Suburban					
GVWR (lbs.)→		4900		5400		5800 & 6300		5200		5800		6400		6200		6800		7300	
Tire	Load Range	FR	R	FR	R	FR	R	FR	R	FR	R	FR	R	FR	R	FR	R	FR	R
E78-15	B	32	32	—	—	—	—	—	—	—	—	—	—	—	—	—	—	—	—
G78-15	B	—	—	32	32	—	—	32	32	—	—	—	—	—	—	—	—	—	—
6.50-16LT	C	—	—	45	45	45	45	45	45	45	45	—	—	45	45	—	—	—	—
H78-15	B	—	—	32	32	32	32	32	32	32	32	—	—	32	32	—	—	—	—
7.00-15LT	C	—	—	45	45	45	45	45	45	45	45	45	45	45	45	—	—	—	—
10-15LT	B	—	—	30	30	30	30	30	30	30	30	30	30	30	30	—	—	—	—
L78-15	B	—	—	32	32	32	32	32	32	32	32	32	32	30	32	30	32	—	—
7.00-16LT	C	—	—	45	45	45	45	45	45	45	45	45	45	45	45	45	45	—	—
LR78-15	C	—	—	34	34	34	34	34	36	34	36	34	36	34	36	—	—	34	36
L78-15	D	—	—	—	—	—	—	—	36	—	—	—	—	34	40	—	—	34	40

		K20, 25 Pickup & Suburban					
GVWR (lbs.)→		6800		7500		8400	
Tire	Load Range	FR	R	FR	R	FR	R
8.75-16.5	C	40	45	40	—	—	—
8.75-16.5	D	40	60	40	60	—	—
9.50-16.5	D	30	60	—	—	30	60
10-16.5	D	30	60	—	—	30	60
7.50-16LT	C	35	45	35	—	35	—
7.50-16LT	D	35	60	35	60	35	—
7.50-16LT	E	35	75	—	—	35	75
9.50-16.5	E	—	—	—	—	—	—

Note: The tire pressures shown are for original equipment tires. Because of the wide variety of tire types and makes available for 4-wheel drive, it is impractical to set down all of the tire pressures in this table. When buying tires other than original equipment sizes, check with manufacturer for recommended pressures. In all cases, never exceed the maximum pressure embossed on the side of the tire.

3

within a couple of inches of the floor. The level should be ¼ in. below the lower edge of each opening (**Figure 4**). If the level is lower than recommended, clean the area around the filler cap and remove it. Add brake fluid clearly marked SAE 70R3, SAE J1703 (which supersedes 70R3), or DOT 3, only to bring the level up to that recommended. In some cases, where the level is extremely low, it may be necessary to bleed the brake hydraulic system as described in Chapter Eight. However, before the system is filled and bled, refer to *Brake Lines and Hoses* in this chapter and check for and correct any leaks that are found.

When the system has been filled (and bled if necessary), install the filler cap and pump the brake pedal several times to restore system pressure.

Brake Adjustment

Most brakes are self-adjusting (refer to Chapter Eight). Front disc brakes (installed on some of the vehicles covered in this manual) are self-adjusting in that as the brake pads wear, fluid is drawn into the wheel circuits from the master cylinder supply reservoir to compensate for the increased piston travel required. For this reason it is important that the fluid in the reservoir be maintained at the recommended level (see *Brake Fluid Level* above).

Brake Pad and Lining Condition

Disc brake pads and drum brake shoe linings should be checked for oil or grease on the friction material and measured to determine their serviceability every 6,000-10,000 miles or when long pedal travel indicates the likelihood of extreme wear. Material thickness and service limits are shown in **Table 2**.

Table 2   BRAKE MATERIAL SERVICE LIMITS

	Service Limit
Disc brake lining	$\frac{1}{32}$ in. above the shoe table or rivet head
Drum brake lining	
Bonded	$\frac{1}{16}$ in.
Riveted	$\frac{3}{16}$ in.

If the friction material is oily or greasy, the pads and linings must be replaced no matter how much material remains. Replacement is covered in Chapter Eight.

The condition of disc brake rotors should be checked at the same time the pads are inspected. If the rotors are scored deeply enough to snag a fingernail, they should be referred to a dealer or brake specialist for resurfacing or replacement.

Parking Brake Adjustment

Adjustment of parking brakes is covered in Chapter Eight.

Brake Lines and Hoses

Brake lines and hoses should be routinely checked for signs of deterioration, chafing, and kinks. This is particularly important following rough, off-road use where the likelihood of brush and rock damage is high. Any line that is less than perfect should be replaced immediately.

Check all the connections for tightness and look for signs of leakage which may indicate a cracked or otherwise unserviceable connection. As with lines and hoses, any connections that are less than perfect should be replaced.

When a line has been replaced, or in any situation where a brake line or hose has been disconnected, refer to Chapter Eight and fill and bleed the brake system.

Manual Transmission Oil Level

The transmission oil level must be checked with the vehicle sitting level. If you do not have access to a hydraulic hoist, a mechanic's "creeper" will be helpful to get beneath the vehicle.

Prior to checking the transmission oil level, the vehicle should be driven for several miles to warm up the oil. Then, unscrew the level plug on the transmission case (**Figure 5**). If the level is correct, a small amount of oil should seep out of the level hole. If necessary, carefully add fresh oil up to the bottom edge of the hole and install the fill/level plug and tighten it securely.

> NOTE: *If the vehicle has been operated in deep water, pay particular attention to the condition of the oil. If water droplets are present, indicating that water has entered the transmission, change the oil immediately.*

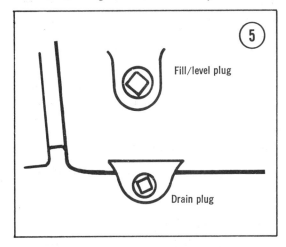

Fill/level plug

Drain plug

Automatic Transmission Oil Level

The transmission oil level must be checked with the vehicle sitting level and the engine and transmission warmed up to operating temperature. If the level is checked with the transmission cold the level will appear to be low.

1. Set the handbrake, select PARK with the transmission control lever, start the engine and allow it to run for a couple of minutes to ensure the fluid coupling is full of fluid. Shift the lever through all positions and return it to PARK.

2. Wipe the transmission dipstick handle and filler tube clean with a dry rag. Withdraw the dipstick and wipe it with a clean lint-free cloth. *Do not use the rag that was used to clean the tube and handle.* Any contamination that might find its way into the transmission—even lint from a rag—could cause serious damage.

3. Insert the clean dipstick all the way into the filler tube and then withdraw it again and check the level. The level should be above the ADD mark on the dipstick (**Figure 6**). If the level is below the ADD mark, add fresh Dexron automatic transmission fluid. The distance between the marks on the dipstick represent about one pint. Use a clean funnel fitted with a fine-mesh filter to direct the fluid into the filler tube. Slowly add the fluid, with the engine running, a little at a time. Periodically recheck the level as described above while adding fluid.

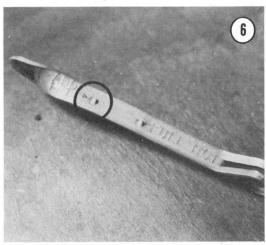

If the fluid level is extremely low, foaming (caused when the fluid pump draws air into the transmission) may prevent an accurate reading on the dipstick. In this case, shut off the engine and allow several minutes for the foaming to subside. Then, add oil as described above—about ¼ quart at a time—checking the level after each addition, until the level is correct. Then, hold the footbrake down and select each of the gear positions for several seconds to allow the servo pistons to fill. Recheck the level as described above and correct it once again if necessary.

> NOTE: *If the vehicle has been operated in deep water, pay particular attention to the condition of the oil. If*

water droplets are present, indicating that water has entered the transmission, change the oil immediately.

Intake/Exhaust Manifold Nuts and Bolts

The intake/exhaust manifold nuts and bolts should be checked for broken or missing lockwashers and for looseness. Nuts that are snug need be tightened no further, but loose nuts should be tightened to the appropriate torque shown in **Table 3**. Overtightening of nuts can cause studs to break or castings to crack, requiring expensive repairs.

Drive Belts

Check the alternator, water pump, fan, air pump, air conditioning, and steering and brake pump belts for fraying, glazing, or cracking of the contact surfaces (vee). Belts that are damaged or deteriorated should be replaced before they fail and cause serious problems from engine overheating, electrical system failure, or reduction of steering and brake control. Belt replacement is described in Chapter Seven.

In addition to being in good condition, it is important that the drive belts be correctly adjusted. A belt that is too loose will cause the driven components to operate at less than optimum, and a belt that is adjusted too tightly will wear rapidly and place unnecessary side loads on the bearings of the driven components, possibly resulting in their premature wear or failure. See Chapter Seven for drive belt adjustment.

Vacuum Fittings and Hoses

Check the vacuum fittings and connection to make sure they are tight, and inspect the hoses for cracking, kinking, or deterioration. Any damaged or deteriorated lines should be replaced.

Coolant Condition

Remove the radiator cap and check the condition of the coolant. If it is dirty, drain and flush the radiator and cooling system and fill it with fresh coolant as described in Chapter Seven. In any case, the coolant should be changed every 24 months regardless of condition or mileage.

Coolant Hoses

Inspect the heater and radiator hoses. Replace any that are cracked, deteriorated, extremely soft, or extremely hard. Make sure the hoses are correctly routed and installed and that all the clamps are tight.

Radiator

Check the radiator for leaks and damage. Blow bugs and dirt out of the fins, from the rear of the radiator, with compressed air. Carefully

Table 3   INTAKE AND EXHAUST MANIFOLD FASTENER TORQUE

Engine	Fastener	Torque
In-line 6 1967-1972	Exhaust manifold to intake manifold	25 ft.-lb.
1973-1975	Exhaust manifold to intake manifold	30 ft.-lb.
V6 1967, 1969	Intake manifold to cylinder head	30-35 ft.-lb.
	Exhaust manifold to cylinder head	15-20 ft.-lb.
V8 (all) 1967-1975	Intake manifold to cylinder head	30 ft.-lb.
	Exhaust manifold to cylinder head	20 ft.-lb.

straighten bent fins with a small screwdriver. Have a service station pressure test the radiator cap. This is a simple test that takes only a few minutes (see Chapter Seven) with the test equipment on hand at most stations. The cap should maintain pressure and the relief valve remain closed to 13 psi.

The radiator should also be pressure tested, as described in Chapter Seven.

Wheel Alignment

Wheel alignment should be checked periodically by a dealer or an alignment specialist. Misalignment is usually indicated first by incorrect tire wear (see *Tire Wear Analysis*, Chapter Two). Wheel alignment specifications are provided as reference in Chapter Nine.

Steering

1. With the vehicle on level ground, and with the front wheels lined up straight ahead, grasp the steering wheel and turn it from right to left and check for rotational free-play. The free-play should not be greater than about one inch (**Figure 7**). If it is, the front wheel bearings should be checked for condition and adjustment (see Chapter Nine), and the kingpins, steering linkage, and steering arm should be checked as possible causes of excessive play. These checks should be referred to a dealer.

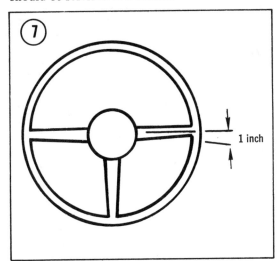

1 inch

2. Try to move the steering wheel in and out and check for axial play. If any play is felt,

check the tightness of the steering wheel center nut.

3. Attempt to move the steering wheel from side to side without turning it. Movement is an indication of loose steering column mounting bolts or worn column bushings. Check and tighten the mounting bolts if necessary, and if the movement is still present, the vehicle should be referred to a dealer for corrective service.

POWER STEERING FLUID LEVEL

The power steering fluid level can be checked cold or with the engine and fluid warmed up to operating temperature.

1. Turn the steering wheel to right and left lock several times and then turn the wheels straight ahead. Shut off the engine.

2. Remove the dipstick from the pump reservoir, wipe it clean with a lint-free cloth, reinsert it all the way into the tube, and withdraw it. If the fluid is at operating temperature (hot to the touch) the level should be between the HOT and COLD marks (**Figure 8**). If the fluid is "cold" (about 70°F) the level should be between the ADD and COLD marks. If the level is not correct, carefully add GM Power Steering Fluid or Dexron automatic transmission fluid, or an equivalent, and recheck the level. Do not overfill the reservoir. If the level after filling is above the FULL mark, fluid must be siphoned off until the level is correct.

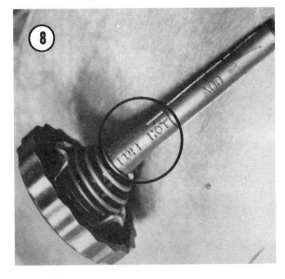

CHAPTER FOUR

LUBRICATION

Strict adherence to a detailed lubrication schedule is at least as important as timely preventive maintenance. The recommended lubrication schedule (**Figures 1 and 2** and **Table 1**) is based on average vehicle use—a combination of highway and urban driving with some light-duty off-road use, in moderate weather and climate. Abnormal use, such as mostly off-road use, in dusty and dirty conditions, or in extremely hot or cold climates, requires that the lubrication schedule be modified so that the lubricants are checked and changed more frequently.

Acids that form in the engine, transmission, and differential oil during short-haul driving, or during operation in extremely cold climates will wear out parts as quickly as dirty lubricants.

NOTE: *This chapter covers 1967-1975 models. If you have a 1976 or later model, be sure to check the Supplement at the rear of this book for the latest information.*

ENGINE OIL AND FILTER CHANGE

For average use (see above) the engine oil and filter should be changed at the intervals shown in Table 1. If driving is primarily short distances and in stop-and-go traffic, or if the vehicle is used mostly off-road, the oil and filter should be changed twice as often as for average use. If the vehicle is driven only a few hundred miles each month, the oil and filter should be changed every 6-8 weeks. If the vehicle is driven for long periods in extremely cold climate, where the temperature is frequently below 10°F, the oil and filter should be changed twice as often as for average use.

Recommended oil grades (by operating temperature) are shown in **Table 2**. Use only a detergent oil with an API rating of SE or SD (formerly MS). These quality ratings are stamped on the top of the can.

Try always to use the same brand of oil. If the oil you select to use is not from one of the major oil companies, it may not always be available when you are travelling and when you are operating the vehicle for extended periods off-road. For these reasons, then, it is a good idea to carry a couple quarts of oil in the vehicle.

The use of oil additives is not necessary nor is it recommended.

Table 2 RECOMMENDED GRADES OF OIL

Oil Grade	Temperature Range
5W-20*, 5W-30	20°F and below
10W, 5W-30, 10W-30, 10W-40	0° to 60°F
20W-20, 10W-30, 10W-40, 20W-40, 20W-50	20°F and above

*If the vehicle is being operated at sustained highway speeds, the next heavier grade of oil should be used.

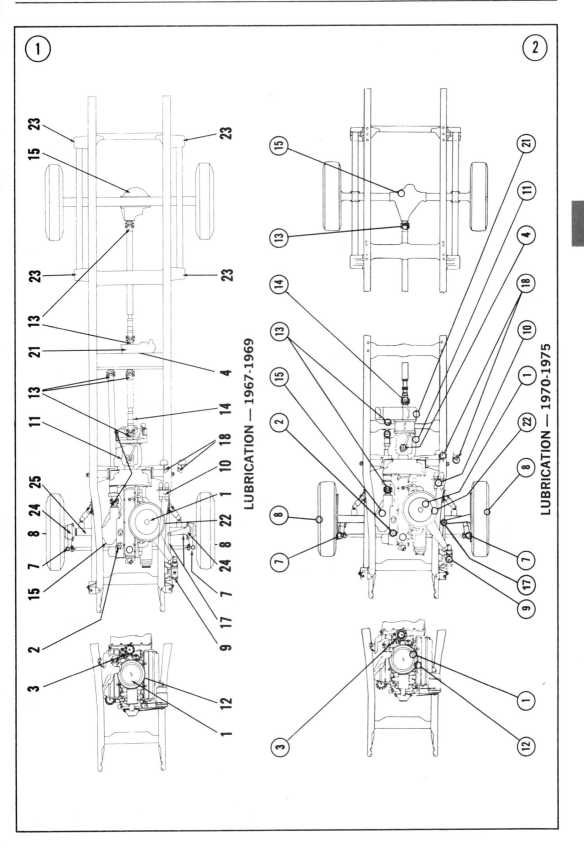

LUBRICATION — 1967-1969

LUBRICATION — 1970-1975

Table 1 LUBRICATION SCHEDULE

1967-1973 Models

No.	Lubrication Points	Lubrication Period	Type of Lubrication	Quantity	Remarks
1	Air cleaner	12,000 miles			Replace L-6. Rotate V8. Replace V8 at 24.000 miles.
2	Distributor—L6	12,000 miles			Replace cam lubricator
3	Distributor—V8	12,000 miles			Replace cam lubricator
4	Control linkage points	6,000 miles	Engine oil	As required	Brush or spray to apply
7	Tie rod ends	6,000 miles	Chassis lubricant	2 places as required	
8	Wheel bearings	30,000 miles	Wheel bearing grease	2 places as required	
9	Steering gear	36,000 miles			Check for grease leak Do not lubricate
10	Master cylinder	6,000 miles	Delco Supreme No. 11 or equivalent	As required	Check—add fluid when necessary
11	Transmission—manual	6,000 miles	GL-5	As required	Keep even with filler plug
	—automatic	6,000 miles	Dexron® or equivalent	As required	
12	Carburetor linkage—V8	6,000 miles	Engine oil	As required	
13	Universal joints	6,000 miles	Chassis lubricant	As required	
14	Drive shaft slip joints	6,000 miles	Chassis lubricant	3 places as required	
15	Front and rear axle	6,000 miles	GL-5	As required	Check
17	Drag link	6,000 miles	Chassis lubricant	2 places as required	
18	Brake and clutch pedal springs	6,000 miles	Engine oil	As required	
21	Transfer case	6,000 miles	GL-5	As required	Check
22	Throttle bell crank—L6	6,000 miles	Engine oil	As required	
23	Spring shackles	6,000 miles	Chassis lubricant	4 places as required	
24	Ball-socket hubs	6,000 miles	SAE 140	As required	
25	Air vents	6,000 miles			Check condition of vent hose

Table 1   LUBRICATION SCHEDULE (continued)

1974 Models

No.	Lubrication Points	Lubrication Period	Type of Lubrication	Quantity	Remarks
1	Air cleaner	12,000 miles			See text
2	Distributor—L6	24,000 miles			Replace cam lubricator**
3	Distributor—V8	24,000 miles			Replace cam lubricator**
4	Control linkage points	12,000 miles	Engine oil	As required	Brush or spray to apply
7	Tie rod ends	6,000 miles	Chassis lubricant	2 places as required	
8	Wheel bearings	24,000 miles	Wheel bearing grease	2 places as required	
9	Steering gear	36,000 miles			Check for grease leak Do not lubricate
10	Master cylinder	6,000 miles	Delco Supreme No. 11 or DOT-3 fluids	As required	Check—add fluid when necessary
11	Transmission—manual	6,000 miles	GL-5	As required	Keep even with filler plug
	—automatic	6,000 miles	Dexron® or equivalent	As required	
12	Carburetor linkage—V8	12,000 miles	Engine oil	As required	
13	Universal joints	6,000 miles	Chassis lubricant	As required	
14	Drive shaft slip joints	6,000 miles	Chassis lubricant	3 places as required	
15	Front and rear axle	6,000 miles	GL-6	As required	Check
17	Drag link	6,000 miles	Chassis B	2 places as required	
18	Brake and clutch pedal springs	6,000 miles	Engine oil	As required	
21	Transfer case	6,000 miles	GL-5	As required	Check
22	Throttle bell crank—L6	12,000 miles	Engine oil	As required	

4

Table 1   LUBRICATION SCHEDULE (continued)

1975 Models

No.	Lubrication Points	Lubrication Period	Type of Lubrication	Quantity	Remarks
1	Air cleaner	15,000 miles		As required	See text
4	Control linkage points	15,000 miles	Engine oil	As required	Brush or spray to apply
7	Tie rod ends	7,500 miles	Chassis lubricant	2 places as required	
8	Wheel bearings	30,000 miles	Wheel bearing grease	2 places as required	
9	Steering gear	30,000 miles			Check for grease leak Do not lubricate
10	Master cylinder	7,500 miles	Delco Supreme No. 11 or DOT-3 fluids	As required	Check—add fluid when necessary
11	Transmission—manual	7,500 miles	GL-5	As required	Keep even with filler plug
	—automatic	7,500 miles	Dexron® II or equivalent	As required	
12	Carburetor linkage—V8	7,500 miles	Engine oil	As required	
13	Universal joints	7,500 miles	Chassis lubricant	As required	
14	Drive shaft slip joints	7,500 miles	Chassis lubricant	3 places as required	
15	Front and rear axle	7,500 miles	GL-5	As required	Check
17	Drag link	7,500 miles	Chassis lubricant	2 places as required	
18	Brake and clutch pedal springs	7,500 miles	Engine oil	As required	
21	Transfer case	7,500 miles	GL-5	As required	Check
22	Throttle bell crank—L6	15,000 miles	Engine oil	As required	

* Replace cam and lubricator at 24,000-mile intervals.
** Replace points at 12,000-mile intervals.

1. Before draining the old oil, thoroughly warm up the engine so the oil will drain freely. Place a drip pan beneath the engine and unscrew the drain plug (**Figure 3**). Allow 10-15 minutes for the oil to completely drain and reinstall the drain plug.

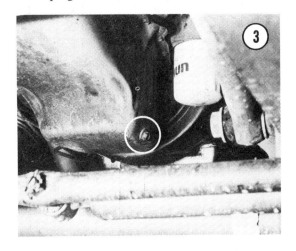

2. On a vehicle equipped with an oil cooler, relocate the drip pan beneath the cooler, remove the drain plug, and allow an additional 5 minutes for draining. Then reinstall the drain plug.

> NOTE: *Not all coolers are equipped with a drain plug. In such case, it will be necessary to disconnect the bottom cooler hose and direct it into the drip pan. When the oil has ceased to drain, be sure to install the hose correctly and tighten the clamp or the union.*

3. Relocate the drip pan beneath the oil filter, unscrew the filter, and allow about 5 minutes for the oil to drain. Discard the filter. When the oil has ceased to drain, thoroughly clean the filter mounting flange with solvent and wipe it dry with a clean cloth. Lightly coat the sealing ring of the new filter with fresh oil and screw the filter onto the block. When it makes contact with the sealing flange, tighten it ¼ turn by hand.

4. Fill the engine with the correct grade (Table 2) and amount (**Table 3**) of fresh oil and install the oil filler cap.

5. Start the engine and allow it to idle for several minutes to ensure that the oil has had a chance to circulate throughout the system. On some vehicles, the oil pressure warning light may re-

Table 3   ENGINE OIL CAPACITY

Engine	Capacity*
292 cid 6	5 quarts
305 cid V6	5 quarts
All other engines (6 and V8)	4 quarts

*Add 1 quart with filter change (e.g., the 292 cid 6 requires 6 quarts for refill after the oil and filter have been changed.

main on for several seconds after the engine is first started; this is normal. While the engine is running, check the drain plugs and the filter for leaks and correct them if necessary. Then, shut off the engine and check the oil level with the dipstick. If necessary, add oil to correct the level.

TRANSMISSION

Procedures for checking the oil (fluid) level in both manual and automatic transmissions are presented in Chapter Three. Oil change in automatic transmissions is recommended at 24,000-mile intervals with normal use. If the vehicle is driven only a few hundred miles each month, or is driven mostly in city traffic, or is used to tow a trailer, the oil should be changed more frequently (12,000 miles), as is the case if the vehicle is operated in extremely cold climate where the temperature is frequently below 10°F. Acids that form in the transmission during short-haul driving or during operation in extremely cold climates damage moving parts. Also, the oil should be changed if water has entered the transmission.

Manual Transmission Oil Change

Prior to draining the transmission, drive the vehicle for several miles to warm the oil so that it will flow freely. Remove the fill/level plug (**Figure 4**). Place a drip pan beneath the transmission and unscrew the drain plug (**Figure 5**). Allow the oil to drain for 10-15 minutes. Clean the drain plug and install it. Tighten the plug firmly but be careful not to overtighten it and risk stripping the threads on the transmission housing.

Refer to **Table 4** and fill the transmission with the correct amount and grade of oil. The trans-

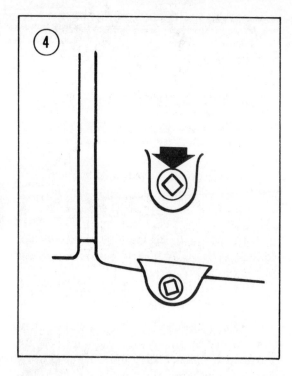

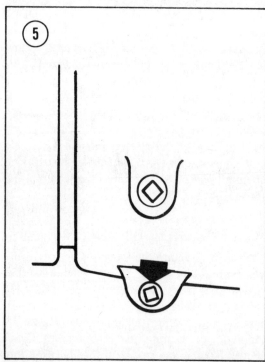

the transmission. Check to make sure the drain plug does not leak.

Automatic Transmission Fluid Change

Prior to draining the transmission, drive the vehicle for several miles to warm up the fluid so it will drain freely. The vehicle must sit level during draining and filling. If a hoist or a pit are not available, a mechanic's "creeper" will be helpful for working beneath the vehicle.

1. Place a drip pan beneath the transmission and unscrew the drain plug from the pan (**Figure 6**). Allow about 5 minutes for the fluid to drain.

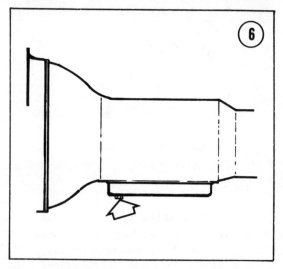

2. When draining is complete, screw in the plug.

3. Using a clean funnel with a fine-mesh filter, pour the correct amount (see Table 4) of fresh Dexron automatic transmission fluid through the filler pipe. Start the engine and allow it to idle for 2 minutes with the gear selector in the PARK position. Increase the engine speed to a fast idle (no more than about 1,200 rpm) and allow the engine and transmission to reach normal operating temperature.

4. With the handbrake set and the service brake depressed, slowly move the selector through all of the gear positions. Return the selector to PARK and recheck the fluid level. If necessary, add fluid to bring the level midway between the ADD and FULL marks on the dipstick. Remember: Do not overfill the transmission; too much fluid is harm-

mission oil level is correct when oil just begins to seep out of the fill/level hole. Screw in and tighten the fill/level plug taking care not to over-tighten, and wipe excess oil from the outside of

Table 4   TRANSMISSION OIL

Transmission	Oil Grade	Capacity
3-speed/4-speed synchromesh	SAE 80W*, SAE 80W-90, GL-5	**
Powerglide/Powerflo	Dexron automatic transmission fluid or equivalent	2 quarts
Turbo Hydra-Matic 350	Dexron automatic transmission fluid or equivalent	2.5 quarts
400	Dexron automatic transmission fluid or equivalent	7.5 pints

*SAE 80W should be used if sustained ambient temperature is below 32°F.
**Fill to bottom of fill/level hole in the side of the transmission.

ful. If the level is above the maximum mark on the dipstick, sufficient fluid must be drained to correct the level.

5. When the fluid level is correct, check for and correct any leaks at the filler tube connection and around the edge of the pan. Then road test the vehicle to ensure the transmission operates correctly. After the vehicle has been driven about 125 miles check the level once again and correct it if necessary.

AXLES

The oil level in the axle differentials should be checked and corrected if necessary every 6,000 miles of road use, every 1,000 miles of off-road use, and daily is the vehicle is operated in deep water. (In this instance, the check is essential to determine if water has entered the axle, in which case the contaminated oil must be drained and the axle filled with fresh oil.)

Oil Level

The vehicle must be sitting level when the axle oil level is checked. Wipe the area around the fill/level plug clean. Unscrew the fill/level plug from the differential case (**Figure 7**—front, **Figure 8**—rear). If the level is correct, a small amount of oil will begin to seep out of the hole. If it does not, slowly add oil to correct the level. For standard differentials, add hypoid gear lubricant (see **Table 5**). For Positraction and Power-Lok (limited-slip) differentials, add hypoid gear lubricant compounded for these units.

When the level is correct, screw in and tighten the fill/level plug and wipe any excess oil from the outside of the differential case.

On models equipped with ball-and-socket hubs, unscrew the filler plug from the hub (**Figure 9**) and check the level. If necessary, add SAE 140 multipurpose lubricant. Each hub holds ½ pint. Install the plugs and tighten them securely.

Table 5   AXLE LUBRICANTS

Ambient Temperature	Viscosity
Below 10°F	SAE 80
Up to 100°F	SAE 90
Consistently above 100°F	SAE 140

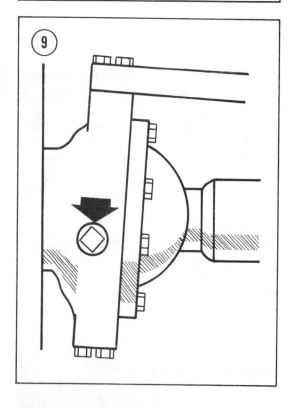

Oil Changing

Prior to draining the oil from the differentials, drive the vehicle for several miles with the transfer case shifted into high 4-wheel drive and the front hubs engaged (if they are lock-out type) to warm up the oil so it will flow freely. With the vehicle sitting level, wipe the area around the fill/level plug clean and unscrew the plug. Place a drip pan beneath the differential being drained and unscrew the bottom cover bolt (**Figure 10**) or the drain plug if fitted. Allow 10-15 minutes for the oil to drain and then install the bottom cover bolt.

Refer to *Oil Level* above and fill the differential with the appropriate type of hypoid gear lubricant until the oil level reaches the bottom of the fill/level hole and just begins to seep out.

Then install the fill/level plug and tighten it securely. Wipe any spilled oil from the differential housing.

After the vehicle has been driven for about 100 miles, check for and correct any leaks around the edge of the cover, particularly in the area of the bottom bolt. If leakage is found, recheck and correct the oil level after the leak has been corrected.

TRANSFER CASE

Oil Level

The vehicle must be sitting level when the transfer case oil level is checked. Wipe the area around the fill/level plug (**Figure 11**) clean and unscrew the plug. On conventional 4-wheel drive vehicles, oil should seep out of the fill/level opening. If it does not, slowly add oil to correct

the level (see **Table 6**). On full-time 4-wheel drive vehicles, the level should be ½ in. from the bottom of the hole. When the level is correct, screw in and tighten the fill/level plug and wipe any spilled oil from the transfer case.

Table 6   TRANSFER CASE LUBRICANTS

Drive System	Viscosity*
Conventional 4-wheel drive	SAE 80, SAE 90 GL-5 gear lubricant
Full-time 4-wheel drive	SAE 10W-30, SAE 10W-40

*The lighter grade should be used in consistently cold climate.

Oil Changing

Prior to draining the oil from the transfer case, drive the vehicle for several miles with the transfer case shifted into high 4-wheel drive and the front hubs engaged (if they are lock-out types) to warm up the oil so it will drain freely.

With the vehicle sitting level, wipe the area clean around the fill/level plug and unscrew it. Place a drip pan beneath the transfer case and unscrew the drain plug (**Figure 12**). Allow 10-15 minutes for the oil to drain and then clean and install the drain plug.

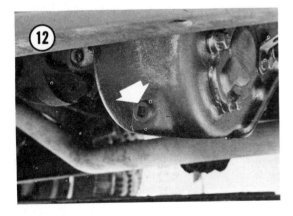

Fill the transfer case with oil (Table 6) until the oil level reaches the bottom of the fill/level hole and just begins to seep out (conventional 4-wheel drive) or is ½ in. from the bottom of the hole (full-time 4-wheel drive). Then install the fill/level plug and tighten it securely. Wipe any spilled oil from the transfer case.

After the vehicle has been driven for about 100 miles, check for and correct any leaks at either plug. If leakage is found, recheck and correct the oil level after the leak has been corrected.

CHASSIS LUBRICATION

Complete chassis lubrication should be performed at the intervals shown in Table 1. For extensive off-road use, the interval should be every 1,000 miles, and if the vehicle is operated in deep water, chassis lubrication should be attended to daily.

Lubrication points and fittings and recommended intervals are shown in Figures 1 and 2. Recommended lubricants are also shown. Equivalent lubricants available through most major oil companies can be used. However, make sure the oil dealer knows the specific application so that he can recommend a suitable substitute.

A simple hand-operated grease gun like the one shown in **Figure 13** is a worthwhile investment, particularly if the vehicle is used extensively off-road and in mud, snow, and water. An adapter like the one shown below the grease gun is required to lubricate the flush-mounted fittings in the double Cardon joints (constant-velocity joints) on the drive shafts.

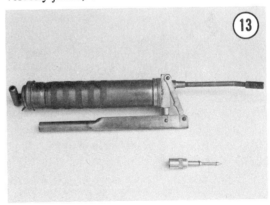

Do not overlook items such as gear selector linkage, clutch linkage, parking brake linkage, speedometer cable, clutch release equalizer, and the steering gearbox. Lack of lubrication on these items will make control operation difficult in addition to causing premature wear. However, lubricants should be used sparingly and excess oil should be wiped away to prevent it from attracting dirt which will also accelerate wear.

BODY LUBRICATION

Door, hood, and tailgate hinges and latches, and front seat tracks should be lubricated at the 6,000-mile intervals to ensure smooth operation and reduce wear.

Apply all lubricant sparingly, operating the mechanism several times to aid penetration.

Then, wipe off the excess lubricant with a clean, dry cloth to prevent it from attracting dirt and from soiling clothing, carpeting, or upholstery.

STEERING GEAR

The steering gearbox on late model vehicles (1971-1975) is permanently lubricated and should require no service other than checking for seal leakage, indicated by thick grease deposits on the steering gearbox around the cover. In such case, the unit should be referred to a dealer for repair.

CHAPTER FIVE

TUNE-UP

To ensure maximum operating economy and service life, and to comply with regulated exhaust emission standards, a complete tune-up should be performed at the intervals shown in **Table 1**.

Table 1   TUNE-UP INTERVALS

Year	Interval
1969-1974	12,000 miles or 12 months
1975	22,500 miles

NOTE: *This chapter covers 1967-1975 models. If you have a 1976 or later model, be sure to check the Supplement at the rear of this book for the latest information.*

These recommended intervals are based on normal use—a combination of highway, city, and off-road driving. If the vehicle is used extensively for stop-and-go city driving, more frequent tune-ups may be required. Extensive off-road use should have little effect on tune and the recommended intervals can generally be followed with little degradation of performance or economy.

EXPENDABLE PARTS

The expendable ignition parts (spark plugs, points, and condenser) should be routinely re-placed during the tune-up. In addition, some expendable emission control devices on some models must also be replaced if the vehicle is to remain within legal emission standards. These devices are shown in Chapter One. You should have all of the necessary parts on hand before you begin a tune-up.

TUNE-UP SEQUENCE

Because different systems in an engine interact, the procedures should be done in the following order.

1. Check cylinder head bolt torque
2. Adjust valve clearance (mechanical lifters)
3. Work on ignition system
4. Adjust carburetor

CYLINDER HEAD BOLTS

It is generally not necessary to tighten the cylinder head bolts of an engine that has been in service for some time, unless leakage is suspected. However, the torque can be periodically checked and corrected if necessary.

1. Note the location of breather hoses and disconnect them and the oil fill cap from the valve cover. Unscrew the bolts which hold the valve cover to the cylinder head and remove the valve cover. It may be necessary to tap the valve cover

rearward, using the heel of your hand or a soft mallet, to break the gasket loose.

2. Tighten the cylinder head bolts in the appropriate pattern shown in **Figure 1** to the torque specified in **Table 2**.

Table 2   CYLINDER HEAD BOLT TORQUE

Engine	Torque
All in-line 6 cylinder	95 ft.-lb.
All V8 except 454 cid	65 ft.-lb.
454 cid (Mark IV)	80 ft.-lb.

Valve Clearance Adjustment

Correct valve clearance in engines equipped with hydraulic lifters is maintained automatically in many cases throughout the life of the engine. However, if incorrect valve clearance is suspected as a possible cause of poor performance or the engine has logged many thousands of miles, the valve clearance should be checked and corrected if necessary by a dealer or automotive specialist.

IGNITION SYSTEM

Two basic types of ignition systems are used on Chevrolet/GMC 4 x 4 vehicles covered in this manual; conventional mechanical contact breaker ignition (1967-1974), and breakerless electronic ignition (1975).

Service to breakerless ignition systems is limited to replacement of spark plugs, checking and correcting ignition timing, and inspection and repair of wiring. Total ignition service is presented for mechanical contact breaker systems. The service procedures are presented separately.

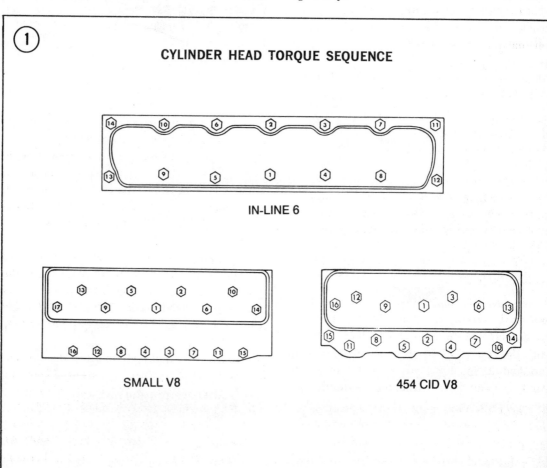

(1) CYLINDER HEAD TORQUE SEQUENCE

IN-LINE 6

SMALL V8

454 CID V8

Mechanical Contact Breaker Ignition

The expendable ignition parts (spark plugs, points, and condenser) should be replaced and the contact breaker dwell angle and ignition timing checked and adjusted if necessary at the intervals shown in Table 1. If the vehicle is used primarily in stop-and-go city driving, or if it is driven extensively at low engine speeds, replacement, or at least cleaning and adjustment of spark plug electrode and contact breaker gaps, should be carried out more frequently.

1. Identify the high-tension spark plug leads and disconnect them from the spark plugs by carefully pulling and twisting the insulated caps; do not pull the leads loose by grasping the wires. Unscrew the spark plugs from the cylinder head(s), keeping them in order. Examine the spark plugs and compare their condition to **Figure 2**. The condition of the spark plugs is an indication of engine condition, and can warn of developing trouble. For this reason, it is important that the spark plugs be kept in order until they have been inspected so that unsatisfactory conditions can be further isolated by cylinder.

2. Remove the distributor cap and rotor. Clean the high-tension spark plug and coil leads and check them for chafing, melting, or cracked insulation and replace any that are deteriorated or damaged. Clean the distributor cap and rotor and inspect them for cracks, burnt contacts, and carbon tracking (**Figure 3**). Pitting of the rotor contact and arc-over between the contacts in the cap generally indicate the presence of resistance, either in the cap or the rotor or both. If excessive pitting or arcing are found, it is a good idea to replace both parts.

3. Unplug the quick disconnect terminal (**Figure 4**). Unscrew the retaining screw from the condensers and the contact set attaching screw. Note the location of the ground wire so it may be installed in the same place, and remove the condenser and breaker from the distributor.

4. Check the movement of the centrifugal advance mechanism by carefully turning the contact breaker cam clockwise by hand and releasing it. It should snap back against spring tension. If it does not, the distributor should be checked

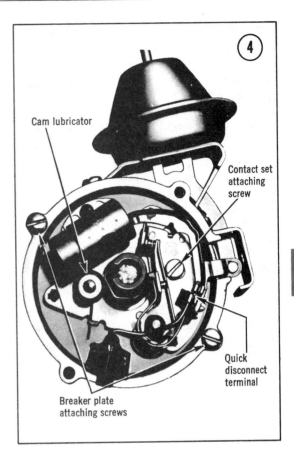

Cam lubricator

Contact set attaching screw

Quick disconnect terminal

Breaker plate attaching screws

for wear or damage. This is a job for a dealer or an automotive electrical specialist.

5. Wipe cam and breaker plate clean. Lightly coat the cam with special distributor cam grease. Never use oil or common grease; they will break down under the high-temperature and frictional load and are likely to find their way onto the contacts.

6. Install the new contact breaker assembly and condenser in the distributor. Make sure the ground lead, condenser lead, and primary lead are installed exactly as they were before. Double check the connections and screw to ensure they are tight.

7. Rotate the crankshaft to close the breaker contacts and check their alignment (**Figure 5**). The breaker must be accurately aligned to ensure full service life and performance. If alignment is not correct, carefully bend the stationary contact; do not bend movable arm (**Figure 6**).

8. Rotate the crankshaft until the breaker contacts are at their maximum opening and the lifter

(2)

SPARK PLUG CONDITION

NORMAL
• Identified by light tan or gray deposits on the firing tip.
• Can be cleaned.

GAP BRIDGED
• Identify by deposit buildup closing gap between electrodes.
• Caused by oil or carbon fouling. If deposits are not excessive, the plug can be cleaned.

OIL FOULED
• Identified by wet black deposits on the insulator shell bore electrodes.
• Caused by excessive oil entering combustion chamber through worn rings and pistons, excessive clearance between valve guides and stems, or worn or loose bearings. Can be cleaned. If engine is not repaired, use a hotter plug.

CARBON FOULED
• Identified by black, dry fluffy carbon deposits on insulator tips, exposed shell surfaces and electrodes.
• Caused by too cold a plug, weak ignition, dirty air cleaner, defective fuel pump, too rich a fuel mixture, improperly operating heat riser, or excessive idling. Can be cleaned.

LEAD FOULED
• Identified by dark gray, black, yellow, or tan deposits or a fused glazed coating on the insulator tip.
• Caused by highly leaded gasoline. Can be cleaned.

WORN
• Identified by severely eroded or worn electrodes.
• Caused by normal wear. Should be replaced.

FUSED SPOT DEPOSIT
• Identified by melted or spotty deposits resembling bubbles or blisters.
• Caused by sudden acceleration. Can be cleaned.

OVERHEATING
• Identified by a white or light gray insulator with small black or gray brown spots and with bluish-burnt appearance of electrodes.
• Caused by engine overheating, wrong type of fuel, loose spark plugs, too hot a plug, low fuel pump pressure, or incorrect ignition timing. Replace the plug.

PREIGNITION
• Identified by melted electrodes and possibly blistered insulator. Metallic deposits on insulator indicate engine damage.
• Caused by wrong type of fuel, incorrect ignition timing or advance, too hot a plug, burn valves, or engine overheating. Replace the plug.

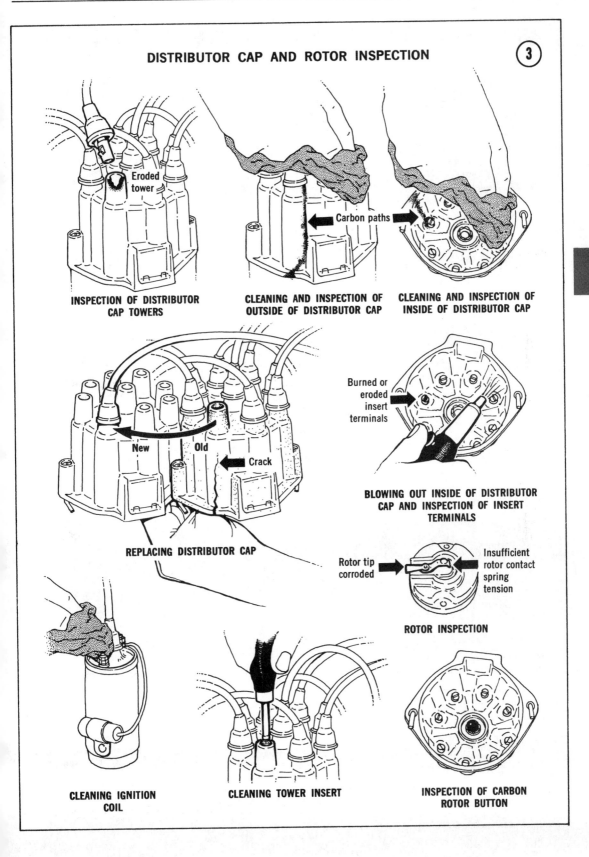

DISTRIBUTOR CAP AND ROTOR INSPECTION ③

Eroded tower

INSPECTION OF DISTRIBUTOR CAP TOWERS

Carbon paths

CLEANING AND INSPECTION OF OUTSIDE OF DISTRIBUTOR CAP

CLEANING AND INSPECTION OF INSIDE OF DISTRIBUTOR CAP

New **Old** **Crack**

REPLACING DISTRIBUTOR CAP

Burned or eroded insert terminals

BLOWING OUT INSIDE OF DISTRIBUTOR CAP AND INSPECTION OF INSERT TERMINALS

Rotor tip corroded **Insufficient rotor contact spring tension**

ROTOR INSPECTION

CLEANING IGNITION COIL

CLEANING TOWER INSERT

INSPECTION OF CARBON ROTOR BUTTON

5

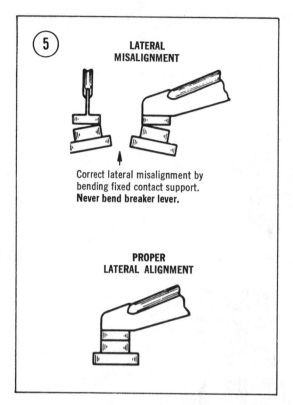

LATERAL
MISALIGNMENT

Correct lateral misalignment by
bending fixed contact support.
Never bend breaker lever.

PROPER
LATERAL ALIGNMENT

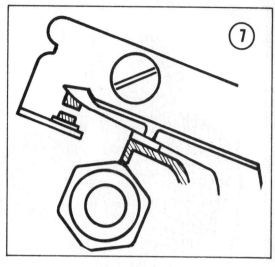

moving the contact breaker plate, tighten the screw and recheck the gap. If a dwell meter is available, connect it in accordance with the manufacturer's instructions and measure the dwell angle of the contacts. If the dwell angle is below that shown in **Table 3** the contact gap is too large, and if the dwell angle is greater than specified, the contact gap is too small. If necessary, readjust the contacts.

9. Set the electrode gap on the new spark plugs (Table 3). Adjust the gap by bending only the side (ground) electrode (**Figure 9**). Screw the spark plugs into the cylinder head and tighten them to 15 ft.-lb.

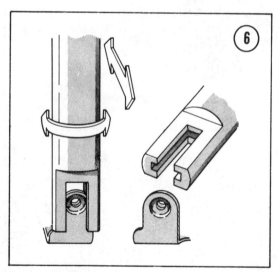

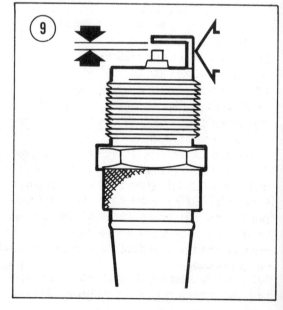

heel rests on the peak of one of the cam lobes (**Figure 7**). Check the gap with a flat feeler gauge. The gap for new points should be 0.019 in. and for used points 0.016 in. To adjust the contact gap, loosen the screw which attaches the contact breaker assembly to the distributor (**Figure 8**) and move the fixed plate as required until the gap is correct. Then, without further

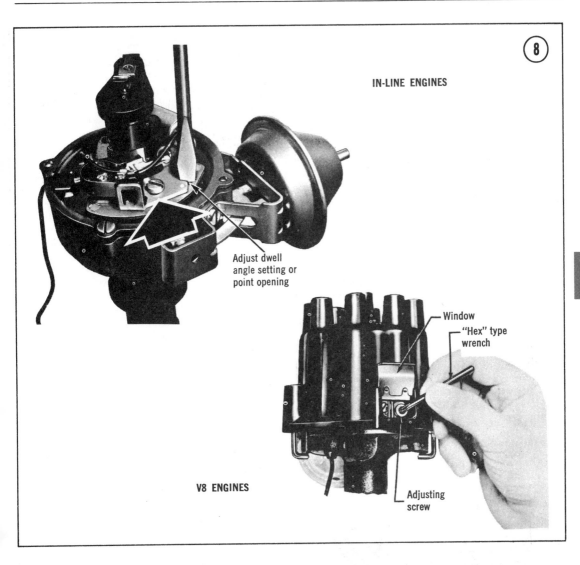

⑧

IN-LINE ENGINES

Adjust dwell angle setting or point opening

Window

"Hex" type wrench

V8 ENGINES

Adjusting screw

10. Install the rotor and the distributor cap. Connect the high-tension leads to the spark plugs as shown in **Figure 10**.

11. Adjust the ignition timing using a timing light and a tachometer. Connect the instruments according to the manufacturer's instructions. (The timing light must be connected to the No. 1 cylinder spark plug. This is the front cylinder on 6-cylinder engines and the front left cylinder on V8 engines.) Clean the timing marks on the crankshaft pulley and the timing plate (**Figure 11**) and mark them with chalk so they can easily be seen. Disconnect and plug the vacuum lines at the distributor.

12. Start the engine and set the idle at 600 rpm with the throttle stop screw (**Figure 12**). This

⑫

Table 3   IGNITION SPECIFICATIONS

230 CID SIX	1967	1968	1969	250 CID SIX	1967	1968	1969
Initial ignition timing	4° BTDC (all)	4° BTDC (except syn w/AIR=0°)	0° BTDC (syn) 4° BTDC (auto)	Initial ignition timing	4° BTDC (all)	4° BTDC (except syn w/AIR=0°)	0° BTDC (syn) 4° BTDC (auto)
Spark plug Type Gap	AC-46N 0.035 in.	AC-46N 0.035 in.	AC-R46N 0.035 in.	Spark plug Type Gap	AC-46N 0.035 in.	AC-46N 0.035 in.	AC-R46N 0.035 in.
Dwell angle	31-34°	31-34°	31-34°	Dwell angle	31-34°	31-34°	31-34°
Distributor point gap	0.016 in. (used) 0.019 in. (new)	0.016 in. (used) 0.019 in. (new)	0.016 in. (used) 0.019 in. (new)	Distributor point gap	0.016 in (used) 0.019 in. (new)	0.016 in (used) 0.019 in. (new)	0.016 in (used) 0.019 in. (new)
Idle speed	w/o AIR 500 (s & a) w/AIR 700 (s) 500 (a)	w/o AIR 500 (s & a) w/AIR 700 (s) 500 (a)	700 (s) 550 (a)	Idle speed	w/o AIR 500 (s & a) w/AIR 700 (s) 500 (a)	w/o AIR 500 (s & a) w/AIR 700 (s) 500 (a)	700 (s) 550 (a)

250 CID SIX	1970	1971	1972	1973	1974	1975
Initial ignition timing	0° BTDC (syn) 4° BTDC (auto)	4° BTDC (all)	4° BTDC (all)	6° BTDC (lt dty) 4° BTDC (hvy dty)	See engine decal	See engine decal
Spark plug Type Gap	AC-R46N 0.035 in.	AC-R46TS 0.035 in.	AC-R46T 0.035 in.	AC-R46T 0.035 in.	AC-R46T 0.035 in.	AC-R46TX 0.060 in.
Dwell angle	31-34°	31-34°	31-34°	31-34°	31-34°	See engine decal
Distributor point gap	0.016 in (used) 0.019 in. (new)	0.016 in (used) 0.019 in. (new)	0.016 in (used) 0.019 in. (new)	0.016 in (used) 0.019 in. (new)	0.016 in (used) 0.019 in. (new)	See engine decal
Idle speed	700 (s) 550 (a)	550 (s) 500 (a)	700 (s) 600 (a)	700 (s) 600 (a)	850 (s-LD) 600 (s-HD) 600 (a-LD & HD)	See engine decal

Legend:

- syn or (s) = standard (synchromesh) transmission
- auto or (a) = automatic transmission
- AIR = Air Injection Reactor system (emission control)
- lt dty or LD = Light duty
- hvy dty or HD = Heavy duty
- Fed or F = Federal emission control standards or regulations

- Cal or C = California emission control standards or regulations
- "10" = Series 10 vehicles
- "200", "185", "220", etc. = Refers to horsepower rating within a given displacement engine
- trk = Truck (including Blazer and Jimmy)
- sub = Suburban (carryall)

Table 3   IGNITION SPECIFICATIONS (continued)

283 CID V8	1967	292 CID SIX	1967	1968	1969	1970
Initial ignition timing	4° BTDC (all)	Initial ignition timing	4° BTDC (all)	4° BTDC (except syn w/AIR=0°)	0° BTDC (syn) 4° BTDC (auto)	0° BTDC (syn) 4° BTDC (auto)
Spark plug Type Gap	 AC-44 0.035 in.	Spark plug Type Gap	 AC-44N 0.035 in.	 AC-44N 0.035 in.	 AC-CR44N 0.035 in.	 AC-CR44N 0.035 in.
Dwell angle	28-32°	Dwell angle	31-34°	31-34°	31-34°	31-34°
Distributor point gap	0.016 in. (used) 0.019 in. (new)	Distributor point gap	0.016 in. (used) 0.019 in. (new)	0.016 in. (used) 0.019 in. (new)	0.016 In. (used) 0.019 in. (new)	0.016 in. (used) 0.019 in. (new)
Idle speed	w/o AIR 500 (s & a) w/AIR 700 (s) 500 (a)	Idle speed	w/o AIR 500 (s & a) w/AIR 700 (s) 500 (a)	w/o AIR 500 (s & a) w/AIR 700 (s) 600 (a)	700 (s) 550 (a)	700 (s) 550 (a)

292 CID SIX	1971	1972	1973	1974	1975
Initial ignition timing	4° BTDC (all)	4° BTDC (all)	4° BTDC (Fed) 8° BTDC (Cai)	See engine decal	See engine decal
Spark plug Type Gap	 AC-R44T 0.035 in.	 AC-R44T 0.035 in.	 AC-R44T 0.035 in.	 AC-R44T 0.035 in.	 AC-R44TX 0.060 in.
Dwell angle	31-34°	31-34°	31-34°	31-34°	See engine decal
Distributor point gap	0.016 in. (used) 0.019 in. (new)	0.016 in. (used) 0.019 in. (new)	0.016 in. (used) 0.019 in. (new)	0.016 in. (used) 0.019 in. (new)	See engine decal
Idle speed	550 (s) 500 (a)	700 (s & a)	700 (s & a) (Fed) 600 (s & a) (Cal)	600 (s & a)	See engine decal

Legend:
- syn or (s) = standard (synchromesh) transmission
- auto or (a) = automatic transmission
- AIR — Air Injection Reactor system (emission control)
- lt dty or LD = Light duty
- hvy dty or HD = Heavy duty
- Fed or F = Federal emission control standards or regulations
- Cal or C = California emission control standards or regulations
- "10" = Series 10 vehicles
- "200", "185", "220", etc. = Refers to horsepower rating within a given displacement engine
- trk = Truck (including Blazer and Jimmy)
- sub = Suburban (carryall)

Table 3   IGNITION SPECIFICATIONS (continued)

307 CID V8	1968	1969	1970	1971	1972
Initial ignition timing	2° BTDC (all)	2° BTDC (all)	2° BTDC (all)	4° BTDC (except 200 (a) = 8° BTDC)	4° BTDC (except "10" (a) = 8° BTDC)
Spark plug Type Gap	AC-44S 0.035 in.	AC-R44 0.035 in.	AC-R44 0.035 in.	AC-R45TS 0.035 in.	AC-R44T 0.035 in.
Dwell angle	28-32°	28-32°	28-32°	31-34°	29-31°
Distributor point gap	0.016 in. (used) 0.019 in. (new)	0.016 in. (used) 0.019 in. (new)	0.016 in. (used) 0.019 in. (new)	0.016 in. (used) 0.019 in. (new)	0.016 in. (used) 0.019 in. (new)
Idle speed	w/o AIR 500 (s & a) w/AIR 700 (s) 600 (a)	700 (s) 600 (a)	700 (s) 600 (a)	600/550 (s & a-200) 550/500 (s & a-215)	900 (s) (F) 950 (s) (C) 600 (a) all

307 CID V8	1973	327 CID V8	1967	1968
Initial ignition timing	4° BTDC (s) LD; 8° BTDC (a) LD; TDC = HD	Initial ignition timing	0° BTDC w/AIR (all) 8° "185" 2° "220"	0° BTDC w/AIR (s) 4° BTDC w/AIR (a) 8° BTDC w/o AIR ("185" only)
Spark plug Type Gap	AC-R44T 0.035 in.	Spark plug Type Gap	AC-C43 ("185") AC-44 ("220") 0.035 in.	AC-C43 ("185") AC-44 ("220") 0.035 in.
Dwell angle	29-31°	Dwell angle	28-32°	28-32°
Distributor point gap	0.016 in. (used) 0.019 in. (new)	Distributor point gap	0.016 in. (used) 0.019 in. (new)	0.016 in. (used) 0.019 in. (new)
Idle speed	900 (s) (F) 600 (s) (C) 600 (a) all	Idle speed	w/o AIR 500 (s & a) w/AIR "220" 700 (s) 600 (a)	700 (s) all 600 (a) "220" 500 (a) "185"

Legend:
- syn or (s) = standard (synchromesh) transmission
- auto or (a) = automatic transmission
- AIR = Air Injection Reactor system (emission control)
- lt dty or LD = Light duty
- hvy dty or HD = Heavy duty
- Fed or F = Federal emission control standards or regulations
- Cal or C = California emission control standards or regulations
- "10" = Series 10 vehicles
- "200", "185", "220", etc. = Refers to horsepower rating within a given displacement engine
- trk = Truck (including Blazer and Jimmy)
- sub = Suburban (carryall)

Table 3   IGNITION SPECIFICATIONS (continued)

350 CID V8	1969	1970	1971	1972	1973
Initial ignition timing	4° BTDC (except "255" (s) = 0° BTDC)	4° BTDC "215" (s) & "255" (a); TDC "255" (s)	4° BTDC (s) 8° BTDC (a)	4° BTDC (s) 8° BTDC (a)	8° BTDC LD (s) 12° BTDC LD (a) 4° BTDC-HD
Spark plug **Type** **Gap**	AC-CR43 "215" AC-R44 "255" 0.035 in.	AC-R44 (all) 0.035 in.	AC-R44TS 0.035 in.	AC-R44T 0.035 in.	AC-R44T 0.035 in.
Dwell angle	28-32°	28-32°	31-34°	29-31°	29-31°
Distributor point gap	0.016 in. (used) 0.019 in. (new)	0.016 in. (used) 0.019 in. (new)	0.016 in. (used) 0.019 in. (new)	0.016 in. (used) 0.019 in. (new)	0.016 in. (used) 0.019 in. (new)
Idle speed	500 "215" (s & a) 700 "255" (s) 600 "255" (a)	700 (s) 600 (a)	600 (s) 550 (a)	800 (s) 600 (a)	900 LD (s) 600 LD (a) & HD (s & a)

350 CID V8	1974	1975	454 CID V8	1975
Initial ignition timing	①	See engine decal	Initial ignition timing	See engine decal
Spark plug **Type** **Gap**	AC-R44T 0.035 in.	AC-R44TX 0.060 in.	Spark plug **Type** **Gap**	AC-R44TX 0.060 in.
Dwell angle	29-31°	See engine decal	Dwell angle	See engine decal
Distributor point gap	0.016 in. (used) 0.019 in. (new)	See engine decal	Distributor point gap	See engine decal
Idle speed	900 LD (s) 600 LD (a) & HD (s & a)	See engine decal	Idle speed	See engine decal

① 12° BTDC (a) F-all   8° BTDC (a) C trk
  8° BTDC (s) F-trk   6° BTDC (a) C sub
  6° BTDC (s) F-sub   4° BTDC (s) C all

Legend:
- syn or (s) = standard (synchromesh) transmission
- auto or (a) = automatic transmission
- AIR = Air Injection Reactor system (emission control)
- lt dty or LD = Light duty
- hvy dty or HD = Heavy duty
- Fed or F = Federal emission control standards or regulations
- Cal or C = California emission control standards or regulations
- "10" = Series 10 vehicles
- "200", "185", "220", etc. = Refers to horsepower rating within a given displacement engine
- trk = Truck (including Blazer and Jimmy)
- sub = Suburban (carryall)

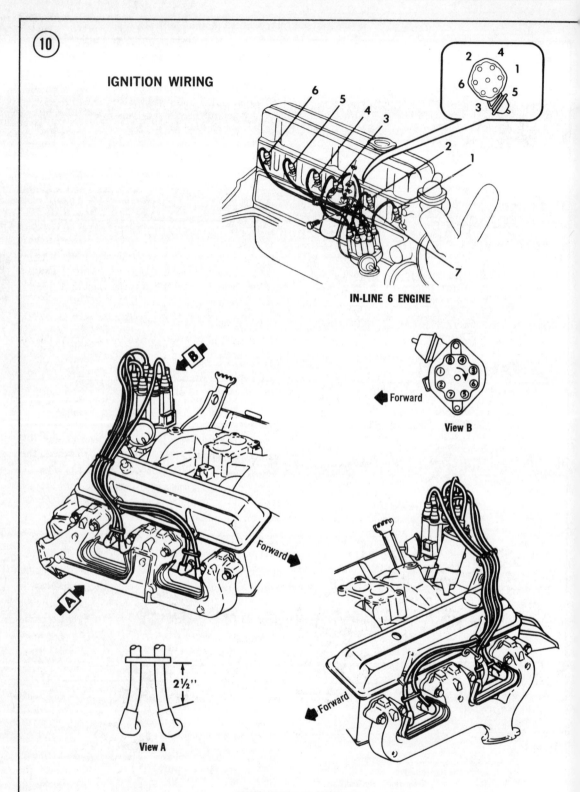

⑩

IGNITION WIRING

IN-LINE 6 ENGINE

Forward

View B

Forward

2½"

View A

Forward

SMALL BLOCK V8 ENGINE

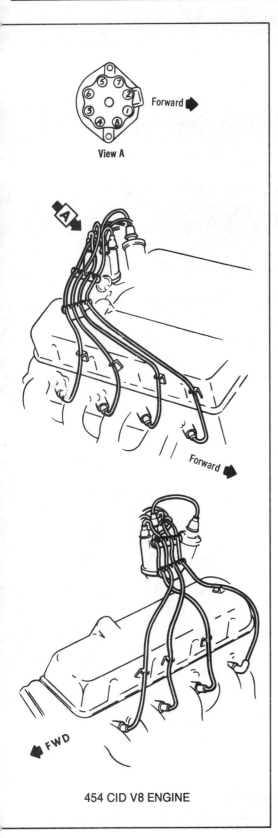

View A

454 CID V8 ENGINE

ensures that the centrifugal advance has not begun to work and that the timing indicated is the basic timing. Point the timing light at the timing marks. The timing mark on the pulley should line up with the appropriate mark on the timing plate (see Table 3).

13. If the timing is incorrect, shut off the engine and loosen the distributor lock bolt just far enough so the distributor can be turned by hand with some resistance. Start the engine and recheck the idle speed and correct it if necessary. Point the timing light at the timing marks and slowly rotate the distributor lock bolt without further moving the distributor and disturbing the setting. Start the engine, recheck the idle speed, and double-check the timing to ensure that the distributor did not move when the lock bolt was tightened.

14. After the initial timing has been set, check the operation of the centrifugal advance mechanism. Start the engine and slowly increase the speed while directing the timing light at the timing marks. Refer to Table 3 for the speed at which advance should begin, the maximum amount of advance, and the speed at which it occurs. If the timing does not advance, or if the values are appreciably lower than specified, the distributor should be entrusted to a dealer or an automotive ignition specialist for bench testing and repair.

15. Check the operation of the vacuum advance. Connect the vacuum line to the distributor vacuum advance unit. Slowly increase the engine speed from idle to the maximum centrifugal advance rpm and observe the timing marks with the timing light. Advance should begin sooner and continue farther than it did during the centrifugal advance test.

If either advance functions fail to work correctly, the distributor must be checked on special test equipment. In such case, refer the work to a dealer or an automotive ignition specialist.

Breakerless Ignition System

The spark plugs should be replaced and the timing checked and adjusted at the intervals shown in Table 1. Procedures are the same as those given under *Mechanical Contact Breaker*

TIMING MARKS

IN-LINE 6

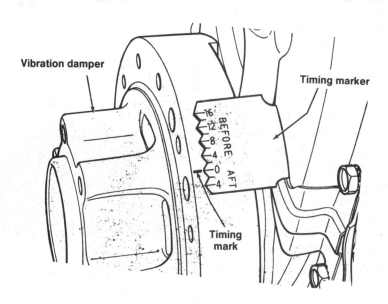

V-8

Ignition. If the vehicle is used primarily in stop-and-go city driving, or if it is driven extensively at low engine speeds, replacement, or at least cleaning and adjustment of the spark plugs should be carried out more frequently.

The only adjustments possible on the breaker-less ignition system are centrifugal and vacuum advance, both of which should be entrusted to a dealer or automotive ignition specialist. Also, suspected ignition trouble should be referred to a dealer or specialist; testing of the electronic module requires special equipment and skills and an otherwise good electronic circuit can be irreparably damaged by an incorrect test hookup.

CARBURETOR

Carburetor adjustments include normal idle and fast idle settings. Idle fuel/air mixture settings are not recommended; this affects exhaust emissions levels and cannot be accurately adjusted without the use of an exhaust gas analyzer. On many models, the idle air mixture screw is fitted with a limiter cap which prevents adjustments being made that will produce an out-of-specification idle mixture. If the idle cannot be correctly set with the idle speed screws, the carburetor should be referred to a dealer or an automotive tune-up specialist certified to make emission level related adjustments.

Accelerator Pump Discharge Test

1. Unscrew the wing nut from the top of the air cleaner assembly and remove the top cover.
2. Open the throttle smoothly and at the same time look in the top of the carburetor and observe the discharge from the accelerator pump nozzle (2 nozzles on 2- and 4-throat carburetors). A quick, steady stream of fuel should be discharged from the nozzle. If the stream is weak or erratic, it is likely that the accelerator pump is faulty and the carburetor should be referred to a dealer or automotive specialist for major service.

Basic Idle Setting (Engine Off)

1. Remove the air cleaner assembly. Carefully turn the idle mixture limiter caps clockwise until they stop (**Figure 13**).

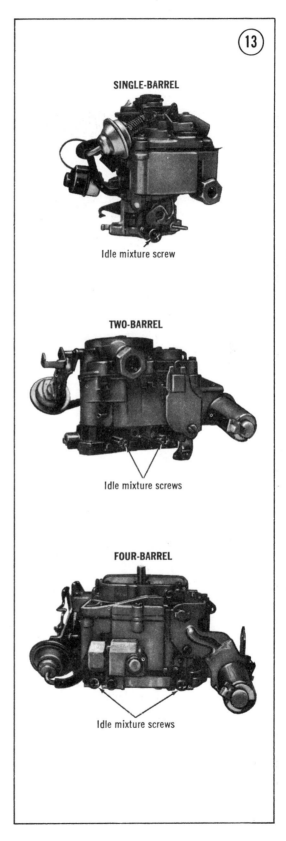

(13)

SINGLE-BARREL

Idle mixture screw

5

TWO-BARREL

Idle mixture screws

FOUR-BARREL

Idle mixture screws

2. Turn the idle speed adjusting screw (Figure 12) counterclockwise until the throttle butterfly seats in the throttle bore. If the butterfly does not seat with the idle speed screw backed out, check the plunger on the dashpot or solenoid (**Figure 14**) to make sure it is not holding the butterfly open. If the plunger is preventing the butterfly from seating, loosen the locknut on the dashpot and screw the dashpot into the bracket until the butterfly seats.

3. Turn the idle speed screw clockwise until it just touches its stop. Then turn the screw 1½ additional turns to set the basic idle.

Idle Setting (Engine On)

1. Set the parking brake, start the engine, and allow it to warm up for 20 minutes at 1,500 rpm by positioning the fast idle cam at the center notch (**Figure 15**). Do not touch the throttle during warm-up or the cam will release and return to normal idle.

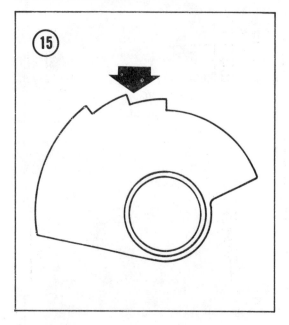

Idle speed (solenoid) screw

Idle speed (solenoid) screw

Idle speed (solenoid) screw

2. Connect a tachometer in accordance with the manufacturer's instructions. On vehicles with a standard transmission the selector must be in neutral, and on vehicles with automatic transmission the selector should be set at DRIVE. *Double check to make sure the parking brake will prevent the vehicle from moving with the*

transmission set in DRIVE. If it will not, shut off the engine and adjust the parking brake before proceeding. Check the choke butterfly to make sure it is fully open.

3. Turn on the headlights and select high beam to place a normal alternator load on the engine. If the vehicle is equipped with air conditioning make sure it is turned off.

4. Reinstall the air cleaner assembly. Set the curb idle speed by turning the idle speed adjusting screw as required, referring to Table 3 for the correct engine rpm. For carburetors equipped with a solenoid throttle modulator (Figure 14), turn the solenoid plunger in or out until the idle is correct. Then, disconnect the solenoid lead near the loom. Turn the idle speed screw as required to bring the idle to that specified in Table 5. Reconnect the solenoid lead and open the throttle slightly. The plunger should extend and remain extended as long as the ignition is on. Check the operation of the solenoid by turning off the engine and restarting it.

5. When the correct idle has been set with the idle speed screw(s), turn the idle mixture limiter (one on single-throat carburetors, 2 on 2- and 4-throat carburetors) until the idle is smooth.

NOTE: *On 2- and 4-throat carburetors, the 2 idle mixture limiters must be turned the same amount.*

Additional Checks

If the correct carburetor idle speed cannot be achieved as described above, and after the preceding recommended tune-up steps have been performed, the vacuum lines and fittings should be carefully inspected for leaks, and if leaks are found, they should be corrected before idle speed adjustment is attempted again.

If the above idle speed adjustment procedure is being used only to correct an unsatisfactory idle condition, the following areas (covered earlier in *Tune-Up*) must also be checked before the idle speed adjustment is attempted.

1. Electrical continuity in the ignition system
2. Spark plug condition and electrode gap
3. Contact breaker and condenser condition and adjustment (dwell angle)
4. Ignition timing
5. Valve clearance
6. Engine compression

If, after all of the services and adjustments described above have been accurately carried out and the idle speed is still not adjustable within specifications, 3 probable areas of investigation remain—carburetor fuel level, crankcase ventilation system condition, and idle air/fuel ration. The vehicle should then be referred to a dealer or automotive tune-up specialist for diagnosis and correction.

AIR CLEANER

Remove the air cleaner cover (**Figure 16**) and remove the filter element. Clean the inside of the filter case thoroughly and inspect the sealing gasket for breaks and deterioration. If the seal is less than perfect, it should be replaced.

The filter element should be replaced at 24,000-mile (V8) and 12,000-mile (in-line 6) intervals under normal driving conditions. If the vehicle is operated under extremely dusty conditions, the filter element should be replaced more frequently, when clogging is evident.

If the filter is equipped with a polyurethane band, this piece can be reused, provided it is not torn. Clean the band in solvent, not carburetor cleaner or acetone, and carefully squeeze it dry. Dip the band in a container of fresh engine oil and then carefully squeeze out the excess. Install the band as shown in **Figure 17**. Reassemble the air cleaner assembly making sure the cover seats completely around its circumference.

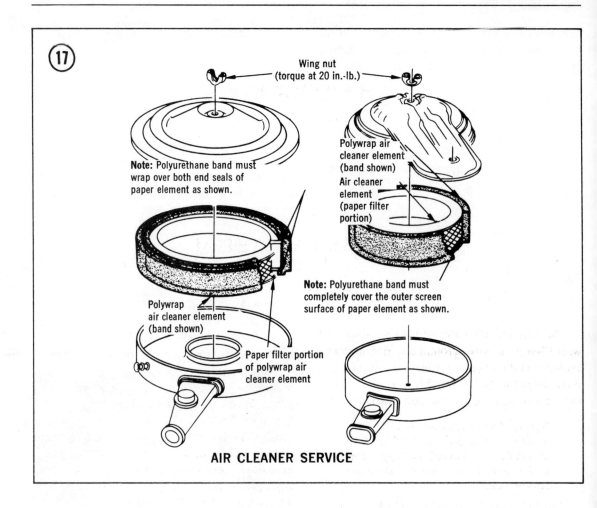

AIR CLEANER SERVICE

CHAPTER SIX

ELECTRICAL SYSTEM

Chevrolet/GMC 4 x 4 vehicles are equipped with 12-volt, negative-ground electrical systems. Included in this chapter are service and checkout procedures for the battery, fuses, starter, charging system, lighting system, and instruments.

NOTE: *This chapter covers 1967-1975 models. If you have a 1976 or later model, be sure to check the Supplement at the rear of this book for the latest information.*

When trouble is experienced in the electrical system, Chapter Two can prove valuable as a guide to isolating problem areas as well as explaining the functions and uses of electrical test equipment. Very often, electrical trouble can be traced to a simple cause, such as a blown fuse, a loose or corroded connection, a loose alternator drive belt, or a frayed wire. But, while these problems are easily correctible and of seemingly no major importance, they can quickly lead to serious difficulty if they are allowed to go uncorrected.

If you plan to do much of your own electrical work, a multimeter (described in Chapter One) combining an ohmmeter, ammeter, and voltmeter, is essential to locating and sorting out problems.

Above all, electrical system repair requires a patient, thorough approach to find true causes of trouble and to correct all of the faults that are involved.

BATTERY

The battery is perhaps the single most important component in the electrical system—and commonly it is the most neglected. In addition to checking and correcting the battery electrolyte level at each gas stop, as described in Chapter Three, the battery should be frequently cleaned with a solution of baking soda and water to remove corrosion from the terminals. Liberally coat the entire top of the battery as well as the terminals with the solution and allow it to stand for several minutes. Carefully flush the residue away with clean water. While the baking soda will neutralize the acids in the corrosion deposits, there is no need to risk getting unneutralized acid onto painted surfaces by rinsing the battery with a high-pressure water spray. When the battery has been thoroughly flushed, dry it with an old rag.

Inspect the battery case for damage, chafing, and cracks. Pay particular attention to moisture on the outside of the case; often this is an indication that the case is damaged and leaking electrolyte.

Periodically test the condition of the battery with a hydrometer. If you don't have a hydrometer but would consider buying one (a nominal investment), select one with numbered graduations rather than with a color-band scale; it's important to know the true condition of the battery—not just good, bad, or so-so. Draw

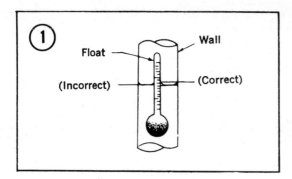

enough electrolyte from each cell, one at a time, to float the float in the hydrometer. Read it as shown in **Figure 1**. If the specific gravity is less than that indicated in **Table 1** (taking into account the temperature), and if the differences in specific gravity from one cell to another are close (less than 0.050), the battery requires a charge.

Table 1   ELECTROLYTE SPECIFIC GRAVITY

	Permissible Value	Full Charge Value at 68°F
Moderate climate	Over 1.20	1.26
Cold climate	Over 1.22	1.28
Warm climate	Over 1.18	1.23

However, if the difference in specific gravity from one cell to another is greater than 0.050, one or more cells may be sulphated or otherwise poor. In such case, the battery should be replaced before it causes trouble.

> NOTE: *When testing the battery with a hydrometer, always return the electrolyte to the cell from which it was removed before testing the next cell.*

Charging

There is no need to remove the battery from the vehicle to charge it. Just make certain that the area is well ventilated and that there is no chance of sparks or open flame being in the vicinity of the battery; during charging, highly explosive hydrogen is produced by the battery.

Disconnect the ground lead from the battery. Remove the caps from the battery cells and top up each cell with distilled water. Never add electrolyte to a battery that is already in service.

The electrolyte level in the cells should be about ¼ in. above the plates.

Connect the charger to the battery—negative to negative, positive to positive (**Figure 2**). If the charger output is variable, select a low setting (5-10 amps), set the voltage selector to 12 volts, and plug the charger in. If the battery is severely discharged (below 1.125), allow it to charge for at least 8 hours. Less charge deterioration requires less charging time.

> NOTE: *If time permits, it is recommended that the battery be charged at at the lower rate and for a longer period of time; however, if there is not sufficient time for slow charging, the high-rate charging times and rates shown in* **Table 2** *should be followed.*

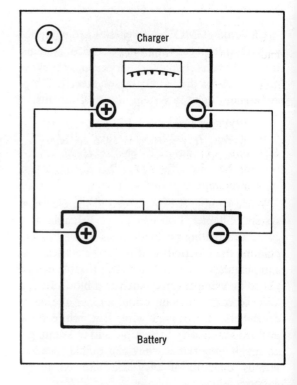

After the battery has been charged for a suitable period of time, unplug the charger and disconnect it from the battery. Be extremely careful about sparks. Test the condition of each cell with a hydrometer as described above and compare the results with Table 1.

If the specific gravity indicates that the battery is fully charged, and if the readings remain the same after one hour, the battery can be con-

Table 2   HIGH-RATE CHARGING TIMES

Specific Gravity Reading	Charge Rate Amperes	Battery Capacity — Ampere Hours				
		45	55	70	80	85
1.125 — 1.150 ①	35	65 min.	80 min.	100 min.	115 min.	125 min.
1.150 — 1.175	35	50 min.	65 min.	80 min.	95 min.	105 min.
1.175 — 1.200	35	40 min.	50 min.	60 min.	70 min.	75 min.
1.200 — 1.225	35	30 min.	35 min.	45 min.	50 min.	55 min.
Above 1.225	5	②	②	②	②	②

① If the specific gravity is below 1.125, use the indicated high rate of charge for the 1.125 specific gravity, then charge at 5 amperes until the specific gravity reaches 1.250 at 80°F.

② Charge at 5 ampere rate only until the specific gravity reaches 1.250 at 80°F.

Warning: At no time during the charging operation should the electrolyte temperature exceed 130°F.

sidered to be in good condition and fully charged. Check the electrolyte level and add distilled water if necessary, install the vent caps, and reconnect the ground lead.

Removal/Installation

1. Loosen the bolts in the terminal clamps far enough so the clamps can be spread slightly. Lift straight up on the clamps (negative first) to remove them from the posts. Twisting or prying on the clamps or posts can result in serious damage to a battery that may otherwise be in good condition.

2. Unscrew the nuts from the hold-down bolts (**Figure 3**) and remove the hold-down frame. For batteries retained with a hold-down lug (**Figure 4**), unscrew the bolt and remove the lug. Lift the battery out of the engine compartment.

3. Reverse these steps to install the battery. Before setting the battery in place, clean the battery holder with a solution of baking soda and water to neutralize any acids that may have formed. Allow the solution to stand for several minutes, then carefully flush it away with clean water, and dry it with an old rag. Set the battery into the holder making sure it's squarely seated. Install the hold-down frame and screw on the nuts snugly.

Connect the positive lead to the battery first, then the negative. Tighten the clamp bolts securely and check their tightness by trying to rotate them on the posts by hand. Coat the

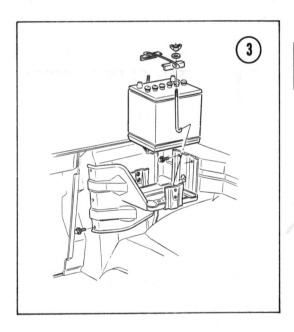

terminals liberally with Vaseline to inhibit corrosion and formation of ash-like acid deposits.

ALTERNATOR

The alternator is a self-rectifying, 3-phase current generator consisting of a stationary armature (stator), a rotating field (rotor) and a 3-phase rectifying bridge of silicon diodes. The alternator generates alternating current which is converted to direct current by the silicon diodes for use in the vehicle's electrical circuits. The output of the alternator is regulated by a voltage regulator to keep the battery in a satis-

factory charged condition. The alternator is mounted on the front of the engine and is driven through a belt by the crankshaft pulley. A typical alternator is shown in exploded view in **Figure 5**.

When working on the alternator make sure the connections are not reversed. Current flow in the wrong direction will damage the diodes and render the alternator unserviceable. The alternator BAT terminal must be connected to battery voltage (**Figure 6**). When charging the battery in the vehicle, disconnect the battery leads before connecting the charger as a precaution against incorrect current bias and heat reaching the alternator.

Performance Testing

The first indication of charging system trouble is usually slow engine cranking speed during starting. This will often occur long before the charge warning light or ammeter indicates that there is potential trouble. When charging system trouble is first suspected, it should be carefully tested, either by a dealer or an automotive electrical specialist. However, before having the system tested, make the following checks.

1. Check the alternator drive belt for correct tension (see Chapter Seven).
2. Check the battery to ensure it is in satisfactory condition and fully charged. Make sure that connections are clean and tight.

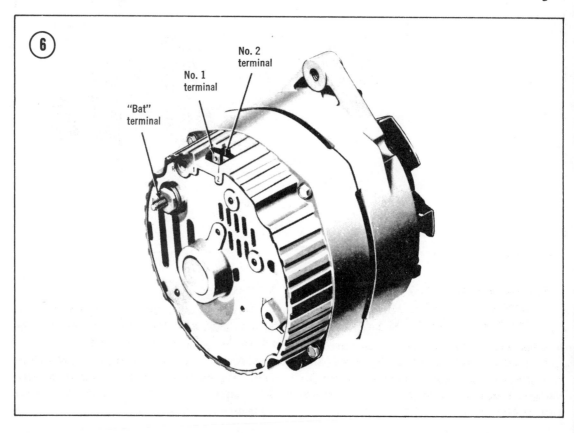

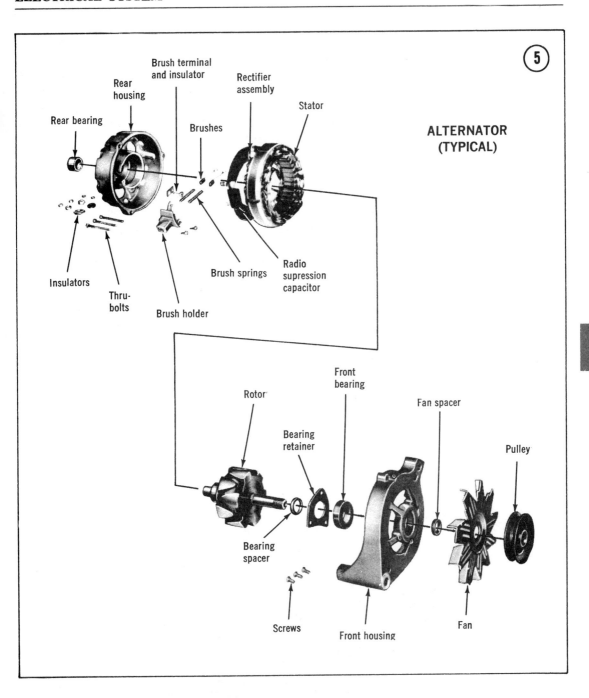

ALTERNATOR (TYPICAL)

Rear bearing
Rear housing
Brush terminal and insulator
Brushes
Rectifier assembly
Stator
Insulators
Thru-bolts
Brush holder
Brush springs
Radio supression capacitor
Rotor
Bearing retainer
Front bearing
Fan spacer
Pulley
Bearing spacer
Screws
Front housing
Fan

5

6

3. Check all of the connections from the alternator and the voltage regulator to ensure that they are clean and tight.

When each of the above points has been carefully checked and unsatisfactory conditions corrected, and there are still indications that the charging system is not performing as it should, have it checked.

Removal/Installation

1. Disconnect the negative battery cable at the battery (**Figure 7**). Unplug the connector from the rear of the alternator (**Figure 8**).

2. Loosen the belt tension adjuster at the alternator (**Figure 9**). Swing the alternator toward the engine and remove the drive belt from the pulley.

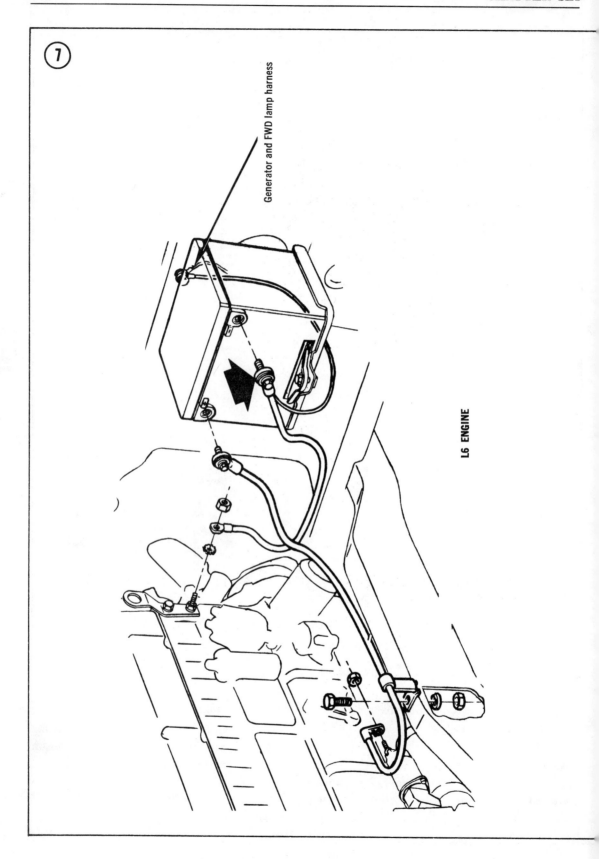

⑦

Generator and FWD lamp harness

L6 ENGINE

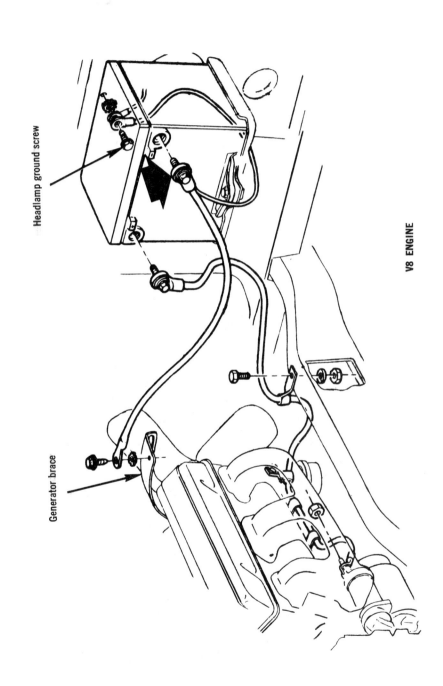

Headlamp ground screw

Generator brace

V8 ENGINE

6

isters discharge, the charge indicator relay, located inside the voltage regulator, must be tested. This is a job for a dealer or an automotive electrical specialist.

STARTER

Service to the starter requires experience and special tools. The service procedure described below consists of removal and installation. Work on the unit itself should be entrusted to a dealer or an automotive electrical specialist.

Removal/Installation

1. Disconnect the negative cable at the battery (Figure 7).

2. Disconnect the positive battery cable and the starter control cable at the starter (**Figure 10**).

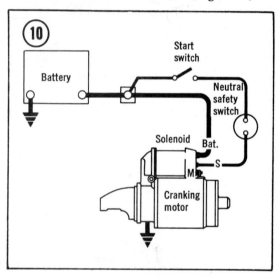

3. Unscrew the adjuster bolt and pivot bolt and remove the alternator.

4. Reverse these steps to install the alternator. Make certain that the alternator plug has been connected before connecting the negative battery lead. Refer to Chapter Seven and adjust the drive belt tension.

CHARGE INDICATOR RELAY

If the alternator and voltage regulator are operating satisfactorily and the charge indicator warning light remains on, or the ammeter reg-

3. Thoroughly clean the outside of the starter and the area at which it attaches to the bell housing. Unscrew the starter mounting bolts (see **Figure 11**) and pull the starter out of the bell housing.

4. Install the starter by reversing these steps. Make sure the connections are tight to ensure good electrical contact.

FUSES

Whenever a failure occurs in any part of the electrical system, always check the fuse box to see if a fuse has blown. If one has, it will be

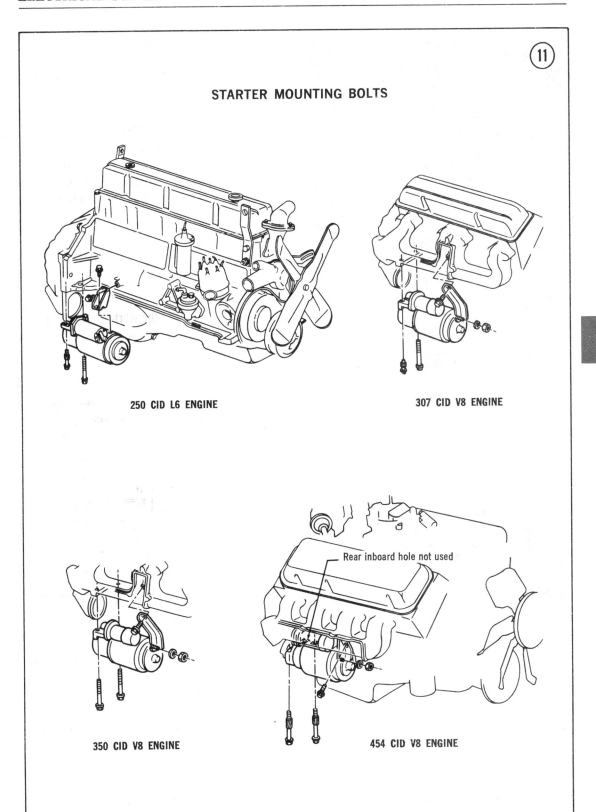

STARTER MOUNTING BOLTS

250 CID L6 ENGINE

307 CID V8 ENGINE

350 CID V8 ENGINE

Rear inboard hole not used

454 CID V8 ENGINE

6

evident by blackening of the fuse or by a break in the metal link in the fuse. Usually the trouble can be traced to a short circuit in the wiring connected to the blown fuse. This may be caused by worn-through insulation or by a wire which has worked loose and shorted to ground. Occasionally, the electrical overload which causes the fuse to blow may occur in a switch or a motor.

A blown fuse should be treated as more than a minor annoyance; it should serve also as a warning that something is wrong in the electrical system. Before replacing a fuse, determine what caused it to blow and then correct the trouble.

WARNING
Never replace a fuse with one of a higher amperage rating than that of the one originally used. Never use tinfoil or other metallic material to bridge fuse terminals. Failure to follow these basic rules could result in heat or fire damage to major parts, or loss of the entire vehicle.

Use the wiring diagrams and the function/color coding charts at the end of this chapter to determine the circuits protected by a particular fuse.

The fuse panel (**Figure 12**) is located at the left end of the firewall, beneath the dashboard.

Fuse ratings are shown in **Table 3**.

The fuse amperage and the circuits protected are shown in Table 3. To replace or inspect a fuse, carefully pry it out of its holder with the end of a pencil or similar non-metallic probe and snap a new one into place.

LIGHTS

All of the lighting elements with the exception of instrument illumination bulbs, are easily replaced. Individual replacement procedures follow, along with a bulb chart in **Table 4**.

Headlight Replacement

The headlights are replaceable sealed-beam units. Both the high- and low-beam circuits and filaments are included in one unit. Failure of one circuit requires replacement of the entire unit.

NOTE: *If both filaments in the lamp unit fail at the same time, it is possible that there is a short in the wiring to that particular lamp. Check the fuse to make sure it is the correct amperage rating and replace it if it is not. Carefully inspect the wiring and connector too for chafing or damage and correct any breaks in the insulation.*

1. Unscrew the screws which hold the headlight trim ring in place and remove the ring (**Figure 13**).
2. Loosen the headlight retaining screws (**Figure 14**). Next, turn the light unit counterclockwise to line up the large cutouts with the

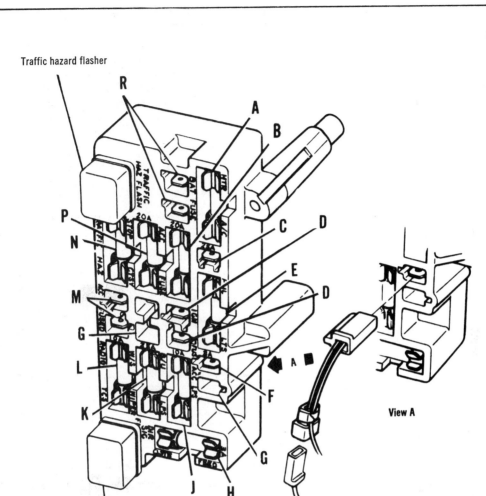

Traffic hazard flasher

Directional signal flasher

View A

FUSE PANEL

A. Fuse—heater/air conditioner
B. Fuse—accessory
C. Receptacle—C62
D. Receptacle—NL2/A33/U16
E. Fuse—panel lights
F. Receptacle—accessory lamps
G. Receptacle—(not used)
H. Fuse—cluster feed

J. Fuse—backup lamps
K. Fuse—windshield wiper
L. Fuse—radio and TCS
M. Receptacle—TP2/M40
N. Fuse—traffic hazard
P. Fuse—tail/stop/courtesy lamps
R. Receptacle—C91/UF2/U35/U37

Table 3   FUSES AND CIRCUIT BREAKERS

1967

Applicability	Location	Amps	Type
Backup lamp	Fuse block	10	3AG, AGC
Windshield wiper motor	Fuse block	20	SAE
Air conditioner	Fuse block	20	SAE
Traffic and hazard flasher	Fuse block	15	Flasher
Dome lamp	Fuse block	15	AG, AGC
Heater and defroster (deluxe)	Fuse block	15	AGC
Heater and defroster (Thrift-Air)	Fuse block	10	AGC
Instrument lamps	Fuse block	3	3AG, AGC
Radio	Fuse block	2.5	3AG, AGC
Spot lamp; license, stop, and tail lamps	Fuse block	15	3AG, AGC
Emergency disability light system	Fuse block	20	SAE
Headlamp and parking lamp circuit	Light switch	15	Circuit breaker

1968-1970

Applicability	Location	Amps	Type
Instrument cluster	Fuse block	3	3AG, AGC
Windshield wiper/washer	Fuse block	20	SAE, SFE
A/C motor	Fuse block	25	SAE, SFE
Heater motor, backup lamps	Fuse block	10	3AG, AGC
Tail, stop, dome, license, marker, park and spot lamp	Fuse block	20	3AG, AGC
Radio	Fuse block	3	3AG, AGC
Hazard flasher	Fuse block	15	SAE, SFE
Ammeter	In-line part of forward generator and forward lamp harness (2 required)	4	3AG, AGC
Headlamps	Light switch (integral)	15	Circuit breaker
Headlamp and parking lamp circuit	Light switch	15	Circuit breaker

Table 3   FUSES AND CIRCUIT BREAKERS   (continued)

1971-1972

Applicability	Location	Amps	Type
Instrument cluster	Fuse block	3	3AG, AGC
Windshield wiper/washer	Fuse block	20	SAE, SFE
A/C motor	Fuse block	25	3AG, AGC
Heater motor	Fuse block	15	3AG, AGC
Backup lamps	Fuse block	10	3AG, AGC
Tail, stop, dome, license, marker, parking, and spot lamps	Fuse block	20	SAE, SFE
Radio	Fuse block	3	3AG, AGC
Hazard flasher	Fuse block	15	3AG, AGC
Ammeter	In-line part of forward generator and forward lamp harness (2 required)	4	3AG, AGC
Headlamps and parking lamp circuit	Light switch (integral)	15	Circuit breaker

1973-1975

Applicability	Location	Amps
Heater, A/C, generator warning lamp	Fuse block	20
Idle stop solenoid, aux. battery, radio, time delay relay, emission control solenoid, transmission downshift	Fuse block	10
Cigarette lighter, clock, dome lamp, cargo lamp	Fuse block	20
Fuel gauge, brake warning lamp, temperature warning lamp, oil pressure warning lamp	Fuse block	3
Courtesy lamp, roof marker lamp, license plate lamp, parking lamp, side marker lamp, tail lamp, clearance lamp	Fuse block	20
Directional signal indicator lamp, stop lamp, traffic hazard	Fuse block	15
Instrument cluster lamp, heater dial lamp, radio lamp, Cruise Control lamp, wiper switch lamp	Fuse block	4
Windshield wiper/washer	Fuse block	25
Cruise Control, rear window, auxiliary fuel tank, tachometer, backup lamp, directional signal indicator lamp, headlamp buzzer	Fuse block	15

Circuit Breakers		
Headlamp and parking lamp circuit	Light switch	15
Windshield wiper motor	Wiper motor	8-10
Tailgate window motor	Engine side of dash	30

6

Table 4   LAMP BULB DATA

1967-1970

Used In	Quantity	Trade No.	Power
Dome lamp	1	211	12 CP
Parking lights	2	67	4 CP
Oil pressure indicator lamp ①	1	194	2 CP
Generator indicator lamp ①	1	194	2 CP
Instrument cluster lamps ④	4	194 or 1895	2 CP
Headlamp beam indicator lamp	1	194	1 CP
Lamp assembly—tail and stop lamp	1	1157	4-32 CP
License light	1	67	4 CP
Directional signal (front park lamps)	2	1157	4-32 CP
Headlamps ④		6012	
Temperature indicator lamp	1	194	2 CP
Cigarette lighter lamp	1	1445	1 CP
Glove box lamp	1	57	2 CP
Tachometer gauge lamp	1	1445	2 CP
Dispatch compartment lamp	1	1895	2 CP
Directional signal indicator lamp	2	168	3 CP
Cab clearance and identification lamps	5	01155	2 CP
Side marker lamps	2	194	2 CP
Brake warning indicator	1	194 or 1895	2 CP

1971-1972

Used In	Quantity	Trade No.	Power
Dome lamp	1	211	12 CP
Oil pressure indicator lamp ①	1	194	2 CP
Generator indicator lamp ①	1	194	2 CP
Instrument cluster lamps	3	194 or 1895	2 CP
Headlamp beam indicator lamp	1	194	2 CP
Lamp assembly-tail and stop lamp	2	1157	3-32 CP
License lamp ③	1	67	4 CP
Directional signal (front park lamps)	2	1157	3-32 CP
Headlamps ②		6014	
Temperature indicator lamp	1	194	2 CP
Directional signal indicator lamp	2	168	3 CP
Cab clearance and identification lamps:			
Suburban models	5	1155	4 CP
Other models	5	194	2 CP
Marker lamps	4	194	2 CP
Brake warning indicator	1	194 or 1895	2 CP
Transmission control	1	1445	.7 CP
Backing lamp	2	1156	32 CP
Heater or air conditioner	1	1445	.7 CP

① On KA 10-30 instrument clusters only.
② Double filament sealed beam; 60W high beam, 50W low beam.
③ 2 lamps used with step bumper.
④ Double filament sealed beam: 37.5W upper, 50W lower.

Table 4   LAMP BULB DATA   (continued)

1973-1974

Used In	Quantity	Trade No.	Power
Dome lamp ④	1	212	6 CP
Oil pressure indicator lamp ①	1	194	2 CP
Generator indicator lamp ①	1	194	2 CP
Instrument cluster lamps	6	194 or 1895	2 CP
Headlamp beam indicator lamp	1	194	2 CP
Lamp assembly—tail and stop lamp	2	1157	3-32 CP
License lamp ③	1	67	4 CP
Directional signal (front park lamps)	2	1157	3-32 CP
Headlamps ②		6014	
Temperature indicator lamp	1	194	2 CP
Directional signal indicator lamp	2	194	2 CP
Cab clearance and identification lamps:			
Suburban models	5	1155	4 CP
Other models	5	194	2 CP
Brake warning indicator	1	194	2 CP
Transmission control	1	1445	.7 CP
Backing lamp	2	1156	32 CP
Heater or air conditioner	1	1445	.7 CP
Corner marker lamps	7	67	4 CP
Cargo lamp	1	1142	21 CP
Radio dial lamp	1	293	2 CP
Cruise Control lamp	1	53	1 CP
Courtesy lamp	1	1003	15 CP

1975

Used In	Quantity	Trade No.	Power
Dome lamps: Cab	1	1003	15 CP
Blazer and Suburban	1	211-1 or 211-2	12 CP
Oil pressure indicator lamp ①	1	168	3 CP
Generator indicator lamp ①	1	168	3 CP
Instrument cluster lamps ⑤	5	168	3 CP
Headlamp beam indicator lamp	1	168	3 CP
Lamp assembly—tail and stop lamp	2	1157	3-32 CP
License lamp ③	1	67	4 CP
Directional signal (front park lamps) ⑥	2	1157	3-32 CP
Headlamps ②	2	6014	
Temperature indicator lamp	1	168	3 CP
Directional signal indicator lamp	2	168	3 CP
Cab clearance and identification lamps	4	168	3 CP
Roof marker lamps	5	194	2 CP
Brake warning indicator	1	168	3 CP
Transmission control	1	1445	.7 CP
Backing lamp	2	1156	32 CP
Heater or air conditioner	1	1445	.7 CP
Corner marker lamps	7	67	4 CP
Cargo lamp	1	1142	21 CP
Radio dial lamp—AM	1	1816	3 CP
—AM/FM	1	216	1 CP

(continued)

6

Table 4   LAMP BULB DATA (continued)

1975			
Used In	Quantity	Trade No.	Power
Cruise Control lamp	1	53	1 CP
Courtesy lamp	1	1003	15 CP
Windshield wiper switch	1	161	1 CP
Clock	1	168	3 CP
Rear identification ⑦	10	1895	2 CP
Underhood lamp	1	93	15 CP

① On KA 10-35 instrument clusters only.
② Double filament sealed beam: 60W high beam, 50W low beam.
③ Two lamps used with step bumper.
④ Two required on utility vehicles.

⑤ Three lamps used on instrument cluster (K series w/o gauges).
⑥ No. 1157 NA, 2.2-24 CP on C & K models.
⑦ Wideside Pickup.

screws, and remove the unit. Unplug the connector from the rear of the light.

> NOTE: *Do not turn headlight beam adjusting screws (**Figure 15**), or the setting will be disturbed and headlight beam will require adjustment.*

3. Reverse the above to install a new light unit. Make sure the connector is firmly seated before installing the unit. Set the light in place, making sure the lugs on the light engage the recesses in the lamp holder (**Figure 16**). Set the retainer ring in place and turn it clockwise so the small

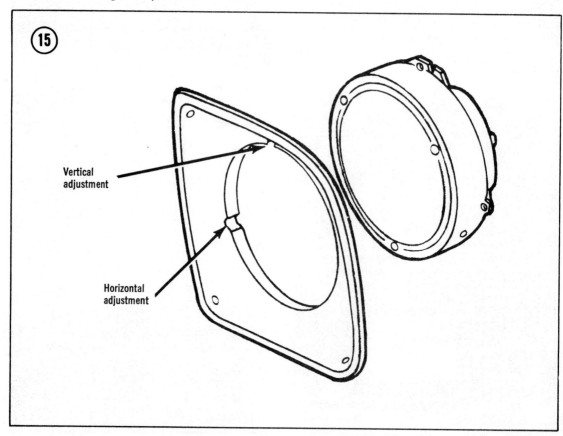

(15)

Vertical
adjustment

Horizontal
adjustment

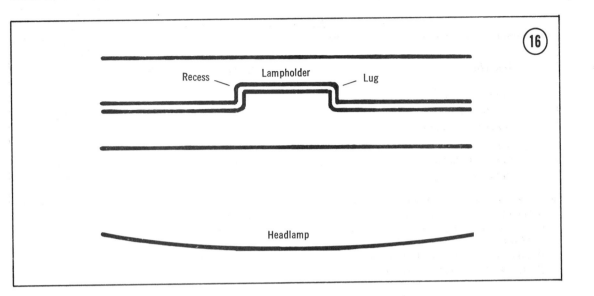

Recess — Lampholder — Lug

Headlamp

⑯

end of each cutout engages a screw. Tighten the screws and install the outer trim ring.

Signal Light Replacement

To change bulbs in a rear combination light (**Figure 17**), license plate light (**Figure 18**), parking/turn indicator lights (**Figure 19**), or side marker lights (**Figure 20**), remove the screws holding the lens in place and replace the bulb.

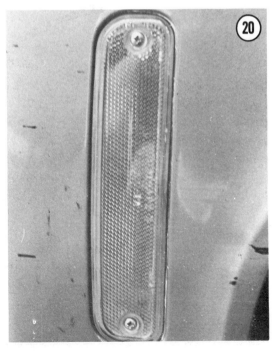

6

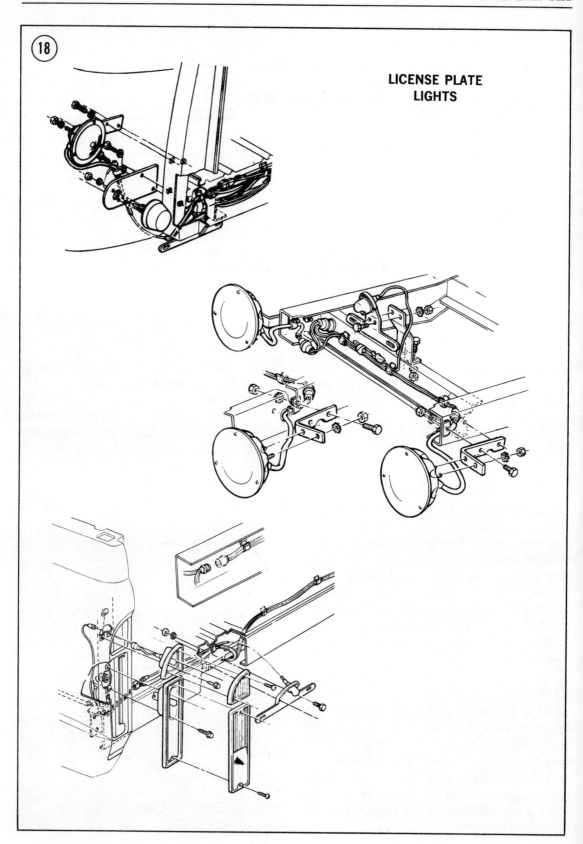

LICENSE PLATE
LIGHTS

CHAPTER SEVEN

COOLING SYSTEM

The cooling system consists of a pressurized radiator, thermostat, water pump, fan, and appropriate plumbing. Included in this chapter are procedures for changing the coolant and replacing and adjusting the water pump and fan drive belts.

COOLANT CHANGE

Chevrolet/GMC 4 x 4 vehicles are cooled with an ethylene glycol based anti-freeze. The anti-freeze can be mixed with water to alter its cooling properties and its resistance to freezing, depending upon the climate in which the vehicle is operated. In most cases, however, anti-freeze can be used undiluted. If it is to be mixed, follow the anti-freeze manufacturer's instructions.

The coolant should be changed every 12 months, regardless of mileage.

Draining

1. Make certain the engine and cooling system are cool. Loosen the radiator cap to its first notch and release the system pressure. Then unscrew the cap completely and remove it.

2. Move the heater temperature control to the WARM position to drain the heater radiator. Place a drip pan beneath the radiator and unscrew the radiator drain plug (**Figure 1**).

3. When the radiator has ceased to drain, relocate the drip pan beneath the engine and open the engine drain taps (**Figure 2**). Loosen the clamp on the IN line to the heater at the engine (**Figure 3**), disconnect it, and bend it down to aid draining the heater. Allow several minutes for the system to drain.

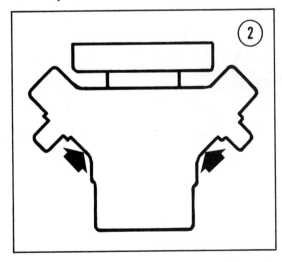

Filling

1. Reconnect the heater hose, making sure the clamp is tight. Close the engine taps and screw in the radiator drain plug. Set the heater controls at WARM.

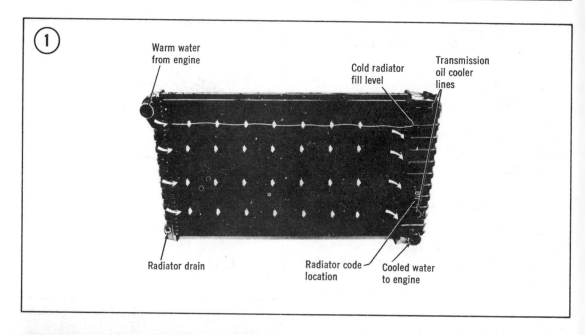

① Warm water from engine / Cold radiator fill level / Transmission oil cooler lines / Radiator drain / Radiator code location / Cooled water to engine

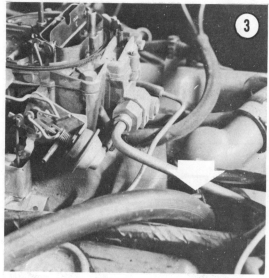

2. Slowly pour coolant into the radiator until the level is at the mark in the filler neck. Start the engine and allow it to idle for about one minute with the radiator cap off.

3. Check the level in the radiator and top it up as required. Install the radiator cap and check for and correct any leaks.

PRESSURE CHECK

If the cooling system requires repeated topping up, it probably has a leak. One of the most likely causes of cooling system leakage is the radiator cap which can be tested as described in Chapter Three. The cooling system test described below can also be made at the time the radiator cap is tested. Have it done by a dealer or a service station if you do not have access to a tester.

CAUTION
The engine cooling system must be cold when pressure test is carried out.

1. Remove the radiator cap and, if necessary, top up the coolant to the level mark in the filler neck.

2. Install the pressure tester and pump it to pressurize the system to 18-21 psi.

3. Thoroughly inspect the radiator, hoses, and all the connections for leaks. If any leaks are found at the hose connections, tighten the clamps and pressurize the system again. If a leak is found in a hose, replace the hose and pressure test the system again.

CAUTION
Any hoses that are brittle, spongy, or swollen should be replaced routinely. If they do not leak now, they soon will; they could even rupture. This type of hose failure, particularly dur-

ing high-speed or off-road driving, could result in extensive engine damage.

If a leak is found in the radiator core or in the top and bottom tanks, have the radiator repaired by a dealer or radiator specialist. When the repaired radiator has been reinstalled, pressure test the system to make sure all of the connections are tight.

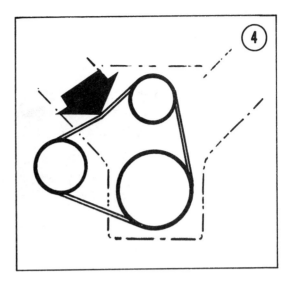

DRIVE BELTS

The water pump/fan drive belt, as well as the belts which drive the alternator, air conditioning, power steering pump, etc., should be inspected monthly for condition and adjustment.

Worn, frayed, cracked, or glazed belts should be replaced at once. The components to which they direct power are essential to the safe and reliable operation of the vehicle. If correct adjustment is maintained on the belts they will usually all enjoy the same service life. For this reason, and because of the labor involved in replacing an inboard belt (requiring the removal of the outer belts), it's a good idea to replace all of the belts as a set. The low added expense is well worth the time involved in doing the job twice, to say nothing of the consequences of a failed belt.

Tension Adjustment

In addition to being in good condition, it's important that the drive belts be correctly adjusted. A belt that is too loose does not permit the driven components to operate at maximum efficiency. In addition, the belt wears rapidly because of increased friction caused by slipping. A belt that is adjusted too tight wears prematurely and overstresses bearings in driven components.

Drive belt tension (adjustment) is measured by deflection of the belt midway between 2 pulleys at the belt's longest run (**Figure 4**).

Alternator/Fan-Water Pump Belt (Without Air Conditioning)

For maximum belt life and component efficiency, the belt tension should be checked with a tester like that shown in **Figure 5**. The tension

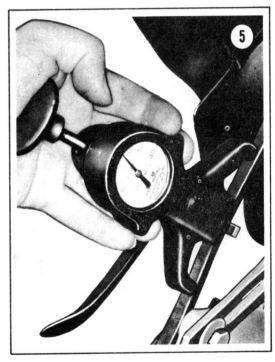

for a new belt should be 125 ± 5 lb. and for a used belt (one that has been in operation for more than 10 minutes) the tension should be 75 ± 5 lb. As a temporary setting, until the actual tension can be adjusted, a deflection of about ½ in. with moderate force applied to the belt is a reasonable compromise.

To adjust the tension, loosen the pivot bolt located beneath the alternator and then loosen the lock bolt (**Figure 6**). Move the alternator

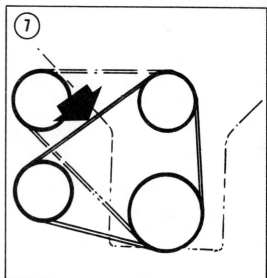

toward or away from the engine as required until the tension is correct, then tighten the lock bolt and then the pivot bolt without further moving the alternator. When the adjustment has been made, double check to ensure that it is correct.

To replace the belt, loosen the alternator bolts as just described and swing the alternator toward the engine as far as it will go so the belt can be removed from the pulleys.

Alternator Belt
(With Air Conditioning)

Adjust the alternator drive belt as described above, using a belt tension tester (Figure 5). The tension for a new belt should be 125 ± 5 lb. and for a used belt (one that has been in operation for more than 10 minutes), the tension should be 75 ± 5 lb.

Fan-Water Pump/Air Conditioning Belt

Measure the belt tension with a tester, midway between the fan-water pump pulley and the air conditioning compressor pulley (**Figure 7**). The tension for a new belt should be 140 ± 5 lb. and for a used belt (one that has been in service for more than 10 minutes), the tension should be 95 ± 5 lb.

To adjust the belt tension, loosen the pivot and lock bolts (**Figure 8**) and move the com-

pressor as required until the tension is correct. Then, without further moving the compressor, tighten bolts securely and recheck the tension.

To replace the belt, loosen the compressor bolts and swing the compressor toward the engine as far as it will go so the belt can be removed.

Power Steering Pump Belt

Measure the tension of the power steering pump belt with a tester, midway between the fan-water pump pulley and the power steering pump pulley (**Figure 9**). The tension for a new

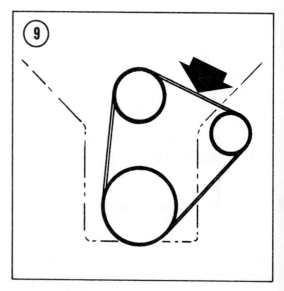

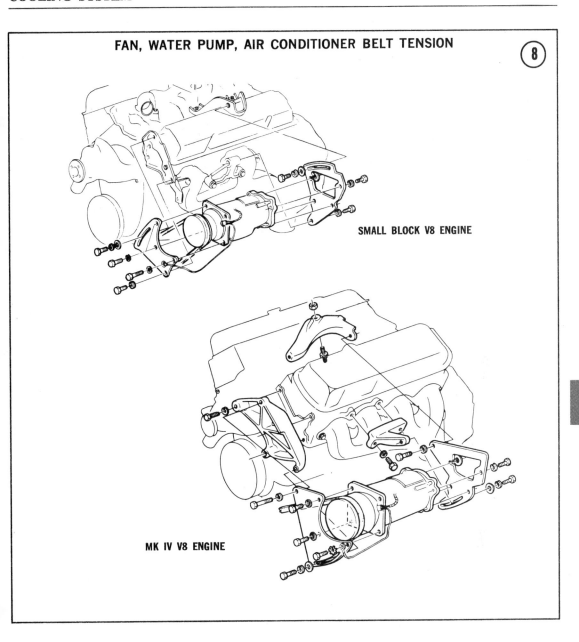

FAN, WATER PUMP, AIR CONDITIONER BELT TENSION

⑧

SMALL BLOCK V8 ENGINE

MK IV V8 ENGINE

7

belt should be 125 ± 5 lb. For a used belt (one that has been in service for more than 10 minutes), the tension should be 75 ± 5 lb.

To adjust the tension of the belt, loosen the bolts which attach the pump or pump mounting bracket to the adjusting bracket (**Figures 10 and 11**) and move the pump by applying pressure at the web behind the pulley.

CAUTION
Do not apply pressure to the reservoir; it will bend and leak.

When the tension is correct, tighten the bolts without further moving the pump. Then recheck the tension to make sure it has not changed.

To replace the belt, loosen the adjusting and pivot bolts and swing the pump toward the engine as far as it will go so the belt can be removed.

Air Injection Pump Belt

Check the tension of the air injection pump belt as shown in **Figure 12**. The tension for a new

⑩ POWER STEERING BELT TENSION

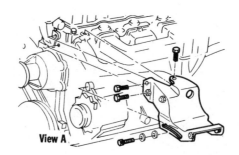

View A

250 CID IN-LINE 6 ENGINE

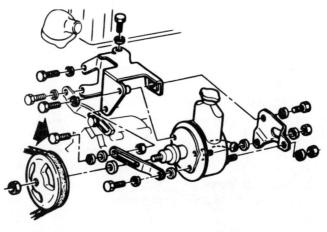

292 CID IN-LINE 6 ENGINE

POWER STEERING BELT TENSION

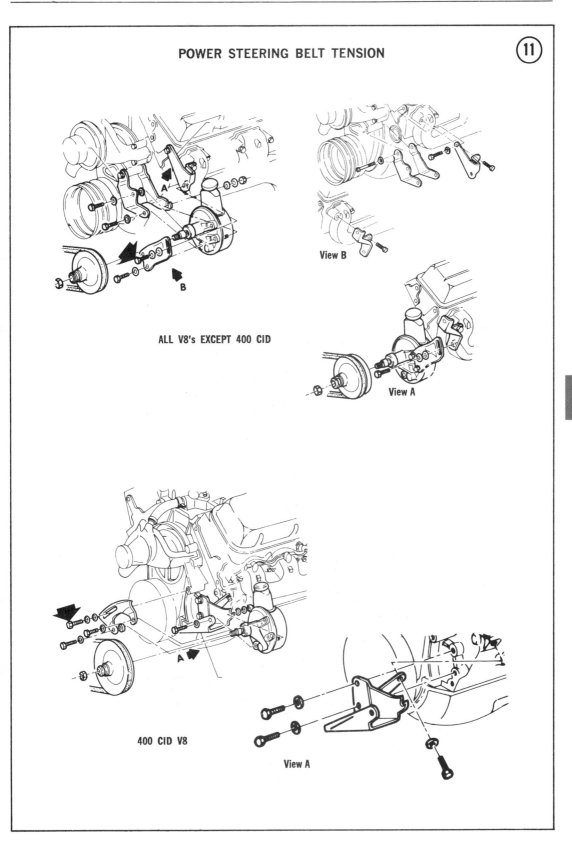

ALL V8's EXCEPT 400 CID

View B

View A

400 CID V8

View A

7

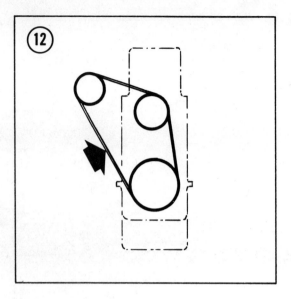

belt should be 75 ± 5 lb. For a used belt (one that has been in service for more than 10 minutes), the tension should be 55 ± 5 lb.

To adjust the tension of the belt, loosen the pump mounting bolt and the adjusting bolt and move the pump as necessary.

CAUTION
Do not pry on the pump body.

When the tension is correct, tighten both bolts without further moving the pump and then recheck the tension.

To replace the belt, loosen both bolts and move the pump toward the crankshaft pulley as far as possible so the belt can be removed.

CHAPTER EIGHT

BRAKES, CLUTCH, AND TRANSMISSION

BRAKES

The brake system on all Chevrolet/GMC 4 x 4 vehicles covered in this handbook have 2 independent hydraulic circuits. One circuit operates the front brakes and the other circuit operates the rear brakes. Failure of one of the brake circuits will normally be indicated by the brake warning light turning on. However, if the light is burned out or the wiring faulty, the first indication of a brake failure may occur when the brakes are applied, requiring much more pedal pressure than normal.

If the warning light comes on, carefully slow and stop the vehicle, taking into account that the braking effectiveness is greatly reduced. Remove the cap from the master cylinder reservoir (**Figure 1**) and check to see if there is fluid in both reservoirs. If the level is low in one, or it is empty, check further for leaks along the brake lines and at each wheel. If the level is correct in both reservoirs, the fault may lie in the switch, wiring, or the differential pressure valve in the master cylinder. In any case, drive the vehicle with extreme care until the system can be checked and the trouble corrected.

This chapter describes routine inspections and services. Major work such as brake shoe replacement and drum reconditioning, and wheel and master cylinder rebuilding, should be en-

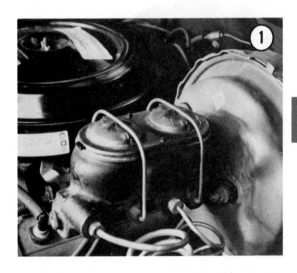

trusted to a dealer or automotive brake specialist.

Brake Fluid Level

The brake fluid level in the master cylinder reservoir should be checked routinely every 6,000 miles or at any time there is suspected leakage in the brake hydraulic system.

The fluid level must be within ¼ in. of the lower edge of the filler opening (**Figure 2**). If the fluid level is extremely low in one or both reservoirs, inspect the lines and fittings for leakage, and check wheel cylinders as described in

Chapter Three, *Brake Lining Inspection*. Correct any leaks before adding fluid and bleed the system as described later.

Add only GM Hydraulic Brake Fluid (Supreme No. 11) or an equivalent fluid (DOT-3). This fluid grade is identified by "DOT-3" embossed on the container and is recommended for all conditions.

WARNING
Never add low-temperature brake fluid to the fluid that is already in the system. The fluid could vaporize causing total brake failure.

Brake Fluid Changing

After long usage, brake fluid absorbs sufficient atmospheric moisture to significantly reduce its boiling point and make it prone to vapor lock during repeated hard brake applications (such as in mountain driving). While no hard and fast rule exists for changing the fluid in the system, it should be checked at least annually by bleeding fluid from one of the wheel cylinders and inspecting it for signs of moisture. If moisture is present, the entire system should be drained and bled as described below.

Bleeding the Brake System

The brake system must be bled following any repairs in which a portion of the system is disconnected, after a leak has been corrected, or when water is present in the hydraulic fluid. The system can be bled using a pressure tank type

bleeder or manually with the aid of an assistant. Because it is unlikely that a hobbyist mechanic will have a pressure tank bleeder, the second method is described.

It is a good idea to bleed the system beginning with the brake located closest to the master cylinder and then working away from the master cylinder. As with adding fluid to the system, use only the fluid specified earlier.

1. Check the brake fluid level in the reservoirs and top them up to within ¼ in. of the lower edge of the filler opening with fresh fluid. Leave the cap and diaphragm off the master cylinder but cover it with clean, lint-free shop rags to prevent fluid from being ejected and getting onto painted surfaces.

2. Wipe any dirt or oil from the bleeder screw (**Figure 3**) of the first brake to be bled and attach a length of hose to the screw. The hose must fit snugly over the screw. Place the other end of the hose in a container partially filled with fresh brake fluid.

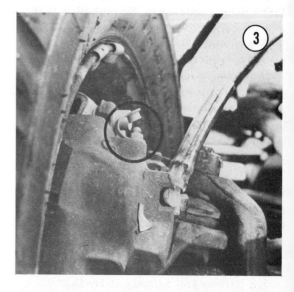

3. Using an assistant, open the bleeder valve about ¾ turn and have your assistant depress the brake pedal and hold it. Just before the pedal bottoms, close the bleeder valve and instruct the assistant to release the brake pedal. When the brake pedal is all the way up, open the bleeder valve and have the brake depressed once again. Close the bleeder valve and have the brake released. Continue this sequence until the brake

fluid running out of the hose and into the container is free of air bubbles. Then close the bleeder valve and tighten it and remove the bleeder hose. Top up the fluid in the master cylinder reservoirs and re-cover the reservoirs with the rags.

4. Bleed the other brakes in the same manner, topping up the reservoir with fresh fluid after each unit has been bled. When the entire system has been bled and the fluid levels in the master cylinder reservoirs topped up to within ¼ in. of the lower edge of the filler opening, check the feel of the brake pedal. If it is not firm, some air remains in the system and it must be bled again in the manner just described.

5. When the pedal feel is correct, road test the vehicle to ensure the brakes operate correctly. Begin checking at low speed until you are confident that the braking action is good.

Service Brake Adjustment

Front disc brakes are self-adjusting. As the brake lining wears down, more fluid is drawn into the caliper cylinders from the master cylinder to compensate for the increased volume in the caliper cylinders.

Drum type service brakes are adjusted when the vehicle is driven in reverse and the brakes are applied. If the brake pedal can be pushed within a couple of inches of the floor, the brakes should be adjusted by backing the vehicle up several times and sharply applying the brakes. Test the adjustment by driving the vehicle at about 20 mph and then braking to a smooth stop. If the pedal travel is still long, adjust them once again as just described.

Parking Brake Adjustment

The parking brake should be adjusted whenever the foot control can be depressed 6 or more clicks. Before adjusting the parking brake, adjust the service brakes as just described.

1. Depress the parking brake pedal one click.

2. Tighten the adjuster nut (**Figure 4**) until there is a slight drag on the rear wheels when they are rotated forward.

3. Release the parking brake control and rotate the wheels. There should be no drag.

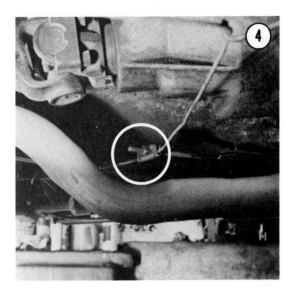

Brake Inspection and Cleaning

The brake inspections described below should be performed every 6,000 miles for disc brakes and 12,000 miles for drum brakes, provided the vehicle is not used extensively under adverse road and weather conditions. For extremely adverse conditions, such as deep sand or mud, the brakes should be inspected and cleaned more frequently, such as at 1,000-mile intervals or each time the wheel bearings are cleaned, repacked, and adjusted.

Disc Brakes

1. Slightly loosen the front wheel lug nuts. Raise the front of the vehicle and support it on frame stands as described in Chapter One. Remove the front wheels.

2. Check the thickness of the lining at both ends of the outboard shoes. If the lining is worn to within 1/32 in. of the shoe on bonded linings, or to within 1/32 in. of the rivet heads on riveted linings, the shoes should be replaced as a set on both front wheels. Also check the thickness of the inboard lining through the inspection hole in the center of the caliper. The minimum lining for the inboard shoe is the same as for the outboard (**Figure 5**).

3. Check the linings for grease, oil, or brake fluid. If they are soaked, they must be replaced in spite of the amount of brake lining material remaining.

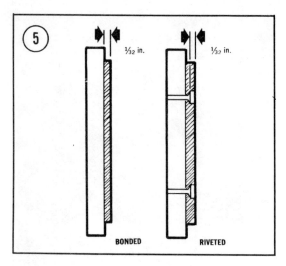

BONDED   RIVETED

4. Inspect the brake rotors for scratches and grooves. If grooves are deep enough to snag a fingernail, the rotors should be serviced by a dealer or a brake specialist.

Drum Brakes

1. Raise the vehicle and support it on frame stands. Remove both wheels from one side. To remove the front drum, first remove the outer grease cup from the hub, remove the cotter key, unscrew the axle nut, and pull out on the drum to remove it. For rear brakes, remove the screws that attach the drum to the axle flange, pull out sharply on the drum, and remove it. If the drum is difficult to remove, loosen the parking brake adjuster; the shoes may be in contact with the drum.

> NOTE: *If the brakes are simply being inspected for lining condition and remaining service life, it is not necessary to remove the drums and wheels from both sides; the condition of the linings and drums on one side is indicative of the condition of those on the opposite side. However, if the drums and linings on the first side require cleaning and dressing, this service should be carried out on the opposite side also.*

2. Wipe the brake shoes and insides of the drums with a clean dry cloth to remove sand, dirt, and any other foreign matter. *Do not use solvent.* Inspect the drums for scoring and scratches. Any score deep enough to snag a

fingernail is reason for having the drums turned and the linings replaced. Minor scoring and scratches can be removed with fine emery cloth, following which the drum must be thoroughly cleaned with compressed air to remove any abrasive.

Inspect the linings for dirt, oil, grease, and brake fluid. Dirt and foreign particles that are imbedded in the lining can be removed with a wire brush, but if the lining is soaked with grease, oil, or brake fluid, it must be replaced.

Measure the depth of the rivet holes with a depth gauge (**Figure 6**). If the lining is worn to within 1/32 in. of the rivet heads, it must be replaced.

> NOTE: *It is important that brakes be reconditioned at least in pairs—both fronts or both rears—or all 4 at the same time. In addition, if the linings are replaced, they must be arced to the contour of the drums which in most cases require truing. This is a job for a • dealer or automotive brake specialist.*

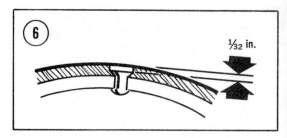

3. Refer to Chapter Nine. Install the wheels and drums and adjust the wheel bearings.

CLUTCH

The clutch in Chevrolet/GMC 4 x 4 vehicles covered in this handbook is a mechanically operated, single-disc type. One adjustment—clutch pedal free travel—will compensate for normal clutch wear. To check the free travel, start the engine and allow it to idle. Depress the clutch pedal to within about ½ in. of the floor and move the gear selector between first gear and reverse several times. If the selector can be moved smoothly without resistance the free travel in the pedal is all right. However, if the selector movement is not smooth the clutch is probably not engaging completely and the pedal should be adjusted.

Before making the adjustment, check the pedal bushings for wear. Also, check the cross shaft, levers, and support bracket for damage. Also check the engine mounts to ensure they are tight; loose mounts will allow the engine to move and bind clutch linkage at cross shaft.

Adjustment

1. Disconnect the clutch return spring from the clutch fork (**Figure 7**).

2. Remove the cotter key and washers from the swivel.

3. Rotate the cross shaft until the clutch pedal contacts the rubber stop on the pedal bracket.

4. Push the clutch arm to the rear until the throwout (release) bearing can be felt to just touch the fingers on the clutch. Loosen the locknut on the rod and turn the adjuster until the swivel can be engaged with the gauge hole (**Figure 8**) and the end of the rod rests firmly against the clutch arm.

5. Pull the swivel out of the gauge hole and reinstall it in the lower hole in the lever. Install

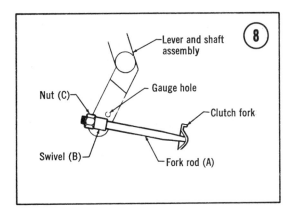

the washers and the cotter key and tighten the locknut without further changing the adjustment.

6. Install the return spring and check the free travel of the clutch pedal. It should be $1\frac{3}{8}$-$1\frac{5}{8}$ in. When the free travel is correctly adjusted, road test the vehicle to ensure that the clutch releases and engages correctly.

TRANSMISSION

Transmission service is limited to checking, adding, or changing oil. Refer to Chapter Three for these procedures.

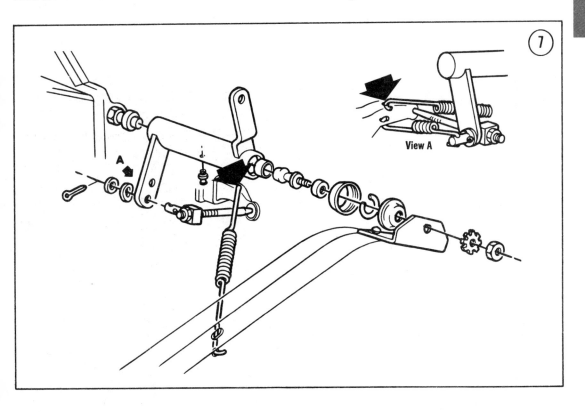

CHAPTER NINE

CHASSIS

Major work on Chevrolet/GMC 4 x 4 chassis frequently requires the use of special tools that are available only to dealers. In addition, a great deal of specialized experience is required that places such work beyond the abilities of a hobbyist mechanic.

Chassis work should be confined to the procedures described below. All other work should be entrusted to a dealer or a qualified specialist.

SHOCK ABSORBERS

The shock absorbers can be routinely checked while installed on the vehicle. However, this is only a general indication of their condition; if there is any doubt about their serviceability, they should be removed as described later and checked more accurately.

To check their general condition, bounce first the front and then the rear of the vehicle up and down several times then release it. The vehicle should not continue to bounce more than twice. Excessive bouncing is an indication of worn shock absorbers. Keep in mind, however, that this test is not conclusive; the spring stiffness of a 4 x 4 vehicle makes it difficult to detect shock absorbers in marginal condition. If there is doubt about the condition of the units, remove them and have them tested.

Removal/Installation (Front)

1. Jack up the front of the vehicle and support it on frame stands (see Chapter One). Remove the front wheels.
2. Unscrew the nut and bolt from the lower mount (**Figure 1**).

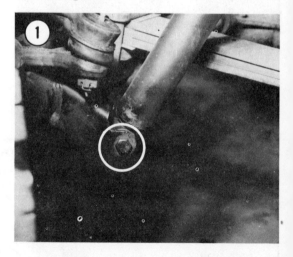

3. Unscrew the nut and bolt from the upper mount, remove the washer and bushings, and pull the shock absorber out of the mount.
4. Install the new shock absorbers with new rubber bushings. Install the upper end of the shock absorber first, but do not tighten the nut

until the bottom has been installed. Then, tighten both nuts and bolts to 65-75 ft.-lb.

Removal/Installation (Rear)

1. Jack up the rear of the vehicle and support it on frame stands (see Chapter One). Remove the rear wheels.

2. Unscrew the upper mounting nut (**Figure 2**) and remove the washer and bushing. Unscrew the nut from the bottom bolt and tap the bolt out with a soft mallet. It may be necessary to drive the bolt out with a soft drift such as a hardwood dowel.

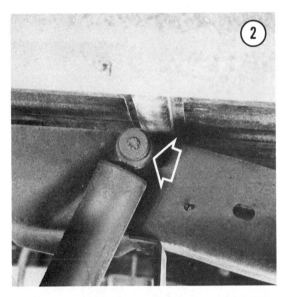

3. Install the new shock absorbers with new bushings. Install the upper end of the shock absorber first, but do not tighten the nut until the lower end has been lined up with the bracket and the bolt installed. Then, tighten the nuts to the values shown in **Table 1**.

Table 1   REAR SHOCK ABSORBER
TIGHTENING TORQUES

Year	Torque
1967-1972	
Upper	65 ft.-lb.
Lower	65 ft.-lb.
1973-1975	
Upper	140 ft.-lb.
Lower	115 ft.-lb.

Inspection

1. Check the piston rod for bending, galling, and abrasion. Any one of these conditions is reason for replacement.

2. Check for fluid leakage. A light film on the rod is normal, but severe leakage is reason for replacement.

3. With the shock absorber in the installed position, completely extend the rod, then invert the shock absorber and completely compress the rod. Do this several times to expel trapped air. Clamp the lower end of the shock absorber in a vise fitted with jaw protectors. Compress and extend the piston rod as fast as possible and check the damping action. The resistance should be smooth and uniform throughout each stroke, and the resistance during extension should be greater than during compression. Also, the action of both shock absorbers in a pair should feel the same. If the damping action is erratic, or resistance to quick extension and compression is very low, or if resistance is the same in both directions, the shock absorbers should be replaced, preferably as a set. The exception here would be for a shock absorber that has failed because of physical damage while the opposite unit performs satisfactorily.

> NOTE: *Comparison of a used shock absorber, that is believed to be good, to a new shock absorber is not a valid comparison; the new shock absorber will seem to offer more resistance because of the greater friction of the new rod seal.*

WHEEL ALIGNMENT

Wheel alignment should be checked periodically by a dealer or an alignment specialist. Misalignment is usually indicated first by incorrect tire wear (see *Tire Wear Analysis*, Chapter Two), or steering or handling difficulties.

Camber and caster are designed into the front axle and are not adjustable. Wheel alignment specifications (**Table 2**) are included, however, so that they may be used to determine if either factor has been disturbed by hard usage or an accident. Toe-in is adjustable (see below).

9

Table 2   FRONT WHEEL ALIGNMENT SPECIFICATIONS (CHECKING)

Year	Caster	Camber	Toe-In
1967	+ 3°	1½°	¹⁄₁₆-⅛ in. per wheel
1968	+ 3°	1 ± ½°	³⁄₃₂-³⁄₁₆ in. total
1969	+ 3°	1 ± ½°	³⁄₃₂-³⁄₁₆ in. total
1970	3° 15′	1 ± ½°	³⁄₃₂-³⁄₁₆ in. total
1971	+ 4°	1½°	¹⁄₁₆-⁵⁄₁₆ in. total
1972	+ 4°	1½°	³⁄₁₆ in. total
1973	+ 4°	1½°	³⁄₁₆ in. total
1974	+ 4°	1½°	0
1975	− 4°	1½°	0

NOTE: *Precision frame and wheel alignment equipment is required to accurately measure caster, camber, and toe-in. If steering, handling, and tire wear difficulties can not be corrected by the checks and corrections presented below, the vehicle should be entrusted to a Chevrolet dealer or an automotive alignment specialist.*

Inspection

Steering and handling problems which may appear to be caused by misalignment may very well be caused by other factors which are readily correctable without expensive equipment. The checks and inspections which follow should be carried out if steering, handling, or tire wear problems exist, and also before toe-in is adjusted.

1. Check all tire pressures and correct them if necessary, referring to Table 1, Chapter Three. It is essential that the pressures be checked when the tires are cold.

2. Raise the front of the vehicle and support it with frame stands as described in Chapter One. Check the end-play of the wheel bearings by grasping the tire front and rear and attempting to move it in and out. If bearing end-play can be felt, refer to the section on wheel bearing service in this chapter and inspect and adjust the bearings.

3. Refer to the section on steering service in this chapter and check the steering components for wear and all of the fasteners for looseness.

Pay particular attention to the steering gear mounting bolts.

4. Check radial and lateral runout of both front tires with a dial indicator (**Figure 3**). Place the indicator against the tread first and slowly rotate the wheel. Then place the indicator against the outer sidewall of the tire and again slowly rotate the wheel. If either the radial or lateral runout is greater than 0.080 in., the tire should be deflated and rotated 90 degrees on the wheel.

NOTE: *It will probably be necessary to soap the wheel rim before the tire can be turned.*

Reinflate the tire to the correct pressure shown in Table 1, Chapter Three, and recheck the runout. If necessary, the tire should be rotated again if the runout is still excessive.

If steering, handling, and tire wear problems cannot be corrected by carrying out the above inspections and adjustments, the vehicle should be referred to a dealer or alignment specialist for a precision inspection and corrective work.

STEERING

Service to the steering gear is limited to checking and correcting the lubricant level (Chapter Four), checking and correcting play in the steering wheel and column (Chapter Three), and checking and tightening the steering gear mounting bolts. The tightening torque for the steering gear mounting bolts (**Figure 4**) is 65 ft.-lb.

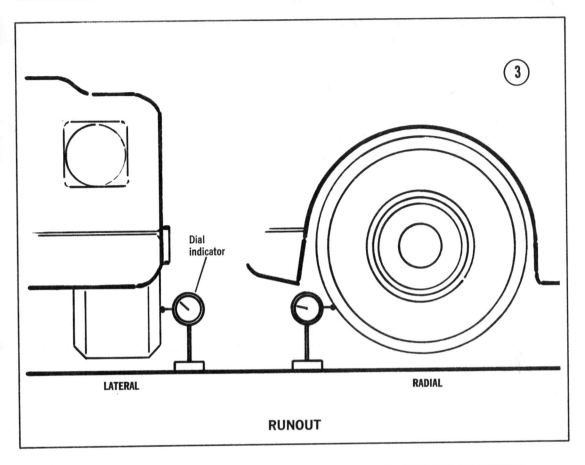

LATERAL   RADIAL

RUNOUT

FRONT WHEEL BEARINGS AND HUBS

The factory-recommended service interval for the front wheel bearings is 12,000 miles or 12 months. This long interval can be virtually disregarded, however, unless the vehicle is operated almost exclusively in dry weather on good roads; in the more likely instance, where the vehicle is used a significant amount off-road, the intervals should be shortened. For moderate off-road use, where the vehicle is not run in water, service intervals of 6,000-10,000 miles are reasonable. However, for vehicles operated in deep water or mud, the bearings should be serviced daily.

The rear wheel bearings are sealed and receive their lubrication from the oil carried in the rear differential. There is no adjustment required for the rear bearings and their expected service life is quite long. A hydraulic press is required to remove and install the bearings and it is recommended that this be referred to a dealer or an automotive machine shop.

FRONT WHEEL BEARING ADJUSTMENT

Check the bearing adjustment with the front of the vehicle raised and supported by frame stands as described in Chapter One. Grasp the wheel front and rear and attempt to move it in and out. If the movement is less than 0.001 in. or greater than 0.010 in., the bearings should be adjusted.

Standard Hubs (Non-Lockout Type)

1. Rotate the wheel to ensure the brake is not dragging in the drum. If it is, loosen the brake adjuster (**Figure 5**) several turns.

2. Refer to **Figure 6** and remove the hub cap. Remove the snap ring and pull out the splined driving hub and the spacer located behind it. On K20/K2500 hubs (**Figure 7**) unscrew the bolts which attach the driving flange to the hub.

3. Using GM tool No. J-6893-01, unscrew the locknut from the axle and remove the lock ring

9

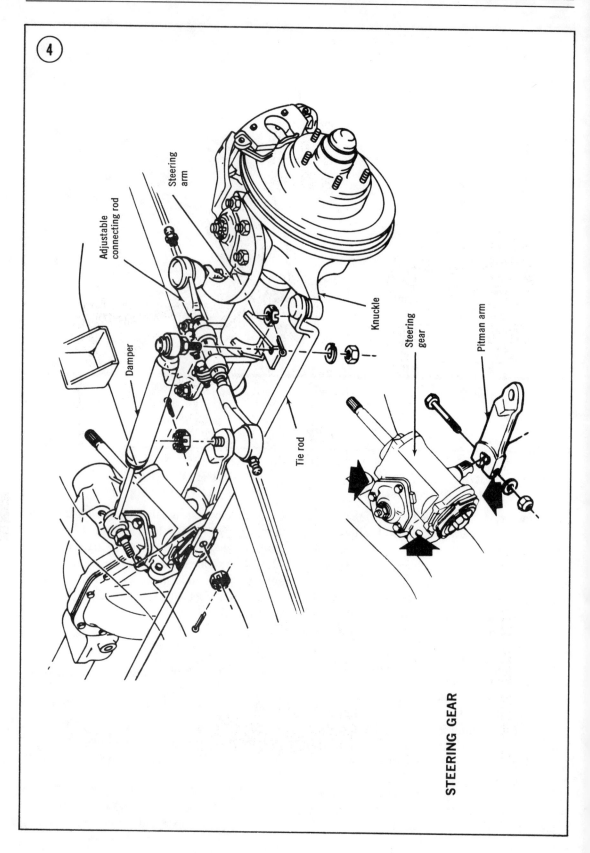

STEERING GEAR

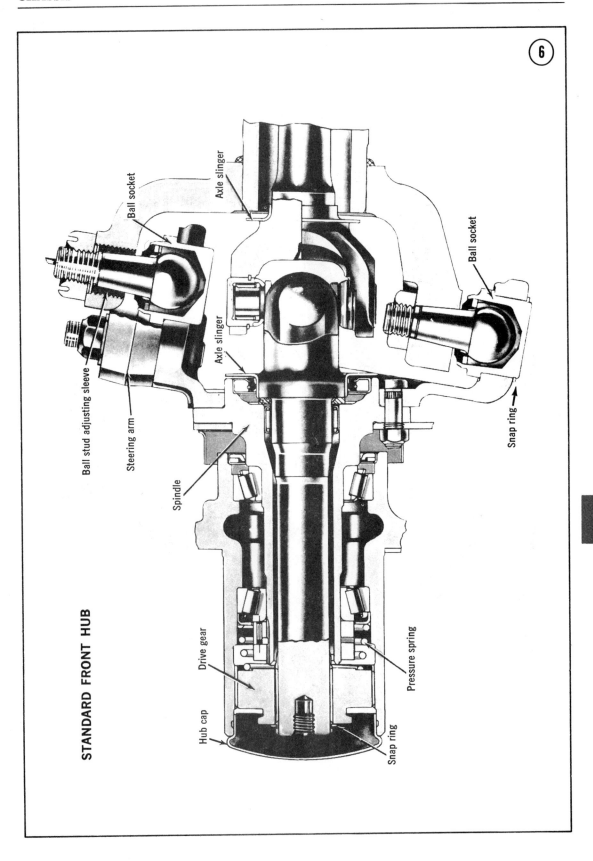

STANDARD FRONT HUB

Ball socket

Axle slinger

Ball socket

Ball stud adjusting sleeve

Steering arm

Axle slinger

Spindle

Snap ring

Drive gear

Pressure spring

Hub cap

Snap ring

9

6

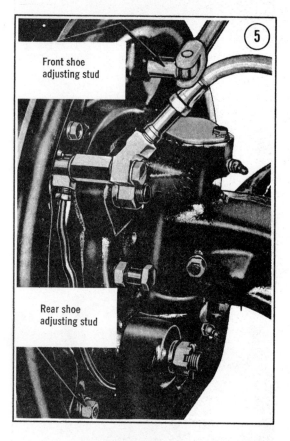

Front shoe
adjusting stud

Rear shoe
adjusting stud

(**Figure 8**). Attach the tool to a torque wrench and tighten the bearing adjusting nut to 50 ft.-lb. while at the same time rotating the wheel back and forth to permit the bearing to seat evenly.

4. Continue to rotate the wheel, loosen the adjusting nut, and retighten it to 35 ft.-lb. Finally, back off the adjusting nut 90 degrees.

5. Install the lock ring and pin, turning the adjusting nut so the pin will engage the nearest notch. Screw on the outer locknut and tighten it with the special wrench to the appropriate value: 1969-1971 models to 50 ft.-lb., 1972-1975 models to 80-100 ft.-lb. Recheck the end-play in the hub as described earlier and repeat the adjustment procedure if it still feels loose.

> NOTE: *If you have access to a dial indicator, measure the end-play of the wheel once it has been adjusted. It should be 0.001-0.010 in.*

6. When the hub end-play has been correctly adjusted, clean and dry the hub drive parts and lubricate all of the splines. Refer to the first part of this procedure and reverse the disassembly

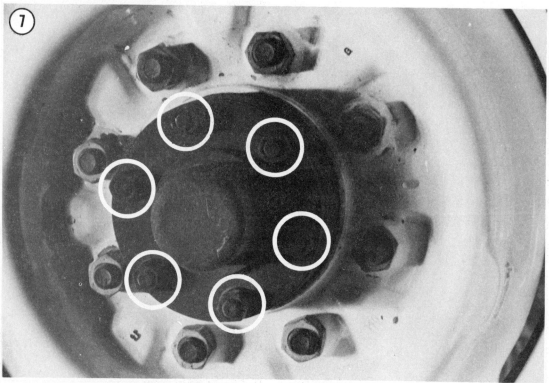

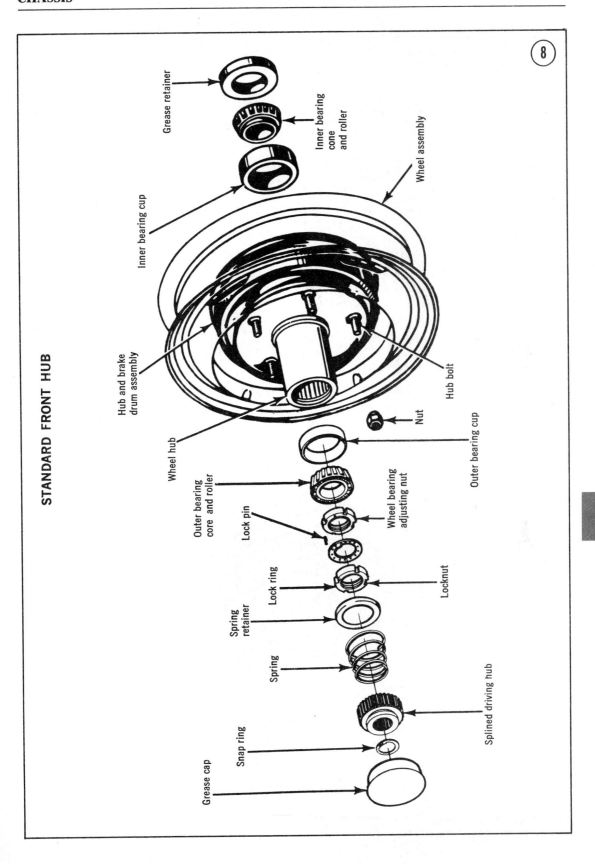

STANDARD FRONT HUB

Grease retainer

Inner bearing cone and roller

Wheel assembly

Inner bearing cup

Hub and brake drum assembly

Wheel hub

Hub bolt

Nut

Outer bearing cup

Outer bearing core and roller

Lock pin

Wheel bearing adjusting nut

Lock ring

Locknut

Spring retainer

Spring

Splined driving hub

Snap ring

Grease cap

9

steps to assemble the drive portion of the hub. Apply a thin coat of non-hardening sealant to the edge of the grease cap before installing it in the end of the hub. Readjust the brake adjuster if it was backed off earlier. Check and correct the end-play of the opposite hub in the manner just described.

Lockout Hubs
(1967 K10, 1967-1968 K20)

1. Rotate the wheel to ensure the brake is not dragging in the drum. If it is, loosen the brake adjuster (Figure 5) several turns.

2. Turn the selector to the free or disengaged position (**Figure 9**).

3. On K10 models, remove the snap ring from the hub (**Figure 10**) and pull the lockout mechanism out of the hub. On K20 models (**Figure 11**), unscrew the 6 bolts from the end of the hub, pull out the lockout mechanism, and remove the extension housing and gaskets. If necessary, tap extension loose with a soft mallet.

4. Remove the circlip from the end of the axle and pull off bushing and inner clutch ring assembly.

5. Refer to Steps 3, 4, and 5 in the procedure for standard hubs (above) and adjust the end-play of the hub as described.

6. Turn the selector to the engaged position to relax the springs in the lockout mechanism. With a drift, drive out the key knob retainer pin and remove the knob and flange from the clutch gear assembly. Remove the circlip from inside the knob and remove it from the flange. Clean and dry all of the hub parts and then thoroughly lubricate them before assemblying by reversing the disassembly steps. Use new gaskets and O-rings. Make certain the circlips are completely seated in their grooves. When assembly is complete, operate the selectors to make sure the hubs lock and unlock.

Lockout Hubs
(Internal Type, 1968-1975)

1. Rotate the wheel to ensure the brake is not dragging in the drum. If it is, loosen the brake adjuster (Figure 5) several turns.

2. Refer to **Figure 12** and unscrew the 6 screws which attach the retaining plate to the hub. Remove the washer and the plate. Pull out the

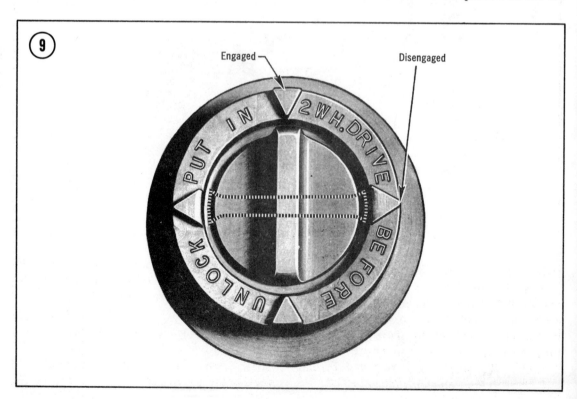

(9)   Engaged   Disengaged

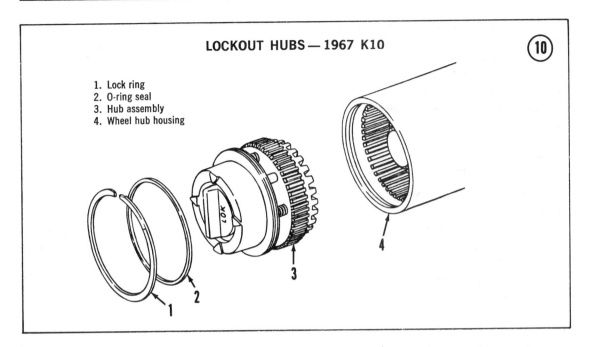

LOCKOUT HUBS — 1967 K10 (10)

1. Lock ring
2. O-ring seal
3. Hub assembly
4. Wheel hub housing

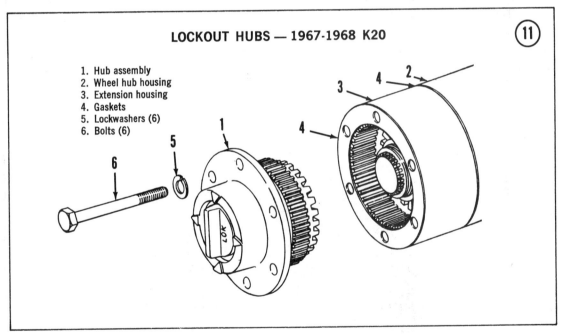

LOCKOUT HUBS — 1967-1968 K20 (11)

1. Hub assembly
2. Wheel hub housing
3. Extension housing
4. Gaskets
5. Lockwashers (6)
6. Bolts (6)

9

actuating knob assembly and remove the O-rings. Remove the internal snap ring and the outer clutch retaining ring. Pull out the actuating cam body. Press in on the axle shaft sleeve and ring assembly and remove the axle shaft snap ring. Remove the axle shaft sleeve and ring assembly, the inner clutch ring and bushing assembly, spring, and spring retaining plate.

3. Refer to Steps 3, 4, and 5 in the procedure for standard hubs (above) and adjust the end-play of the hub as described.

4. When the hub end-play has been correctly adjusted, clean and dry all of the hub parts and apply grease to the points shown in **Figure 13**. Refer to the first part of this procedure and reverse the disassembly steps to assemble the

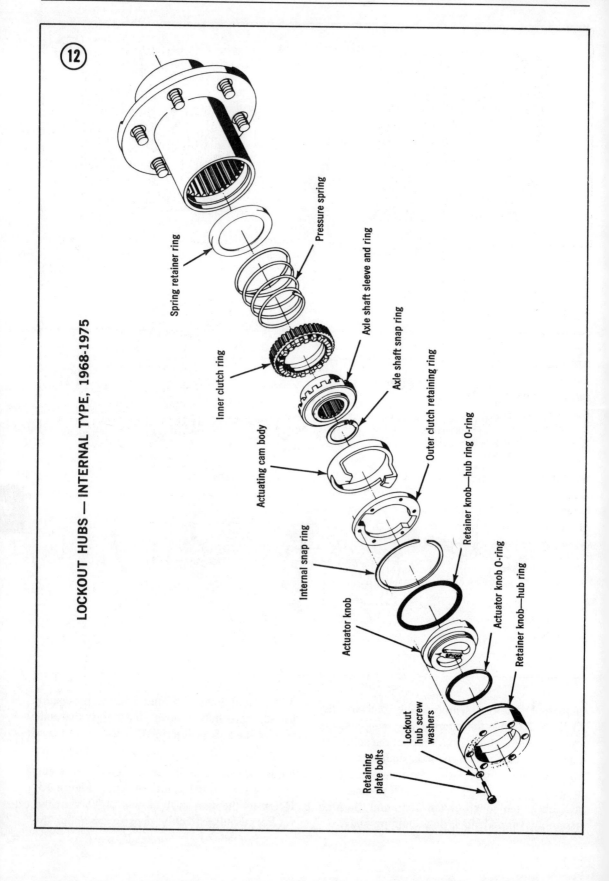

LOCKOUT HUBS — INTERNAL TYPE, 1968-1975

Spring retainer ring

Pressure spring

Inner clutch ring

Axle shaft sleeve and ring

Axle shaft snap ring

Actuating cam body

Outer clutch retaining ring

Retainer knob—hub ring O-ring

Internal snap ring

Actuator knob

Actuator knob O-ring

Retainer knob—hub ring

Lockout hub screw washers

Retaining plate bolts

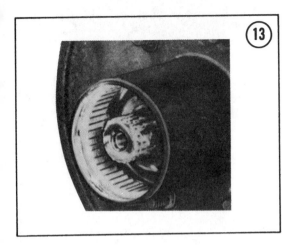

drive portion of the hub. Make sure the spring retainer plate fits firmly against the outer wheel bearing cup. Install the spring with the large coil against the plate (**Figure 14**). Assemble the inner and outer clutch rings (**Figure 15**) and install them in the hub keeping the teeth meshed. Use a new axle snap ring and make sure it is correctly seated in the groove. When installing the internal snap ring, make sure it is also correctly seated in its groove. Coat the large O-ring with O-ring lubricant and install it on the actuating knob and retaining plate assembly before installing this assembly in the hub (**Figure 16**). When the retaining plate has been installed, screw in the 6 screws and tighten them in a criss-cross pattern (**Figure 17**) to 35-40 in.-lb.

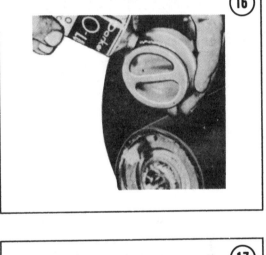

5. Readjust the brake adjuster if it was backed off earlier. Check and correct the end-play of the opposite hub in the manner just described.

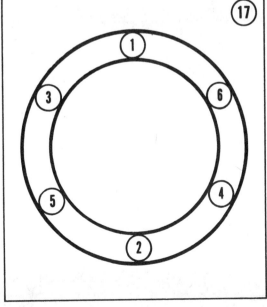

9

Lockout Hubs
(External Type—1969-1975)

1. Rotate the wheel to ensure the brake is not dragging in the drum. If it is, loosen the brake adjuster (Figure 5) several turns.

2. Refer to **Figure 18** and unscrew the screws from the actuating knob retainer. Note the position of the dished washers (**Figure 19**). They must be installed in exactly the same way.

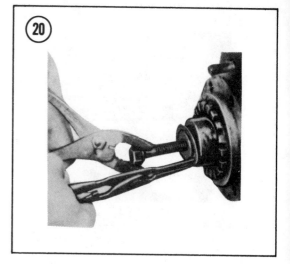

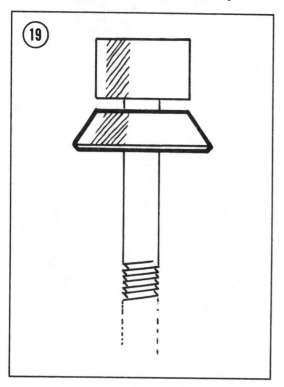

3. Break the gear hub housing loose from the wheel by tapping it with a mallet and remove it from the wheel.

4. Screw a bolt into the end of the axle, pull out on it, and remove the snap ring, inner clutch gear, and the bushing (**Figure 20**). Remove the grease cap.

5. Refer to Steps 3, 4, and 5 in the procedure for the standard hubs (above) and adjust the end-play of the hub as described.

6. When the hub end-play has been correctly adjusted, disassemble the drive portion of the hub and clean and lubricate it as described. Separate the housing from the knob retainer and discard both the inner and outer gaskets. Press

in on the clutch gear and remove the snap ring which attaches it to the actuating cam. Turn the actuator knob to LOCK and slowly release the outer clutch gear and remove it and the spring. Turn the actuator knob to FREE and drive the cam lock pin out of the assembly with a drift and remove the cam. Remove the knob retainer snap ring and then remove the knob from the retainer.

7. Clean all of the parts thoroughly and inspect the spines on the clutch gears for damage. Minor roughness can be removed with fine emery cloth but if damage is severe, the pieces should be replaced. Apply high-speed grease to both faces of the bushing, the splines in the housing and the clutch gears, and both cam grooves. Apply Parker O-ring lubricant to the groove in the actuating knob and install the O-ring. Set the knob in the retainer with the arrow pointing to FREE and install the snap ring (**Figure 21**). Line up the ears on the actuating cam with the grooves in the retainer and set it in place. Install the lock pin making sure both of its ends are flush with the outer surface of the cam. Turn the knob to LOCK and install the spring, outer clutch, and snap ring, making sure the snap ring is correctly seated in its groove. Turn the knob back to FREE and install 2 screws and washers in the retainer. Wipe the retainer to remove any grease and install a new outer gasket. Line up the gear hub housing with the 2 screws and the splines on the outer clutch gear and set it in place on the retainer. Install a new inner gasket over

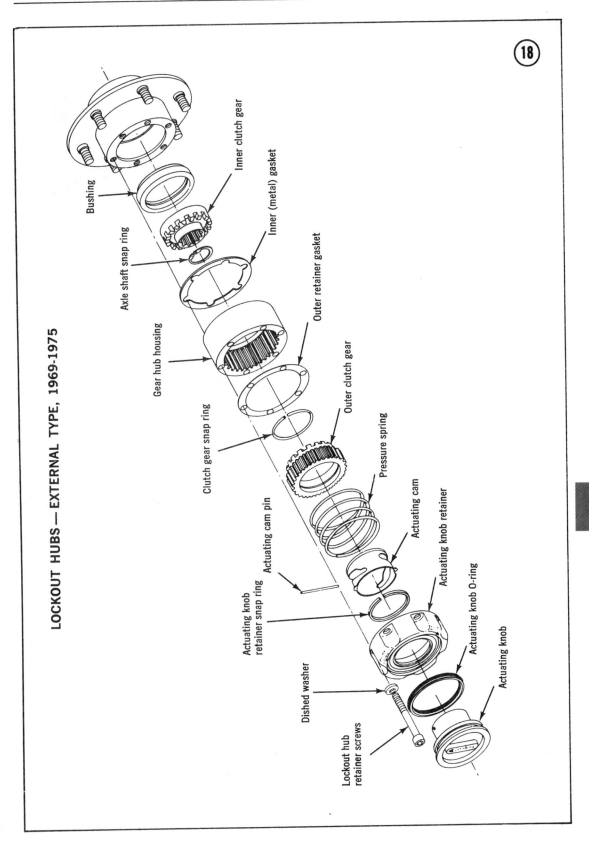

LOCKOUT HUBS — EXTERNAL TYPE, 1969-1975

Bushing

Inner clutch gear

Axle shaft snap ring

Inner (metal) gasket

Gear hub housing

Outer retainer gasket

Clutch gear snap ring

Outer clutch gear

Actuating cam pin

Pressure spring

Actuating cam

Actuating knob retainer

Actuating knob
retainer snap ring

Actuating knob O-ring

Actuating knob

Dished washer

Lockout hub
retainer screws

18

9

the 2 protruding screws. Install the hub bushing and inner clutch gear. Pull out on the bolt in the end of the axle and install the snap ring, making sure it is correctly seated in its groove. Unscrew the bolt from the axle. Install the hub on the wheel and screw in the 2 positioning screws. Turn the knob to LOCK. Install the remaining screws and washers, and tighten them in a criss-cross pattern (**Figure 22**) to 30-35 ft.-lb. Turn the knob back to FREE. It may be difficult to turn at first, but it will loosen after the vehicle has been driven a short distance.

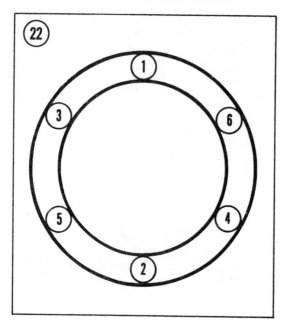

8. Readjust the brake adjuster if it was backed off earlier. Check and adjust the free-play of

the opposite hub, and clean and lubricate the hub drive mechanism in the manner just described.

FRONT HUB AND BEARING LUBRICATION

The front hubs should be serviced at the intervals discussed under *Front Wheel Bearings and Hubs.*

1. Raise the front of the vehicle and support it on frame stands as described in Chapter One.

2. Disassemble the hubs as described under bearing adjustment above. Continue disassembly by unscrewing the bearing adjusting nut.

3. Pull out on the wheel to remove the wheel, brake drum, and hub as an assembly. This will also remove the outer bearing assembly from the axle spindle.

4. Drive the inner bearing cup and the bearing out of the hub using either a bearing driver (**Figure 23**) or soft drift, tapping progressively around the inner edge of the bearing assembly.

5. Thoroughly clean the bearings and the inside of the hub with solvent and blow them dry with compressed air.

WARNING
Do not spin the bearings with the air jet; it is capable of rotating the bear-

ings at speeds far in excess of those for which they were designed. The likelihood of a bearing disintegrating under this condition and causing damage and injury is very real.

Check the bearing rollers and the cups for signs of wear and damage and replace them as a set if they are less than satisfactory. If the bearings are to be replaced, carefully drive the outer cups out of the hub using a soft drift and tapping evenly around the edges of the cups. Seat the new cups squarely in the hub and carefully tap them into place with the drift, evenly around the circumference of each cup.

6. Clean the brake assembly as much as possible, using a stiff, *dry* brush; do not use any solvents to clean any of the brake components and in particular make sure no solvents come in contact with the brake lining material. Solvent will render the lining unserviceable, requiring that it be replaced.

NOTE: *This is a good opportunity to check the serviceability of the brake linings. Refer to Chapter Eight and inspect and measure the lining as described.*

7. When the brake has been cleaned and all of the dirt and foreign matter removed, carefully clean the spindle with solvent, taking care not to get any on the brake.

8. Pack the inside of the hub with a multi-purpose grease until it is level with the inside diameter of the outer bearing cups (**Figure 24**). Thoroughly pack the bearing assemblies with grease, working it in carefully by hand, and apply a film of grease to the inner cone. Install the inner bearing assembly into the outer cup. Set a new seal squarely into the hub and carefully tap it into place evenly around the circumference.

9. Install the wheel, keeping the hub centered around the spindle to prevent damage to the spindle threads and the seal. Install the outer bearing assembly and screw on the bearing adjusting nut. Refer to the procedure for bearing adjustment and adjust the end-play of the hub and complete the reassembly. Repeat the above procedure for the opposite wheel.

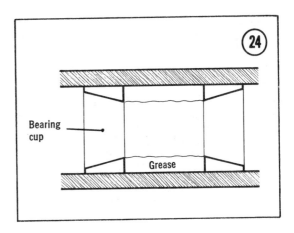

DRIVE SHAFTS

When the vehicle is to be towed for long distances, it is essential that the drive shafts be disconnected (this is not necessary for the front drive shaft on models equipped with lockout type hubs).

1. Mark both halves of the yoke at the axle with light-colored chalk or crayon so the phasing of the drive shaft and differential will be the same when the drive shaft is reconnected (**Figure 25**).

2. Unscrew the 4 nuts at the axle end of the drive shaft (**Figure 26**), carefully back the U-bolts out by tapping them, and disconnect the end of the shaft. Tape the bearing cups in place so they will not fall off.

3. Securely tie the end of the drive shaft up and out of the way of the differential.

4. Before reconnecting the drive shaft, thoroughly clean the yoke, bearing caps, and U-bolts. Line up the end of the shaft with the differential yoke making sure the marks are on the same side.

5. Tap the U-bolts into place and screw on the nuts and tighten them in a criss-cross pattern (**Figure 27**) to 8-15 ft.-lb.

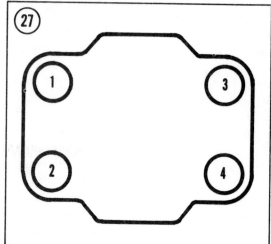

CHAPTER TEN

AIR CONDITIONING

AIR CONDITIONING

Major service and repair to air conditioning systems requires specialized training and tools, and the difficulty of the work is compounded in the late heating/air conditioning systems. However, most air conditioning problems do not involve major repair; they are well within the ability of an experienced hobbyist mechanic, armed with an understanding of how the system works.

SYSTEM OPERATION

A typical air conditioning system is shown in **Figure 1**. (Actual component locations may differ, depending on model.)

The five basic components are common to all air conditioning systems:

a. Compressor
b. Condenser
c. Receiver/drier
d. Expansion valve
e. Evaporator

> *WARNING*
> *The components, connected with high-pressure hoses and tubes, form a closed loop. A refrigerant, dichlorodifluoromethane (more commonly referred to as R-12), circulates through the system under high pressure—as much as 300 psi. As a result, work on the air conditioning system is potentially hazardous if certain precautions are ignored. For safety's sake, **read this entire section** before attempting any troubleshooting, checks, or work on the system.*

A typical system is shown schematically in **Figure 2**. For practical purposes, the cycle begins at the compressor. The refrigerant, in a warm, low-pressure vapor state, enters the low-pressure side of the compressor. It is compressed to a high-pressure hot vapor and pumped out of the high-pressure side to the condenser.

Air flow through the condenser removes heat from the refrigerant and transfers the heat to the outside air. As the heat is removed, the refrigerant condenses to a warm, high-pressure liquid.

The refrigerant then flows to the receiver/drier where moisture is removed and impurities are filtered out. The refrigerant is stored in the receiver/drier until it is needed. Generally, the receiver/drier incorporates a sight glass that permits visual monitoring of the condition of the refrigerant as it flows. This is discussed later.

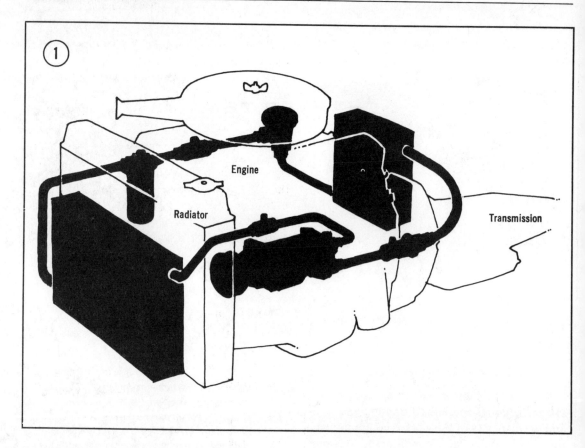

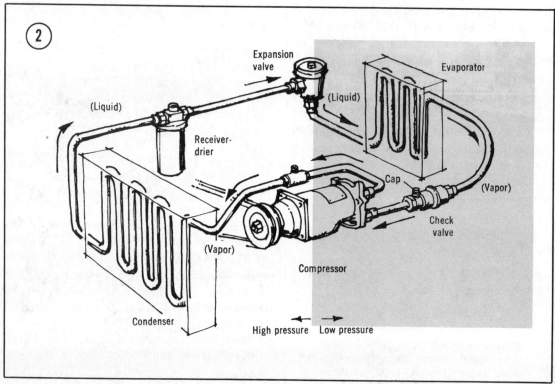

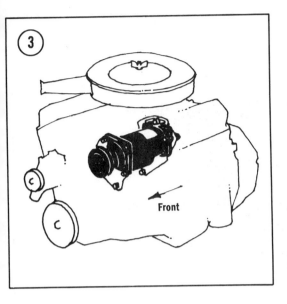

Front

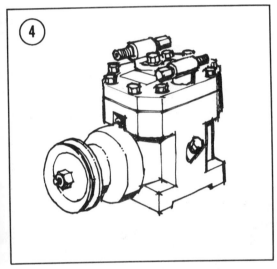

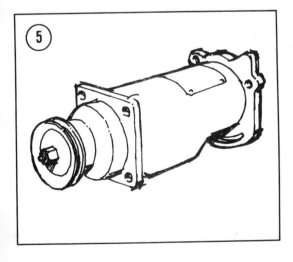

From the receiver/drier, the refrigerant flows to the expansion valve. The expansion valve is thermostatically controlled and meters refrigerant to the evaporator. As the refrigerant leaves the expansion valve it changes from a warm, high-pressure liquid to a cold, low-pressure liquid.

In the evaporator, the refrigerant removes heat from the cockpit air that is blown across the evaporator's fins and tubes. In the process, the refrigerant changes from a cold, low-pressure liquid to a warm, high-pressure vapor which flows back to the compressor where the refrigeration cycle began.

GET TO KNOW YOUR VEHICLE'S SYSTEM

With **Figure 1** as a guide, begin with the compressor and locate each of the following components in turn:

a. Compressor
b. Condenser
c. Receiver/drier
d. Expansion valve
e. Evaporator

Compressor

The compressor is located on the front of the engine, like an alternator, and is driven by one or two drive belts (**Figure 3**). The large pulley on the front contains an electromagnetic clutch that is activated and operates the compressor when the air conditioning controls are switched on. There are two compressor types — piston-and-crank (**Figure 4**) and swashplate (axial plate, **Figure 5**).

Condenser

In most cases, the condenser is mounted in front of the radiator (**Figure 6**). Air passing through the fins and tubes removes heat from the refrigerant in the same manner it removes heat from the engine coolant as it passes through the radiator.

Receiver/Drier

The receiver/drier is a small tank-like unit (**Figure 7**), usually found mounted to one of the

10

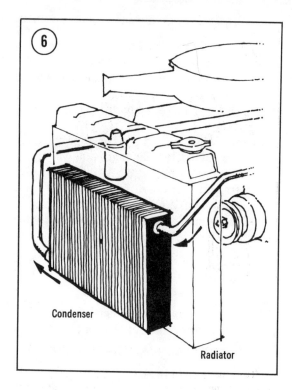

Condenser

Radiator

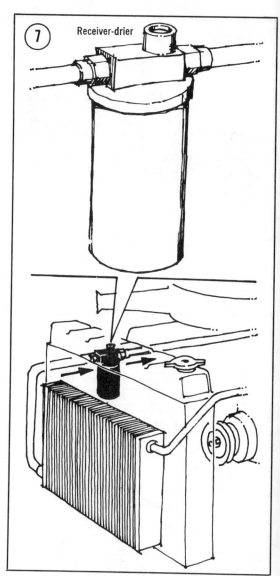

Receiver-drier

wheel wells. Many receiver/driers incorporate a sight glass through which refrigerant flow can be seen when the system is operating (**Figure 8**). Some systems have an in-line sight glass (**Figure 9**). Some early systems do not have a sight glass but it's not essential to system operation — just handy to help diagnose air conditioning problems.

Expansion Valve

The expansion valve (**Figure 10**) is located between the receiver/drier and the evaporator. It is usually mounted on or near the firewall, in the engine compartment. In some very late systems, the valve is concealed in a housing on the firewall.

Evaporator

The evaporator is located in the passenger compartment, beneath the dashboard, and is hidden from view by the fan shrouding and ducting (**Figure 11**). Warm air from the passenger compartment is blown across the fins and tubes in the evaporator where it is cooled and dried and then ducted back into the compartment through the air outlets.

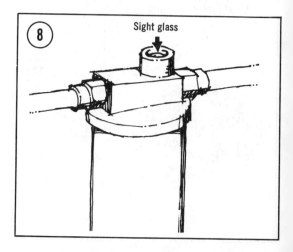

Sight glass

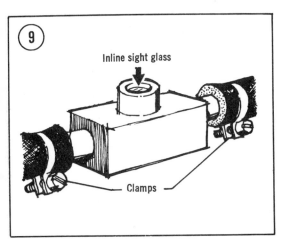

⑨

Inline sight glass

Clamps

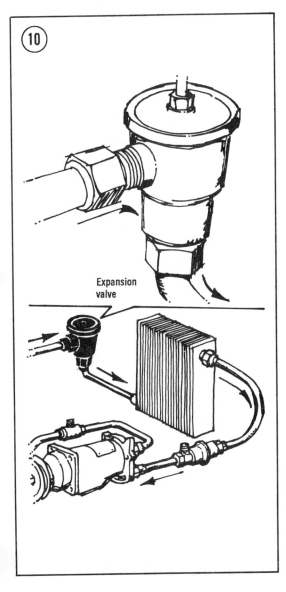

⑩

Expansion
valve

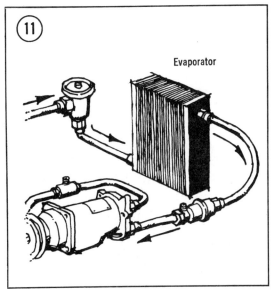

⑪

Evaporator

ROUTINE MAINTENANCE

Preventive maintenance for your air conditioning system couldn't be simpler; at least once a month, even in cold weather, start your engine and turn on the air conditioner and operate it at each of the switch and control settings. Allow it to operate for about five minutes. This will ensure that the compressor seal will not deform from sitting in the same position for a long period of time. If this occurs, the seal is likely to leak.

The efficiency of your air conditioning system depends in great part on the efficiency of your engine cooling system. Periodically check the coolant for level and cleanliness. If it is dirty, drain and flush the system and fill it with fresh coolant and water, following the coolant manufacturer's instructions for coolant/water ratio. Have your radiator cap pressure tested and replace it if it will not maintain 13 psi pressure. If the system requires repeated topping up and the radiator cap is in good condition, it is likely that there is a leak in the system. Pressure test it as described earlier in Chapter Seven.

With an air hose and a soft brush, clean the radiator fins and tubes to remove bugs, leaves, and any other imbedded debris.

Check and correct drive belt tension as described earlier.

10

If the condition of the cooling system thermostat is in doubt, check it as described earlier and replace it if it is faulty.

When you are confident that the engine cooling system is working correctly, you are ready to inspect and test the air conditioning system.

Inspection

1. Clean all lines, fittings, and system components with solvent and a clean rag. Pay particular attention to the fittings; oily dirt around connections almost certainly indicates a leak. Oil from the compressor will migrate through the system to the leak. Carefully tighten the connection, taking care not to overtighten and risk stripping the threads. If the leak persists it will soon be apparent once again as oily dirt accumulates. Clean the sight glass with a clean, dry cloth.

2. Clean the condenser fins and tubes with a soft brush and an air hose, or with a high-pressure stream of water from a garden hose. Remove bugs, leaves, and other imbedded debris. Carefully straighten any bent fins with a screwdriver, taking care not to dent or puncture the tubes.

3. Check the condition and tension of the drive belts and replace or correct as necessary.

4. Start the engine and check the operation of the blower motor and the compressor clutch by turning the controls on and off. If either the blower or the clutch fails to operate, shut off the engine and check the condition of the fuses. If they are blown, replace them. If not, remove them and clean the fuse holder contacts. Then, recheck to ensure that the blower and clutch operate.

Testing

1. With the transmission in PARK (automatic) or NEUTRAL (manual) and the handbrake set, start the engine and run it at a fast idle.

2. Set the temperature control to its coldest setting and turn the blower to high. Allow the system to operate for 10 minutes with the doors and windows open. Then close them and set the blower on its lowest setting.

3. Place a thermometer in a cold-air outlet. Within a few minutes, the temperature should be 35-45°F. If it is not, it's likely that the refrigerant level in the system is low. Check the appearance of the refrigerant flow through the sight glass. If it is bubbly, refrigerant should be added.

REFRIGERANT

The majority of automotive air conditioning systems use a refrigerant designated R-12. However, a commercial grade, designated R-20, is used in heavy-duty systems. The two are not compatible. Look for an information sticker, usually mounted near the compressor, to determine which refrigerant your system uses (**Figure 12**). Also, check the system capacity indicated on the sticker. Capacity can range from two to five pounds, depending on the system.

> WARNING
> *That harmless-looking little can of refrigerant is potentially hazardous. If it is hooked up to the high-pressure side of the compressor, or is hooked up without a gauge set, it becomes almost like a hand grenade.*

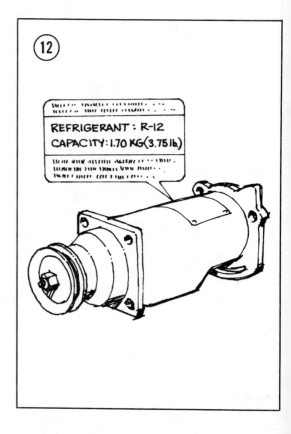

REFRIGERANT : R-12
CAPACITY : 1.70 KG (3.75 lb)

Charging

1. Carefully read and understand the gauge manufacturer's instructions before charging the system.

2. Remove the cap from the Schrader valve on the low-pressure side of the compressor (**Figure 13**). The low-pressure is labelled SUCTION, SUCT., or SUC.

3. Connect the gauge set to the low-pressure Schrader valve. Connect the refrigerant can to the gauge set and hang the gauge set on the hood (**Figure 14**).

4. Start the engine and run it at a fast idle (about 1,000 rpm).

5. Set the temperature control at its coldest setting. Set the blower at its lowest setting.

6. Slowly open the refrigerant feed valve on the gauge set (**Figure 15**). Do not allow the refrigerant pressure to exceed 50 psi.

7. Watch the refrigerant as it flows through the sight glass (**Figure 16**). When it's free of bubbles, the system is charged. Shut off the refrigerant feed valve on the gauge set.

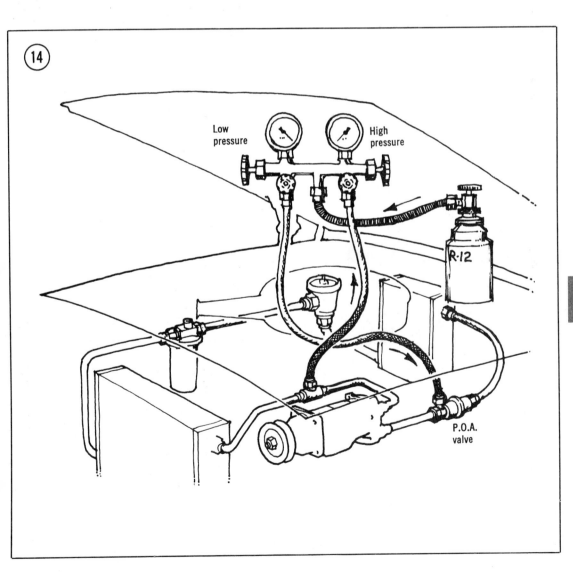

(14)

Low pressure — High pressure

R-12

P.O.A. valve

10

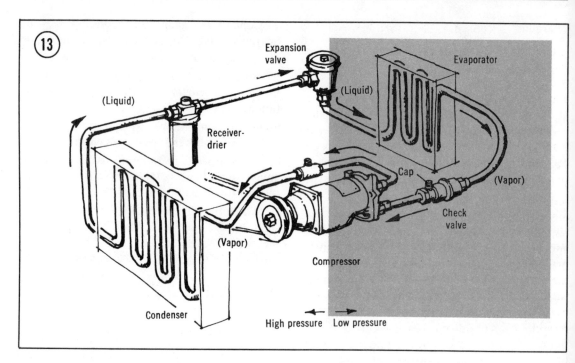

(13)

Expansion
valve

(Liquid)

Evaporator

(Liquid)

Receiver-
drier

Cap

(Vapor)

Check
valve

(Vapor)

Compressor

Condenser

High pressure   Low pressure

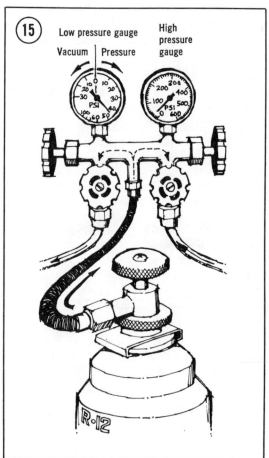

(15)

Low pressure gauge   High
                       pressure
Vacuum | Pressure   gauge

PSI

PSI

R-12

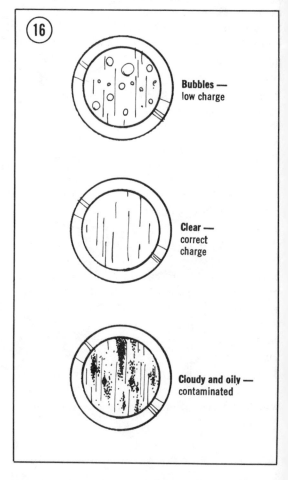

(16)

Bubbles —
low charge

Clear —
correct
charge

Cloudy and oily —
contaminated

TROUBLESHOOTING

Preventive maintenance like that just described will help to ensure that your system is working efficiently. Still, trouble can develop and while most of it will invariably be simple and easy to correct, you must first locate it. The following sequence will help to diagnose system troubles when your air conditioning ceases to cool the passenger compartment.

1. First, stop the vehicle and look at the control settings. One of the most common sources of air conditioning trouble occurs when the temperature control is set for maximum cold and the blower is set on low. This arrangement promotes ice buildup on the fins and tubes of the evaporator, and particularly so in humid weather. Eventually, the evaporator will ice over completely, and restrict air flow. Turn the blower on high and place a hand over an air outlet. If the blower is running but there is little or no air flowing through the outlet, the evaporator is probably iced up. Leave the blower on high and turn off the temperature control or turn it down to its lowest setting — and wait; it will take 10 or 15 minutes before the ice begins to melt.

2. If the blower is not running, the motor may be burned out, there may be a loose connection, or the fuse may be blown. First check the fuse panel for a blown or incorrectly seated fuse. Then, check the wiring for loose connections.

3. Shut off the engine and check the condition and tension of the compressor drive belt. If it is loose or badly worn, tighten or replace it.

4. Start the engine and check the condition of the compressor clutch by turning the air conditioner on and off. If the clutch does not energize, it may be defective, its fuse may be blown, or the evaporator temperature-limiting switches may be defective. If the fuse is defective, replace it. If the clutch still does not energize, refer the problem to an air conditioning specialist.

5. If all components checked so far are OK, start the engine, turn on the air conditioner and watch the refrigerant through the sight glass; remember, if it's filled with bubbles after the system has been operating for a few seconds, the refrigerant level is low. If the sight glass is oily or cloudy, the system is contaminated and should be serviced by an expert as soon as possible. Corrosion and deterioration occur rapidly, and if it's not taken care of at once it will result in a very expensive repair job.

6. If the system still appears to be operating satisfactorily but the air flow into the passenger compartment is not cold, check the condenser and cooling system radiator for debris that could block the air flow. Recheck the cooling system as described under *Inspection*.

7. If the above steps do not uncover the difficulty, have the system checked and corrected by a specialist as soon as possible.

DISCHARGING THE SYSTEM

The pressure in the system must be relieved before any fittings are disconnected. To do this, connect the gauge set in the same manner as though the system were to be charged; however, do not attach a refrigerant can to the center hose. Slowly open both the high- and low-pressure valves on the gauge set. Then, slowly open the valve for the center hose.

WARNING
Route the center hose down through the engine compartment so it will discharge on the ground. Wear safety goggles and take care not to let the refrigerant touch your skin.

When the system pressure has been relieved, disconnect the gauge set. Slowly loosen any fittings that are involved until you are sure the system is not pressurized. *Wear safety goggles.*

Immediately plug any open fittings to keep moisture out of the system; corrosion will begin almost instantly if the system is left open to the atmosphere, and it will quickly make some very expensive components unserviceable.

When all of the system components and lines have been reconnected, charge the system as described earlier.

10

CHAPTER ELEVEN

EMISSION CONTROL SYSTEM

Harmful emissions are minimized by a number of systems, depending on year:

a. Positive crankcase ventilation (PCV)
b. Controlled combustion system (CCS)
c. Air injection reaction (AIR)
d. Combination emission control system (CEC)
e. Fuel evaporation control system (ECS)
f. Exhaust gas recirculation system (EGR)
g. Carburetor calibration
h. Distributor calibration
i. Catalytic converter
j. Early evaporation system (EFE)

POSITIVE CRANKCASE VENTILATION

All vehicles covered have positive crankcase ventilation. Clean air is drawn from the air cleaner; the oil filler cap is not vented. The clean air scavenges emissions (e.g., piston blow-by) from the crankcase, and manifold vacuum draws the emissions into the carburetor. Eventually they can be reburned in the normal combuston process. **Figure 1** shows the closed system.

Either a PCV valve or fixed metered orifice mounted on the carburetor controls the volume of flow from crankcase to manifold.

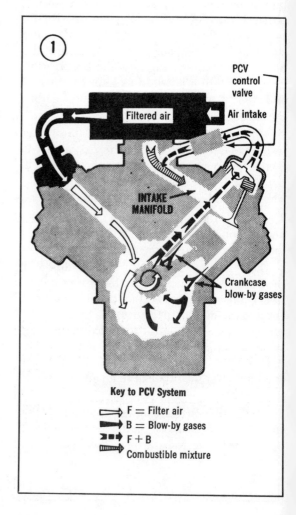

① PCV control valve

Filtered air   Air intake

INTAKE MANIFOLD

Crankcase blow-by gases

Key to PCV System

→ F = Filter air
→ B = Blow-by gases
→ F + B
→ Combustible mixture

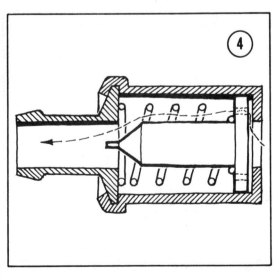

The PCV valve should be checked and replaced, if necessary, at each tune-up. Remove the valve from the rocker cover but leave it connected to the vent hose.

If the valve is clear, a hissing sound will be heard when the engine is idling, and a strong vacuum will be felt when a finger is placed over the valve (**Figure 2**).

Reinstall the valve in the rocker cover and disconnect the crankcase inlet air cleaner from the rocker cover. Hold a stiff piece of paper over the opening (**Figure 3**). After about a minute, when the crankcase pressure has subsided, the paper should be sucked down against the hole. Shut off the engine and once again disconnect the PCV valve from the rocker cover. Shake it and listen for a clicking sound that indicates the valve is free. If it is not, it should be replaced.

When a new valve is installed, check it as before, with a piece of paper held over the inlet. If the force is not considerable, it is necessary to clean the vent hose and the passages in the carburetor. Clean the hose with solvent and blow it dry with compressed air. The carburetor must be removed to clean the passages; this should be entrusted to a dealer. **Figure 4** shows a cross section of a PCV valve.

CONTROLLED COMBUSTION SYSTEM

The controlled combustion system on 1970 and later models includes a special thermostatically controlled air cleaner, special calibrated carburetor and distributor, and a higher temperature thermostat (**Figure 5**).

The thermostatically controlled air cleaner maintains air to the carburetor at a temperature of 100°F or higher. The air cleaner includes a temperature sensor, vacuum motor, and control damper assembly (**Figure 6**).

Operation of the air cleaner is shown in **Figure 7**. When the engine is off, absence of manifold vacuum permits the vacuum motor to close off the hot air pipe. When the engine is running and underhood temperatures are below 85°F, the temperature sensor bleed valve is closed and manifold vacuum operates the vacuum motor. The vacuum motor closes off the underhood air supply and the carburetor

11

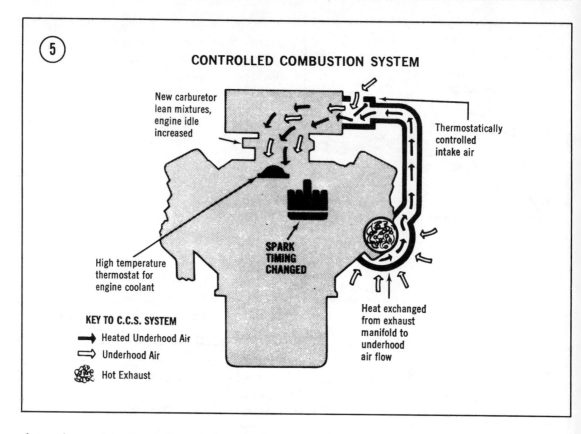

⑤ CONTROLLED COMBUSTION SYSTEM

New carburetor lean mixtures, engine idle increased

Thermostatically controlled intake air

High temperature thermostat for engine coolant

SPARK TIMING CHANGED

Heat exchanged from exhaust manifold to underhood air flow

KEY TO C.C.S. SYSTEM
→ Heated Underhood Air
⇨ Underhood Air
🌀 Hot Exhaust

draws the much hotter air from the hot air pipe. Between 85°F and 128°F, the temperature sensor air bleed is partially open. The vacuum motor opens both the underhood air inlet and the hot air tube inlet. The resulting blend is maintained around 100°F or higher. Finally, if the underhood temperature is above 128°F, the temperature sensor air bleed is fully open, the vacuum motor cannot operate and carburetor air is drawn from the underhood air inlet only.

Inspection

1. Check all heat pipe and hose connections.

2. Check for kinked or deteriorated hoses.

3. Remove the air cleaner cover and place a thermometer as close as possible to the sensor. Install the cover. Lift the cover after temperature stabilizes and read thermometer; temperature must be below 85°F before proceeding. Put cover back in place.

> NOTE: *Use a relatively fast acting thermometer such as a photographic darkroom thermometer. These are available for less than $10.*

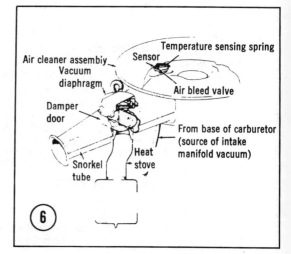

Temperature sensing spring

Air cleaner assembly
Sensor
Vacuum diaphragm
Air bleed valve
Damper door
From base of carburetor (source of intake manifold vacuum)
Snorkel tube
Heat stove

⑥

4. With the engine off, the snorkel passage should be completely open (**Figure 7**, View A). If not, check for binds in the linkage.

5. Start the engine. With the air temperature below 85°F, snorkel passage should close. When the damper door begins to open, remove air cleaner cover and check the temperature; it should be between 85-115°F.

⑦

A—ENGINE OFF

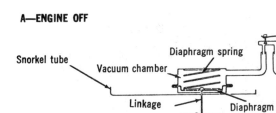

**B—UNDERHOOD TEMPERATURE
BELOW 85°F**

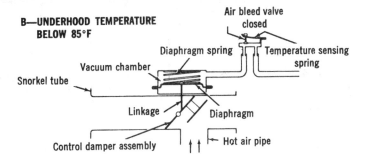

**C—UNDERHOOD TEMPERATURE
ABOVE 128°F**

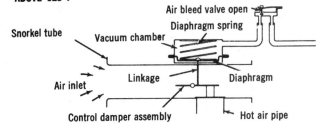

11

**D—UNDERHOOD TEMPERATURE
BETWEEN 85°F AND 128°F**

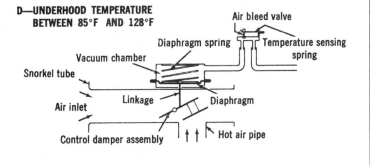

6. If the damper door does not close completely or open at the right temperature, check the vacuum motor as described below.

Vacuum Motor Checking

1. Turn the engine off and disconnect the vacuum hose from the sensor.

2. Suck on the hose. The damper door should completely close. If not, check for a vacuum leak at other end of hose.

3. With vacuum applied, bend or tightly clamp hose. The damper door should remain closed. If not, the vacuum motor leaks and must be replaced.

4. If the vacuum motor is good but the system does not work properly, replace the temperature sensor.

Vacuum Motor Replacement

Refer to **Figure 8** for the following procedure.

1. Remove the air cleaner from engine.

2. Drill out the spot welds that fasten the motor to the snorkel.

3. Unhook the motor from the damper door.

4. Drill a ⁷⁄₆₄ in. hole in the snorkel tube at the center of the motor retaining strap.

5. Connect the motor to the damper door.

6. Fasten the retaining strap to the air cleaner with a sheet metal screw.

7. Install the air cleaner and check the operation of vacuum motor as described above.

Temperature Sensor Replacement

1. Remove the air cleaner from engine and disconnect the vacuum hose at the sensor.

2. Pry up the sensor clip tubes. See **Figure 9**.

3. Remove the clip and sensor from the air cleaner.

4. Install the sensor and gasket in the air cleaner in exactly the same position as the old one.

5. Press the clip on sensor. Hold sensor by its sides only; do not touch control mechanism.

6. Install air cleaner and connect vacuum hoses.

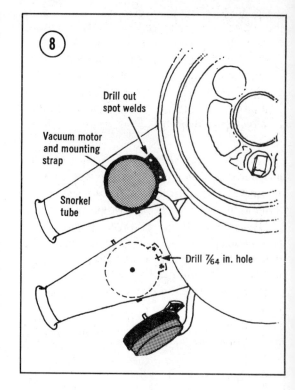

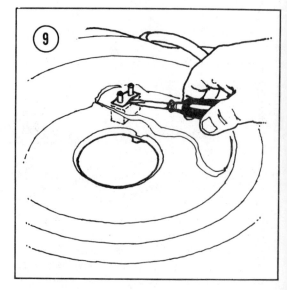

AIR INJECTION REACTOR SYSTEM

The air injection reactor system reduces air pollution by oxidizing hydrocarbons and carbon monoxide as they leave the combustion chamber. See **Figure 10 and 11**.

The air injection pump, driven by the engine, compresses filtered air and injects it at

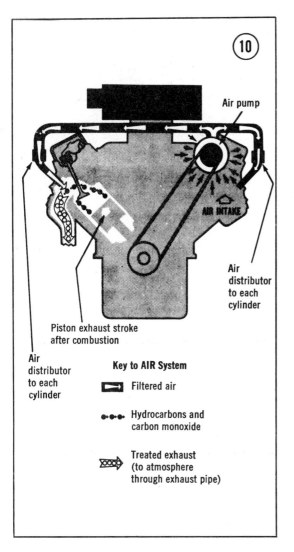

Air pump

Air distributor to each cylinder

AIR INTAKE

Piston exhaust stroke after combustion

Air distributor to each cylinder

Key to AIR System

Filtered air

Hydrocarbons and carbon monoxide

Treated exhaust (to atmosphere through exhaust pipe)

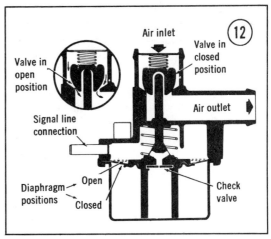

Air inlet

Valve in open position

Valve in closed position

Air outlet

Signal line connection

Diaphragm positions

Open

Closed

Check valve

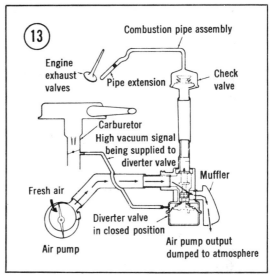

Combustion pipe assembly

Engine exhaust valves

Pipe extension

Check valve

Carburetor

High vacuum signal being supplied to diverter valve

Muffler

Fresh air

Diverter valve in closed position

Air pump output dumped to atmosphere

Air pump

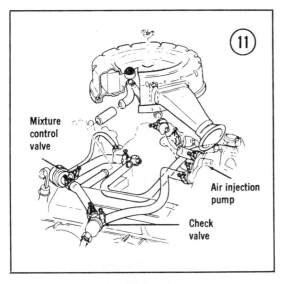

Mixture control valve

Air injection pump

Check valve

the exhaust port of each cylinder. The fresh air mixes with the unburned gases in the exhaust and promotes further burning.

On 1967 systems, the mixture control valve **(Figure 12)** senses sharp increases in manifold vacuum, such as closed throttle deceleration. The increased vacuum opens the valve admitting fresh air into the intake manifold. This leans out the air/fuel mixture and prevents exhaust system backfire.

On 1968 and later systems, a diverter valve performs a function similar to the earlier mixture control valve. However, rather than admitting air from the pump into the intake manifold, backfire is prevented by cutting the fresh air to the exhaust system and diverting the pump output to the atmosphere **(Figure 13)**.

11

The check valves prevent exhaust gases from entering and damaging the air pump if the pump becomes inoperative, e.g., from a drive belt failure. Under normal conditions, the pump delivers sufficient air pressure to prevent exhaust gases from entering the pump.

The air injection reactor system also depends on a special calibrated carburetor, distributor, and other related components.

AIR System Inspection

The inspections to the AIR system can be performed without the aid of special test equipment. Replacement of faulty hoses, check valves, diverter valve, or drive belt are routine. However, when replacing hoses, make sure they are designed for use with the AIR system and will withstand high operating temperatures. Also, use an anti-seize compound on the threads of all connectors that attach to the exhaust manifold or cylinder head.

Drive Belt

Check the condition of the drive belt. If it is cracked, worn, excessively glazed, or if the rubber is deteriorated, replace it. Also check the tension of the belt. If the belt is in good condition, it should be adjusted to a tension of 50 lb. using a belt tension gauge.

If adjustment is required, loosen the pump pivot bolt and the bracket adjustment bolt. Move the pump as required until the tension is correct.

> **WARNING**
> *Do not pry on the pump housing to move it. This can severely damage the pump.*

Air Manifold, Hoses, and Tubes

Inspect the hoses for deterioration and check the hoses and tubes for cracks. Replace any that are not satisfactory. Check the connections to make sure they are tight and leak free. Test the pressure side of the system with a soapy water solution applied to each of the connections with the engine idling (**Figure 14**). Bubbling and foaming are indications that a connection is not tight and leak free. Correct any leaks that are found.

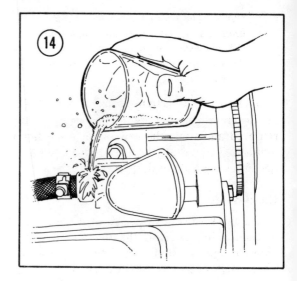

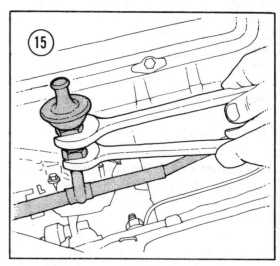

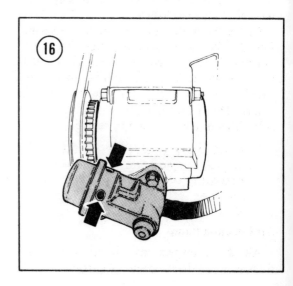

NOTE: *The connectors at the cylinder head (L6 engine) or exhaust manifold (V8 engines) are ¼-in. straight pipe threads; do not use a ¼-in. tapered tap to clean them.*

If a hose or tube is to be replaced, pay careful attention to the routing of the piece being removed and route the new piece in the same manner. Tighten all the connections securely and check for leaks as described above.

Check Valve

If a check valve is suspected of being faulty, disconnect its hose from the diverter valve and blow through it. There should be no resistance. Then, attempt to suck air through the hose. If the valve is in good condition this will not be possible. If the valve fails to perform satisfactorily in either direction, replace it. When removing and installing a check valve be careful not to bend the air manifold. Use two wrenches of comparable shaft length for equal torque (**Figure 15**).

Diverter Valve

Check the condition and tightness of the lines to the diverter valve. Pay particular attention to the vacuum line from the carburetor base plate or manifold to the valve; it must not be kinked, damaged, or deteriorated. With the engine idling, disconnect the vacuum line from the diverter valve and see if vacuum is present. If it is not, the line or the ports in the carburetor base plate may be clogged.

Check the outlets in the diverter valve muffler. At idle, no air should escape through the muffler. Quickly open and close the throttle; a blast of air at least one second in duration should be discharged through the muffler (**Figure 16**). If the valve fails to operate correctly in either mode, it should be replaced.

NOTE: *Make certain a new valve is the same as or equivalent to the one being replaced to ensure that it was designed for your engine and its operating specifications.*

Air Injection Pump

All of the inspections, checks, and corrections just described should be carried out first.

Then, with the air pressure hoses disconnected from the check valves, accelerate the engine to about 1,500 rpm and check the air flow from the hoses. It should increase as engine speed increases. If it does not, or if there is no air pressure at all, the air pump can be assumed to be faulty. Service to or replacement of the pump should be entrusted to a dealer.

NOTE: *If, after inspection and correction of any defects found in the* AIR *system have been carried out, the vehicle performs poorly or does not idle smoothly, the earlier tune-up procedures and inspections should be rechecked. The pump and the pressure-side lines and fittings have no effect on engine performance. Rough idling or poor performance could be caused by a leaking diverter valve vacuum line, or backfiring could be caused by a defective diverter valve or connections. The* AIR *system has no effect on performance other than these points.*

Air Injection Pump
Removal/Installation

1. Disconnect the hoses from the pump.
2. Hold the pump pulley with the belt and loosen the bolts.
3. Loosen the pump mounting bolt and pump adjustment bracket bolt. Swing the pump until the drive belt can be removed.
4. Remove the pump pulley.
5. Remove the pump mounting bolts and remove the pump.
6. Installation is the reverse of these steps.
7. Adjust belt tension (Chapter Three).

Mixture Control Valve Replacement

1. Refer to **Figure 17**. Disconnect the vacuum signal line.
2. Disconnect the air inlet and outlet hoses.
3. Remove the valve.
4. Install a new valve by reversing these steps.

NOTE: *The mixture control valves, though similar in appearance, are designed for a particular engine. Be sure you install the correct valve.*

11

Check Valve Replacement

Refer to **Figure 17** for following procedure.

1. Disconnect pump outlet hoses from valve.

2. Unscrew check valve from air manifold. Be careful not to bend the manifold.

3. Installation is the reverse of these steps.

Air Hose Replacement

To remove any hose or tube, first note the routing, then remove the hose or tube and install a new piece and tighten the connection.

CAUTION
Air reactor system hoses are made from special materials to withstand high temperatures. Do not use substitutes.

COMBINED EMISSION CONTROL SYSTEM

This system reduces exhaust emissions by permitting vacuum spark advance while in high gear only. It also prevents dieseling common to emission controlled engines.

The system consists of an electrically operated solenoid which shuts off the vacuum line between the carburetor and the distributor. See **Figure 18**. A switch on the transmission detects when the transmission is in a high gear.

Figure 19 is a more detailed diagram of the 1970-1971 system. When the solenoid is not energized, vacuum to the distributor vacuum advance unit is shut off. The distributor is vented to atmosphere through a filter at the opposite end of the solenoid. When the solenoid is energized, the vacuum ports uncover and the plunger shuts off the clean air vent.

The solenoid performs another function besides that of a vacuum switch. When idling in a low gear, e.g., during high gear deceleration with throttle closed, the solenoid is energized and the plunger is extended. This provides a higher idle rpm for reduced hydrocarbon emissions during high gear deceleration.

Two switches and two relays control the solenoid. When the transmission is in low gear, the transmission switch contacts are closed and the reversing relay contacts are open and the solenoid is de-energized. When the transmission shifts to high gear, the transmission switch

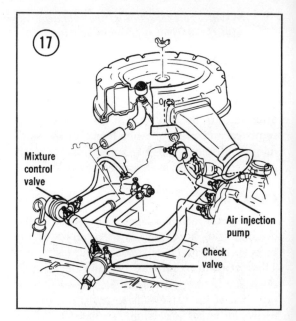

Mixture control valve / Air injection pump / Check valve

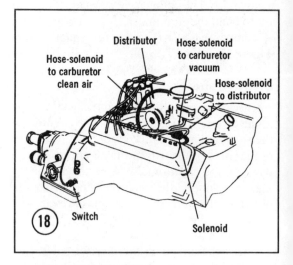

Distributor / Hose-solenoid to carburetor clean air / Hose-solenoid to carburetor vacuum / Hose-solenoid to distributor / Switch / Solenoid

contacts open, the reversing relay de-energizes, and the reversing relay contacts close. The solenoid energizes.

Two other circuits can energize the solenoid. The time delay relay holds its contacts closed for about 15 seconds after the ignition is turned on. The voltage developed across the resistor energizes the solenoid. Full vacuum during this time improves acceleration and eliminates stalling after a start. Finally, the water temperature switch provides an override when the temperature is below 82°F. The switch closes to ground below this temperature and energizes the solenoid.

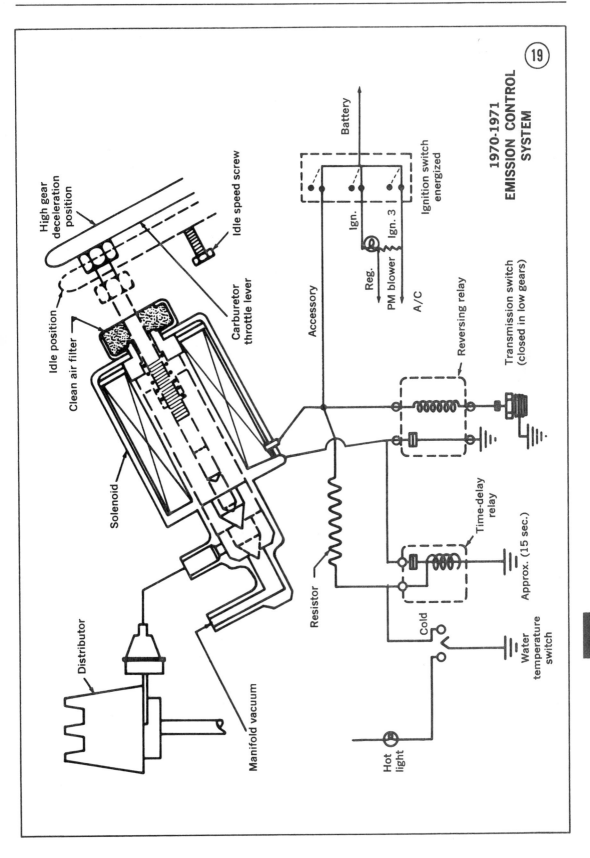

19

1970-1971
EMISSION CONTROL
SYSTEM

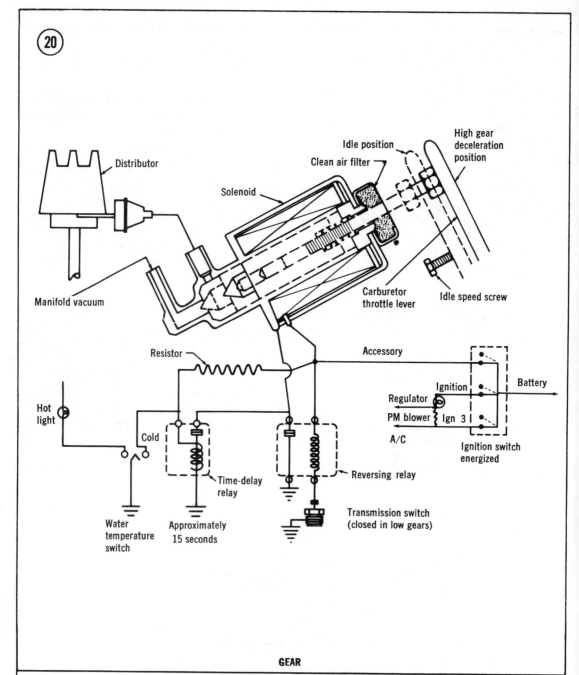

Transmission	Park	Neutral	Reverse	1st	2nd	3rd	4th
3 speed	—	—	—	—	—	Vacuum	—
4 speed	—	—	—	—	—	Vacuum	Vacuum
Torque Drive	—	—	—	—	Vacuum	—	—
Powerglide	—	—	—	—	Vacuum	—	—
Turbo Hydra-Matic 350	—	—	Vacuum	—	—	Vacuum	—
Turbo Hydra-Matic 400	—	—	Vacuum	—	—	Vacuum	—

The combined emission control system also provides methods to prevent dieseling which is a problem with emission controlled engines. One method is a by-product of the much lower "curb" idle rpm which occurs when the CEC solenoid is de-engergized. The engine runs at such a low rpm it cannot diesel.

On air-conditioned vehicles with automatic transmission, the throttle is open more with the engine idling, and the engine tends to diesel if the air conditioner compressor happens to be off. To prevent this, a solid state timer engages the air conditioner clutch for 3 seconds after the ignition is turned off. The additional compressor load stops the engine quicker, reducing its tendency to diesel. **Figures 20 and 21** show the location of components in the 1970-1971 system.

The system on 1972 and later L6 250 and V8 350 cu. in. engines is similar to the earlier system with the following exceptions:

a. The transmission switch is open in low gears, eliminating the need for reversing relay.

b. A separate idle stop solenoid closes throttle completely when ignition is turned off to prevent dieseling.

c. The water temperature override operates below 82°F as before, but also operates above 232°F.

d. No time delay relay operates during startings.

e. A time delay prevents energizing vacuum advance solenoid for 23 seconds after shifting to high gear.

Figure 22 is a simplified schematic of the L6 250 and V8 350 cu. in. systems. When the ignition is turned on, the idle stop solenoid cracks the throttle open to idle. If the engine cools and temperature is below 82°F, the solenoid operates. Vacuum advance when the engine is cold improves acceleration and helps minimize stalling. If the coolant is above 82°F, the solenoid does not energize.

When engine coolant rises above 82°F, the solenoid can energize only when the transmission is in high gear and the 20-second time delay period has passed. In low gear, the transmission switch opens, de-energizing the solenoid. When the transmission is shifted to high gear, the transmission switch closes, but the time delay relay holds its contacts open for 20 seconds, preventing the solenoid from energizing. After 20 seconds, the solenoid energizes. If the

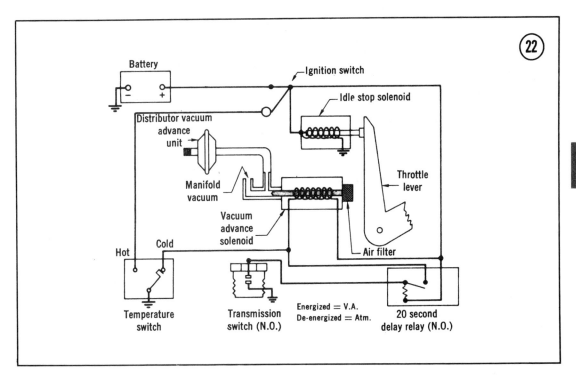

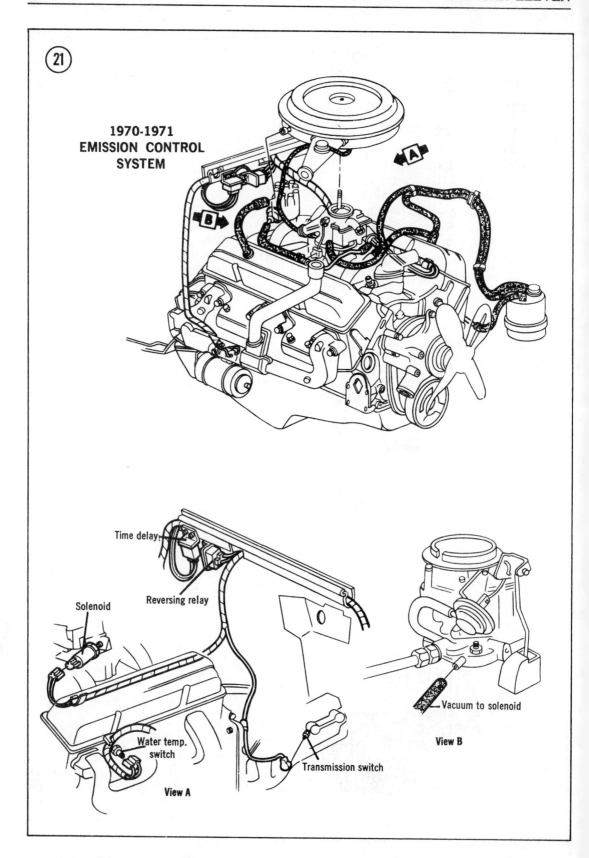

㉑

1970-1971
EMISSION CONTROL
SYSTEM

Time delay

Reversing relay

Solenoid

Water temp. switch

Transmission switch

View A

Vacuum to solenoid

View B

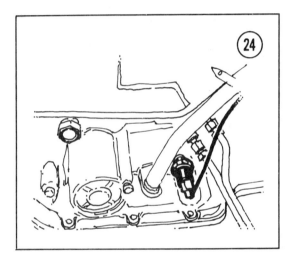

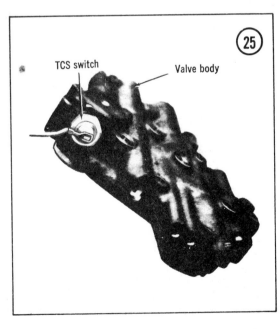

TCS switch   Valve body

transmission downshifts, even momentarily, from high gear, the time delay relay will still prevent energizing the solenoid for 20 seconds.

If coolant temperature exceeds 232°F, regardless of gear, the temperature switch overrides the system and operates the solenoid to supply vacuum advance.

Transmission Switch Replacement (1970-1971)

Refer to **Figures 20 and 21**.

Disconnect the electrical lead, unscrew the switch, and screw in new switch and connect the lead. Test the switch as described above.

Transmission Switch Replacement (1971-1974 Manual and Turbo-Hydramatic 350)

Figures 23 and 24 show location of the switch on the manual and Turbo-Hydramatic 350 transmission, respectively.

Disconnect the electrical lead. Unscrew the switch, screw in a new switch and connect the lead. Test the switch as described above.

Transmission Switch Replacement (1972-1974 Turbo-Hydramatic 400)

The switch is located internally (**Figure 25**). The transmission oil pan must be removed to reach the switch. See Chapter Ten—*Hydramatic Draining/Filling*, and remove the pan.

A wire connects the switch to the externally mounted detent solenoid TCS connector (**Figure 26**). The switch can be tested externally as described in Chapter Three.

CEC Solenoid Replacement (1970-1971)

See *Disassembly* procedure for your carburetor in Chapter Six.

Vacuum Advance Solenoid Replacement (1972-1974)

On 350 engines, the solenoid is located on the right rear portion of the intake manifold. See **Figure 27**. On the 1972 and 1973 L6 engines, the solenoid is located on the carburetor. See **Figure 28**. On 1974 L6 engines, the solenoid is bracket mounted to ignition coil (**Figure 29**).

11

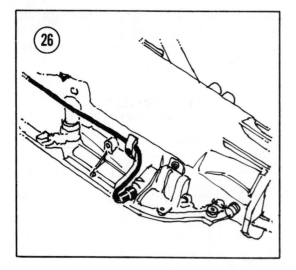

1. Disconnect the vacuum hoses and electrical wires from the solenoid.

2. Remove the solenoid from the bracket.

3. Install a new solenoid. Connect the vacuum hoses and wires.

Idle Stop Solenoid Replacement (1972-1974)

The idle stop solenoid is mounted on the carburetor. See **Figure 30**. Refer to *Disassembly* procedure in Chapter Six for your carburetor.

Relay Replacement (1970-1971)

Refer to **Figures 20 and 21**.

1. Disconnect the cable from the relay.

2. Unscrew the relay bracket.

3. Install a new relay and reconnect the cable.

Time Delay Relay (1972-1974)

The time delay relay is located on the instrument panel reinforcement immediately behind the console instrument cluster assembly (or on the cowl vertical wall on L6 engines).

1. Disconnect the cable from the relay.

2. Unscrew the relay bracket.

3. Install a new relay and reconnect the cable.

Water Temperature Switch Replacement (1970-1974)

The water temperature switch is located on the left cylinder head on 1970-1971 V8 engines

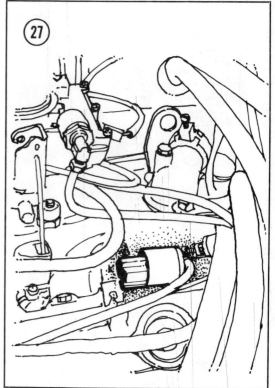

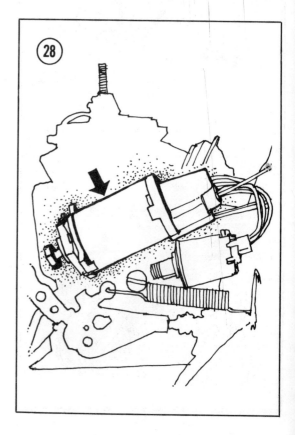

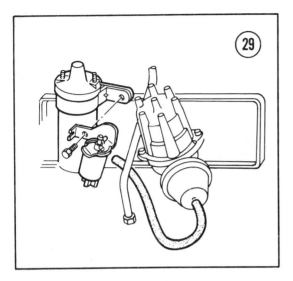

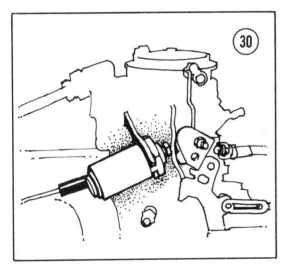

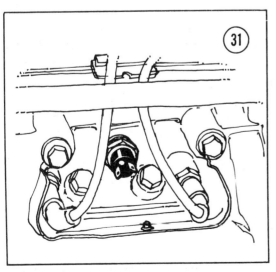

(**Figure 21**) and on the right cylinder head on 1972-1973 V8 engines (**Figure 31**). On L6 engines, the switch is on the left side of the cylinder head.

FUEL EVAPORATION CONTROL SYSTEM

All 1972 and later vehicles (1970 and later in California) are equipped with a fuel evaporation control system which prevents release of fuel vapor into the atmosphere.

Fuel vapor from the fuel tank passes through the liquid/vapor separator to the carbon canister. The carbon absorbs and stores the vapor when the engine is stopped. When the engine runs, manifold vacuum draws the vapor from the canister. Instead of being released into the atmosphere, the fuel vapor takes part in the normal combustion process.

There is no preventive maintenance other than replacing the filter on the bottom of the carbon canister every 12,000 miles and checking tightness and condition of all lines connecting the parts of the system.

Canister Filter Replacement

1. From beneath the vehicle, first note the locations of the canister hoses then disconnect them from the top of the canister.

2. Loosen the canister mounting clamp and remove the canister.

3. Remove the filter from the bottom of the canister.

4. Check the hose connections in the canister and clean them of any obstructions.

5. Install a new filter in the canister and assemble the canister.

6. Set the canister in the clamp and tighten the bolts.

7. Reconnect the lines to the canister.

EXHAUST GAS RECIRCULATION (1973 and LATER)

The Exhaust Gas Recirculation (EGR) system is used to reduce the emission of nitrogen oxides (NOX). Relatively inert exhaust gases are introduced into the combustion process to

11

slightly reduce peak temperatures. This reduction in temperature reduces the formation of NOX.

The exhaust gases are introduced into the intake manifold by way of an EGR valve. See **Figure 32**. This shutoff and metering valve operates on vacuum from the intake manifold via a signal port in the carburetor. On 1974 and later models, a thermal vacuum switch cuts off vacuum to the EGR valve until water temperature reaches 100-130°F. At idle speed, recirculation is not required. Thus, the carburetor signal port is located above the throttle valve and vacuum to the EGR valve diaphragm is cut off at idle speeds. This causes the EGR to close, halting the inroduction of exhaust gas to the intake manifold. As the throttle valve is opened, the signal port is again exposed to manifold vacuum. This actuates the EGR valve diaphragm, which opens the valve and allows exhaust gas to be metered (through an orifice) into the intake manifold. See **Figure 33**.

On L6 engines, the EGR valve is located on the intake manifold next to the carburetor (**Figure 34**). On V8 engines, the valve is located externally on the right side of the intake manifold next to the rocker arm cover (**Figure 35**).

EGR Valve Replacement

1. Disconnect the vacuum line from the valve.

2. Remove the bolt and clamp, then remove valve from manifold.

3. Install the valve on manifold, using new gasket. Tighten the bolt to 25 ft.-lb. and bend the lock tab up over the bolt head. Connect the vacuum line.

EGR Valve Cleaning

CAUTION
Do not wash valve assembly in solvent or degreaser. Permanent damage could result.

1. Use a wire brush or wire wheel to clean the valve base and remove exhaust deposits from the mounting surface.

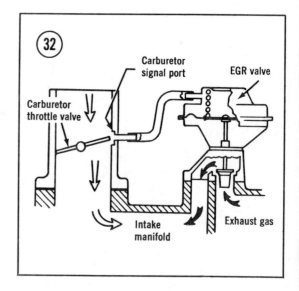

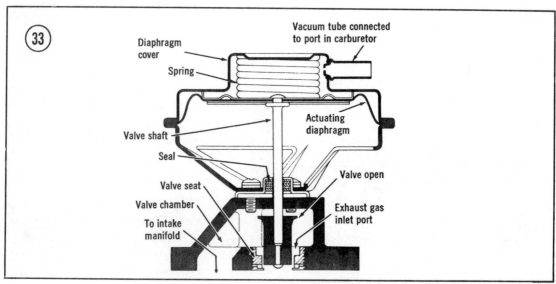

2. A spark plug cleaner (sandblaster) can be used to clean valve seat and pintle. Insert valve and pintle into machine and blast for 30 seconds.

> NOTE: *Many service stations have this type of spark plug cleaner and will clean the valve for a small fee.*

3. Compress the diaphragm spring so the valve is fully unseated and repeat sandblasting for 30 seconds.

4. Make sure all exhaust deposits have been removed. Repeat cleaning if required.

5. Use compressed air to remove all abrasive material from the valve.

Thermal Vacuum Switch Replacement (1974)

1. Disconnect the vacuum lines and remove the switch from the thermostat housing.

2. Apply a sealer to threads and install the switch in the thermostat housing. Tighten the switch to 15 ft.-lb.

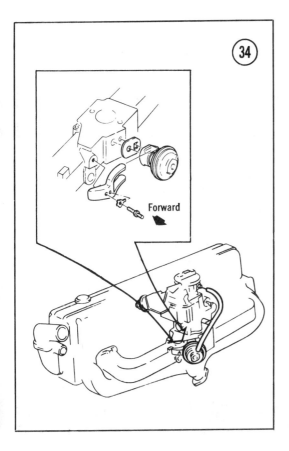

3. Rotate the head of the switch for correct hose routing and install the vacuum hoses.

> NOTE: *The thermal vacuum switch is non-repairable. If defective, replace it.*

CARBURETOR CALIBRATION

In addition to providing the engine with a combustible mixture of air and fuel, the carburetor is also calibrated to maintain proper emission levels. The idle, off-idle, power enrichments, main metering, and accelerating pump systems are all calibrated to provide the best possible combination of performance, economy, and exhaust emission control.

Calibration is especially critical on 1975 and later models, and the tasks involved require special skills and test equipment the home mechanic is not likely to have. Except for the adjustments of idle speed and idle mixture described in Chapter Four, carburetor work on late models should be entrusted to an expert.

DISTRIBUTOR CALIBRATION

Distributor calibration consists of adjusting initial timing, centrifugal advance, and vacuum advance to obtain the best combination of engine performance, fuel economy, and exhaust emission level control. Timing specifications for each engine are given on the Vehicle Emission Control Information (VECI) decal located in the engine compartment. See *Ignition*

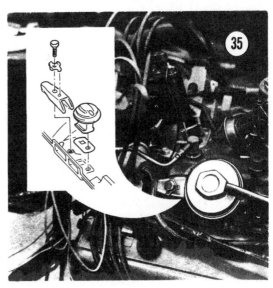

11

Timing Adjustment, Chapter Four, for instructions on how to set the initial timing. Adjustment or repair of the centrifugal and vacuum spark advance systems should be left to an expert.

CATALYTIC CONVERTER

Catalytic converters, used since 1975, reduce air pollutants by promoting further burning of the exhaust gases. The converter is located in the exhaust line ahead of the muffler and contains a material coated with platinum and palladium. Both of these materials are catalysts, and cause the reduction of hydrocarbons and carbon monoxide by burning as the exhaust gases pass over them. The catalytic converter should be checked for general condition at the same time the remainder of the exhaust system is checked (see *Periodic Maintenance*, Chapter Three). See *Catalytic Converter*, Chapter Nine, for replacement procedure.

EARLY FUEL EVAPORATION SYSTEM

The early fuel evaporation (EFE) system, used on 1975 and later models, provides heating to the intake manifold while the engine is cold, to promote vaporization of the fuel. This helps cut down on choke time and also promotes more thorough burning of the fuel. This, in turn, reduces the amount of pollutants released into the air. The heart of the system is the EFE valve, which controls the amount of heat (exhaust gas) directed under the intake manifold. The valve is controlled by a thermostatic switch in the cooling system that applies or removes vacuum to the EFE valve according to the temperature of the engine coolant. Use the following procedure to check operation of the EFE system.

EFE System Check

Refer to **Figure 36** (V8 engines) or **Figure 37** (L6 engines).

1. With the engine cold, place the transmission in NEUTRAL or PARK, apply the handbrake, and start the engine. Observe the movement of EFE actuator rod and heat valve. The valve should move to the closed position.

2. If the valve does not close, remove the vacuum hose from the actuator and check for the presence of vacuum. If vacuum is present, replace the actuator. If no vacuum is present, remove the vacuum input hose at thermo-vacuum switch (TVS) and check for vacuum. If vacuum is present, replace the TVS. If no

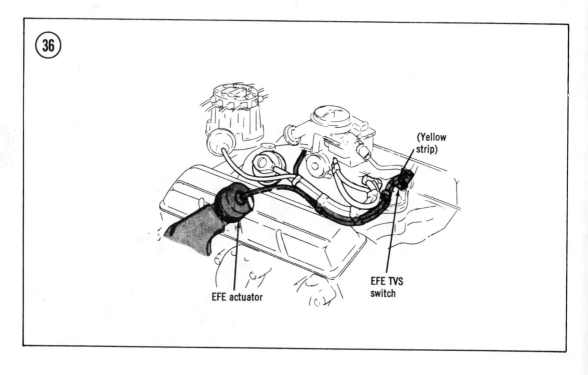

(36)

(Yellow strip)

EFE actuator

EFE TVS switch

vacuum is present, check for damaged vacuum hose and replace it as required.

3. If the valve closes, allow the engine to warm up until coolant temperature reaches 180°F (V8) or 150°F (L6). The exhaust heat valve should move to the open position. If not, remove the hose from the actuator and check for vacuum. If no vacuum is present, replace the actuator. If vacuum is present, replace the TVS.

NOTE: *When replacing the* TVS *on the V8 engines, drain the coolant below the level of the coolant outlet housing. Apply a soft setting sealant to the replacement switch threads before installation, and tighten it to 120 in.-lb.*

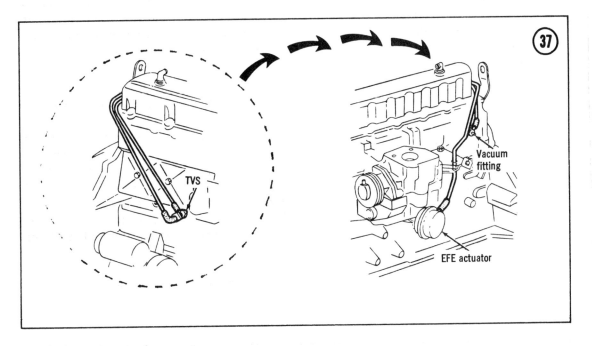

CHAPTER TWELVE

OFF-ROAD PREPARATION

Off-roading's present popularity is due in great part to the state of the art of vehicle design; compare the modern 4x4 with the rugged, uncomfortable military-type rigs of a generation ago and the advances that have been made in design and construction become obvious.

Just as important as the vehicles themselves, the specialized, product-filled aftermarket has further prompted the growth of off-roading. There is a part, an accessory, or a modification for virtually any application that one might dream up for a 4x4. Tires alone are so specialized as to precisely meet any traction requirement. One major off-road equipment supplier stocks more than 40 different makes and types of off-road tires — from high-speed designs that are as smooth as passenger car tires, to sand paddles.

With all of the goodies that are available, it is definitely a shopper's market — but it should be a careful shopper's market. If you are equipping a new 4x4, or are thinking about making some changes to the old model, first analyze your requirements. Not all of those special bits and pieces that are available are suited to all uses. For example, monster mud tires and super heavy-duty suspension are just the ticket for rough going, but their harsh ride characteristics would soon be tiresome on a vehicle that is used primarily for long-distance travel with only occasional easy excursions off the pavement.

Be sure of the quality of the equipment you select before purchasing it. ORV equipment is not cheap. "Bargain" items may save a few dollars in the beginning but usually require replacement earlier than good items. Also, the performance of bargain pieces is often poor. To ensure reasonable value for your time and money, deal with reputable suppliers and manufacturers, such as those shown in the sources list at the end of this chapter.

Off-road preparation, as described in this chapter, deals with tailoring a vehicle to meet personal needs. Guidelines are presented instead of a "recipe" for building a particular vehicle.

Engine performance modifications are avoided; increased horsepower has little to do with the overall vehicle performance. In addition, an entire book would be required to cover the subject to any effect.

TIRES AND WHEELS

Tires have a greater affect on the performance of a 4x4 than any other component. Tire selection is perhaps the most important decision you will have to make when tailoring your vehicle to suit your needs. But tires should not be considered independent of wheels; wheel design and construction are important factors that must be taken into account at the same time. Also, it's a good idea to purchase tires and wheels as a set, correctly mounted and balanced. If trouble is experienced through use, your chances of having it corrected are much greater if you are dealing with a single source. If you purchase tires and wheels separately, it's possible that the wheel seller will blame any trouble on the tires and the tire seller will blame the wheels.

Tires

Tire selection should begin with an honest evaluation of what you need rather than what looks good or is popular. A tire like the Cepek Monster Mudder, with its aggressive tread, looks like it could handle any terrain imaginable — and that's pretty much the case. But, for a 4x4 that is used for daily commuting with occasional long highway trips and only a minor amount of easy off-road use, this tire would be a poor choice. It is noiser than less radical treads and it will wear faster on pavement than one like an Armstrong SD-200.

Tire selection seems like a formidable task when you consider all the makes, patterns, and sizes available. However, it's not really so difficult if you carefully analyze your needs. First, determine the weight category of your vehicle — lightweight, up to 3,200 pounds; medium weight, 3,200 to 5,000 pounds; heavy weight, over 5,000 pounds. Don't guess at the weight and don't assume that the weight on the rating plate is correct. Instead, have the vehicle weighed at a public scale. The cost is usually no more than a couple of dollars. If you have reason to believe the vehicle falls into the heavy category, weigh the front and rear individually to determine actual axle rates.

As much as practical, the vehicle should be weighed loaded and equipped just as it is when it is used. Also, the fuel tank or tanks should be full, as well as auxiliary gas and water cans.

When the true weight is known, use **Table 1** to determine size and rating requirements.

The next step is to determine actual vehicle use. Is the vehicle your primary form of transportation? Does it serve as a second car that is used occasionally off-road? Is it a second car that is used mostly for fun? Or is it used exclusively off-road?

If you are an average owner, your vehicle is probably used as a second car with some off-road driving. Off-road mileage in such a case will be from 5-10%, rarely more. It would appear then that a correct tire in this case would have excellent highway performance, long tread life, with reasonable traction performance off-road. Well, all of this in combination is a big order and the ideal all-around tire just does not exist. What remains, then, is a compromise — a tire that may not be a perfect off-road tire but will still perform acceptably, and will provide smooth, quiet street and highway performance along with good mileage. Such tires are available.

Tire cost should be considered along with performance. Cost is not simply the price of the tire, but the cost per mile as well. Tire mileage depends heavily on vehicle loading and correct pressure, so it is a good idea to talk to owners of vehicles which are similar to yours, similarly equipped, and that use the tires you are interested in.

Tire size is also an important consideration because it will affect gear ratios. First, measure the circumference of one of your present tires. Then measure the candidate tire, mounted on an appropriate wheel and inflated. Determine the difference between the two tires to find the gear ratio change. For instance, say that the original tire has a 92 in. circumference and the new tire is 112 in. The difference — 20 in. — represents an increase of better than 20%. If the axle gear ratio is low (around 4:1), the larger tires would alter it to about 3.2:1. If your engine produces abundant horsepower this might not be bad, although you will notice a performance loss, particularly during acceleration and on long highway grades. As a rule of thumb, the combined gear and tire ratio should permit your vehicle to develop maximum torque at 60-65 mph. If the torque peak occurs significantly higher, performance will suffer. So, if you want super-large tires because they look great or you need some extra clearance,

12

Table 1   TIRE INFLATION/LOAD CAPACITY RELATIONSHIP (TIRES USED AS SINGLES)

Tire Size	Load Range	Maximum Load Capacities Per Tire (lb.) At Cold Tire Inflation Rates (psi)								
		20	25	30	35	40	45	50	55	60
L78-15	B	1520	1715	1900						
7.9-14	C	790	900	1000	1090	1180	1260			
9-15	C	1230	1400	1560	1710	1850	1980			
10-15	B	1390	1580	1760						
10-15	C	1390	1580	1760	1930	2080	2230			
11-15	B	1500	1710	1900						
11-15	C	1500	1710	1900	2080	2250	2410			
12-15	B	1780	2020	2250						
12-15	C	1780	2020	2250	2460	2660	2850			
14-15	C	1780	2020	2250	2460	2660	2850			
16-15	C	1780	2020	2250	2460	2660	2850			
8.00-16.5	D			1360	1490	1610	1730	1840	1945	2045
8.75-16.5	D			1570	1720	1850	1990	2110	2240	2350
9.50-16.5	D			1860	2030	2190	2350	2500	2650	2780
10-16.5	C			1840	2010	2170	2330			
10-16.5	D			1840	2010	2170	2330	2480	2620	2750
12-16.5	B			2370						
12-16.5	D			2370	2590	2800	3000			
12-16.5	E			2370	2590	2800	3000	3190	3370	3550
14-16.5	C	1780	2020	2250	2460	2660	2850			
16-16.5	C	1780	2020	2250	2460	2660	2850			
14-17.5	D			2820	3080	3210	3500	3790	4060	

you had better reconsider; appearance is not nearly as important as performance, and increased clearance can be obtained with a lift kit.

There are a couple of additional points to consider about super tires. First, they will likely require that the wheel openings be enlarged and that flares be added to keep water and mud off the outside of the vehicle. Also, super tires are usually constructed with 6 plies — great for handling consistently heavy loads, but they are heavy and will degrade driving comfort, shorten shock absorber life, and will also require that critical nuts and bolts be checked more often for tightness. If you need the performance of a super tire you won't find anything to take its place. But, if you can get by with a smaller tire you'll be happier about highway performance.

When selecting a mud-and-snow type tire, carefully inspect the tread design. A correctly designed tread, even one as aggressive as that shown in **Figure 1**, does not need to be noisy. Notice the random spacing of the side and interior blocks. This arrangement eliminates the harmonics that are produced by evenly spaced blocks and, consequently, reduces tire "sing."

Wheels

Wheels should be selected as carefully as tires. There are a number of excellent wheel manufacturers in the country — and there are probably an equal number who have little or no knowledge of what is required to produce a safe, quality wheel. As with tires, wheel selection can be simplified if you deal with a manufacturer, distributor, or dealer who is experienced with ORVs. And, as mentioned earlier, it's a good idea to buy wheels and tires as a set, correctly mounted and balanced.

There are several guidelines you can apply to your selection process to determine if the wheels you are considering are correct for your vehicle and your needs, and if they are safely constructed.

First, make sure the rim width is correct for the tires you have selected (**Table 2**). A narrow wheel, when used with a flotation tire, will pull the tire beads too close together and cause the tire to crown. Off-road, crowning will reduce

Table 2   RECOMMENDED WHEEL SIZE FOR VARIOUS TIRES

Tire Size	Wheel Size (Width Bead to Bead)
E or ER 78-14	5–7 in.
F or FR 78-14	5–7 in.
G or GR 78-14	5½–7 in.
H or HR 78-14	5½–8 in.
J or JR 78-14	6–8 in.
F or FR 78-15	5–7 in.
G or GR 78-15	5½–7 in.
H or HR 78-15	5½–7 in.
J or JR 78-15	5½–8 in.
L or LR 78-15	6–8 in.
M or MR 78-15	6–8 in.
N or NR 78-15	6½–9 in.
F or FR 60-14	6–8 in.
G or GR 60-14	6½–9 in.
G or GR 60-15	6–8 in.
L or LR 60-15	7–10 in.
7.9-14LT	6–7 in.
9-15LT	7–8 in.
10-15LT	7–8 in.
11-15LT	8 in.
12-15LT	10 in.
12R-15LT	8–10 in.
14-15LT	10 in.
16-15LT	10–12 in.
8.00-16.5	6 in.
8.75-16.5	6¾ in.
9.50-16.5	6¾ in.
10-16.5	8¼ in.
12-16.5	9¾ in.
14-16.5	9¾ in.
16-16.5	9¾ in.
14-17.5	10½ in.

12

the inherent flotation of the tire. On the highway, crowning will cause the tire to wear rapidly around the center of the tread. A rim that is too wide is vulnerable to rock damage.

Make sure the rim-to-center offset is correct for your vehicle. Outside (positive) offset (**Figure 2**) should be no greater than what is required for inside clearance. If the offset is extreme, excessive loads will be placed on the bearings and spindles, resulting in rapid wear or failure. Some positive offset is necessary because the inside of the wheel and tire must not interfere with tie rods or suspension (**Figure 3**). If you have questions about inside clearance, ask your tire dealer to install a candidate wheel and tire to check the clearance. If he will not do this, or cannot offer complete assurance that the clearance is sufficient, find another dealer.

A search for wheels should begin with an examination of their construction. Surprisingly, wheel design and manufacture are not controlled and regulated, so you can't simply look for a DOT stamp of approval to ensure that what you are buying is safe as well as a good value.

Aluminum wheels, or "mags" as they are commonly but incorrectly called, are still very popular despite the inroads the steel spoke types have made into the market. Cast wheels remain the most popular of the aluminum types, although in spite of the vast amount of technical information that has grown out of their long history, inferior cast wheels are still being manufactured. Brands like Crager, E-T, and Turbo-Vector are safe bets in that they are correctly engineered, heat treated, and machined for balance and roundness. There are good cast wheels other than those mentioned — but beware of bargain wheels.

New to the ORV market is the monocoque wheel, made of two pieces of high-grade aluminum, precision stamped, and riveted together (**Figure 4**). This type of construction has been common in automobile racing for some time. It produces a light, strong wheel that resists cracking better than cast wheels. There is a catch, however, and that is the price. The Centerline Championship wheel, for example, has a retail price of about $180 — each.

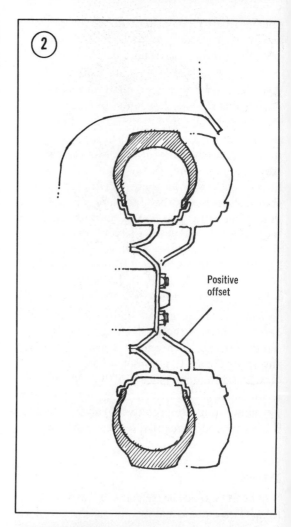

Positive offset

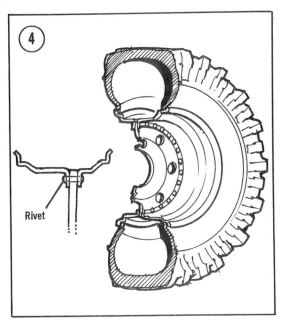

Rivet

The most popular ORV wheel is the steel spoke type, and while they may appear to be all pretty much the same, close inspection reveals that there are manufacturers who know what they are doing and probably just as many who do not. A few simple checks will reveal who is producing a good product.

Check to see if the wheel has a full circumference mating flange (**Figure 5**), rather than stub spokes (**Figure 6**). The full circumference center is stronger, distributes the load better, and allows some necessary flexing.

Check the weld quality; a good weld will be uniform and free of large pits. The weld should be continuous around the circumference, but if it is not, it should be applied between the spokes rather than in line with them (**Figure 7**).

Inspect the wheel centers around the inside of the bolt pattern. The center should be machined or stamped so the wheel will "crush" when the

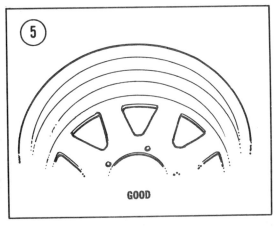

GOOD

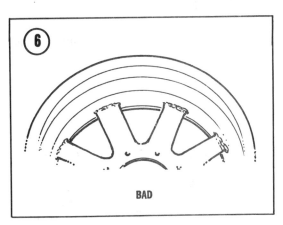

BAD

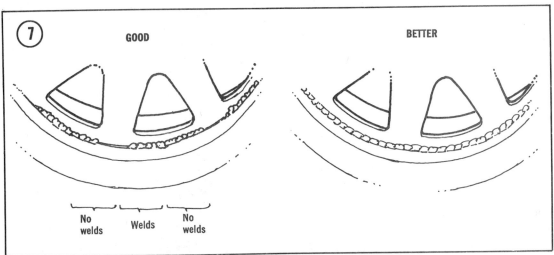

GOOD   BETTER

No welds   Welds   No welds

12

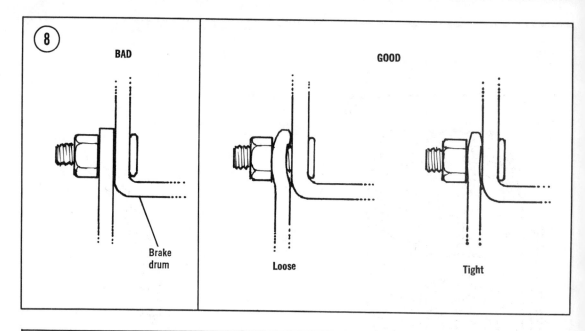

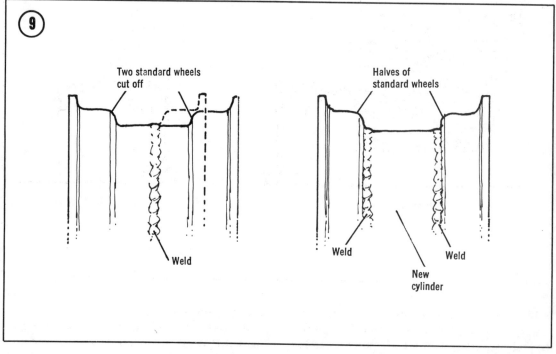

lug nuts are tightened, tensioning the lug nuts so they will not loosen (**Figure 8**). Avoid any wheel with a flat mounting flange on the inside.

Disc wheels are still common and are generally less expensive than aluminum or steel spoke wheels. However, caution should be exercised when selecting disc wheels, despite their safe-looking stock appearance. A common cost saver used by shady manufacturers is a two- or three-piece rim (**Figure 9**). The wheel on the left was made up of two rim halves welded together to obtain a wider rim. The one on the right is made up of two outer sections connected by a straight center section. Both types are invariably made from old wheels. They are

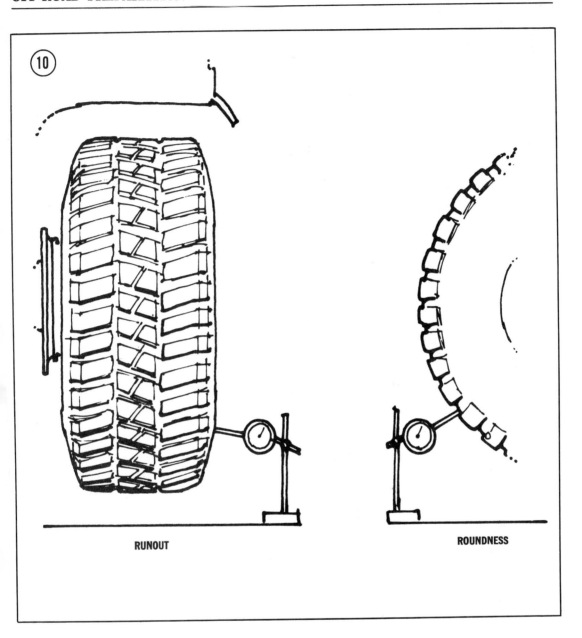

RUNOUT   ROUNDNESS

seldom round, usually have excessive runout, and their strength is questionable. It's possible to build a good wheel in this manner, but costly machining, an expensive jig, and expert welding are required — hardly what you would expect from a manufacturer who is maximizing his profit by using salvage wheels. Not long ago, before wide, one-piece rims were available to wheel manufacturers, this type of construction was common. But today, with new, wide rims available, there is no rational reason to build wheels in this manner — certainly not so far as the consumer is concerned.

Riveted centers in disc wheels are a good indicator that the manufacturer knows what he is doing; because of the equipment required, riveting is much more expensive than welding, although there are many good welded wheels on the market.

As a final check for any wheel you may select, have each wheel in the set checked for runout and roundness (**Figure 10**). Runout and out-of-round should not exceed 0.08 in. Good wheels will pass this test easily.

12

Mounting and Balancing

Correct mounting and balancing of ORV tires is essential. It's wise to have this done by the seller. Be critical, however; he may have a good product yet not know how to handle the task correctly.

Mounting is a straightforward job, but nevertheless it can be botched by an incompetent. The beads and rim should be soaped or lubricated beforehand so the tire can be eased onto the rim without resorting to beating the bead into place with a large hammer. The beads should be evenly and completely seated before the tire is inflated to operating pressure. Misalignment of the tire on the rim will cause it to be out-of-round.

Balancing is a little trickier than mounting. Because of the size and weight of most ORV tires, bubble balancing is ineffective and may, in fact, indicate that weight should be added where it is not needed. The only accurate way of balancing ORV tires is with a spin balancer, with the tire/wheel combination off the vehicle. If this method of balancing is not available from the seller, ask him for an adjustment in the price and then shop around until you find someone who is qualified and equipped to do precision spin balancing. It may cost a little extra to begin, but it will pay off in increased tire mileage and ride comfort.

Don't worry about the appearance of balance weights on the outside of your bright new wheels. Yes, they do look cobby, but if weight is applied only to the inside of the wheel so it won't show, good dynamic balance is difficult to obtain, particularly if a great deal of balance weight is required.

Tire Pressure

A good quality, accurate tire gauge is an essential piece of equipment that should be carried in your vehicle at all times and used *regularly*. Check your tire pressure weekly, with the tires cold. The recommended pressures shown in **Table 1** will serve as a guideline.

Most drivers will correct the tire pressure when increasing the vehicle load, but few remember to reduce pressure after they have unloaded the vehicle. As a result, the ride is harsh and tire mileage is reduced around the center of the tread.

In special situations, such as operating in deep sand or mud when maximum flotation is required, tire pressure can be greatly reduced, to as low as 10 psi to provide a bigger "footprint." However, tires should be run at low pressure for no longer than necessary, and then at very low speeds to prevent overheating caused by increased rolling resistance.

Inspection and Care

Tire and wheel inspection should begin with the weekly pressure check. Incorrect inflation pressures will show up rapidly as incorrect wear patterns, and once this has begun, there's no correcting it — wear will accelerate.

Inspect the tread and the sidewalls — inside and out — for cuts and slices. If the surface is cut deep enough to expose cord, have the tire checked by a specialist to determine if it is still serviceable.

Check also for bubbles, usually on the sidewalls. Bubbles indicate that the plies have separated. If you find a bubble, deflate the tire to a low pressure and press in on the bubble to check for resistance. Compare the bubbled area to an unaffected area of the sidewall. If the bubbled area feels mushy, there is likely to be a star break inside the tire. There is nothing to do for it but replace the tire as soon as possible. If the vehicle must be driven with a tire damaged in this manner, it's a good idea to deflate the tire, break the bead, and install a heavy rubber boot in the damaged area until the tire can be replaced.

Inspect rims for dents and fractures and have them repaired as soon as possible. Periodically, check the wheel and tire for roundness and runout as described under *Wheel Alignment* in the *Chassis* chapter and correct them if they are out of specification.

Tire balance should be checked and corrected if necessary every 15,000 miles. Tires do not wear evenly no matter how well they are cared for, and they tend to "grow" as they wear, creating changes in balance that must be occasionally corrected.

Tires should be rotated every 3,000-5,000

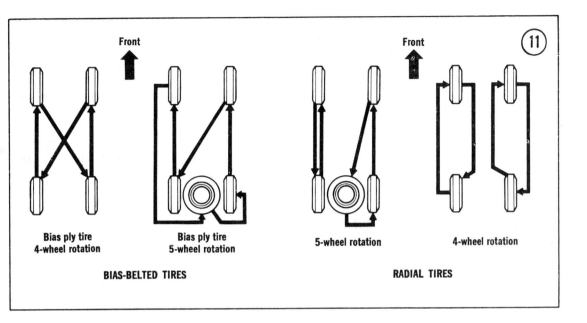

Bias ply tire 4-wheel rotation

Bias ply tire 5-wheel rotation

BIAS-BELTED TIRES

5-wheel rotation

4-wheel rotation

RADIAL TIRES

miles (**Figure 11**) for best service life. On vehicles equipped with a limited-slip differential and bias-ply tires, the rear tires should be switched every 1,500 miles to evenly distribute wear. This is not advised for radial-ply tires which develop a directional "set" that causes them to favor rotation in one direction.

LIGHTS

The selection of off-road driving lights would be easy if manufacturer's claims weren't so confusing. The traditional method of rating the output of a lamp — candlepower — is still the only valid measure of performance. Allusions to "reflective range" are not only vague (reflected off what?), but they are invalid. Not only are there no standards for testing reflective range, there is no clear definition of what is meant by the term.

Claims for candlepower can also be confusing with such references as "cumulative candlepower." There is no criteria for such a measurement.

The performance of a light should be measured as maximum beam candlepower. Maximum beam candlepower is measured 60 feet from the light. At this distance the beam pattern is established. This is the test used by the National Bureau of Standards and state motor vehicle departments.

Most importantly, the performance of a light should be to your satisfaction. Does it provide sufficient power so you are not overdriving or "outrunning" your light? Is the cost reasonable? Actual use is the most important standard by which to judge the performance of a light and all the claims that can be made will not alter reality.

The State of California has recently adopted certain performance standards for off-road driving lights. Manufacturers are required to submit candidate lights to the State for testing, and lights that meet the standards are then approved and added to the *Approved Devices* handbook carried by California Highway Patrolmen. The list is constantly updated to include new equipment that has been approved, and for this reason, the information is not included in this handbook. Before purchasing lights, California residents should make sure the light in question is approved. If a dealer or distributor can't assure you that the light is legal, don't buy it. If you are stopped for an equipment inspection, you can be ordered to remove the light if it isn't approved.

Types

There are two basic types of off-road driving lights — spot beam and flood. Spot beam lights afford maximum range, allowing you to know

12

what is ahead well in advance. However, beam dispersion to the sides is not good and driving with spot beams alone, particularly on a moonless night, is like driving in a well-lit tunnel.

Flood beams offer wide dispersion and light up the sides of the road or trail. Their shortcoming lies in their reduced range.

Ideally, spots and floods should be used in combination. If your budget will permit it, four lights should be used — two spots and two floods. As a minimum, a spot should always be used in conjunction with a flood.

Another major consideration, often overlooked when planning a lighting system, is generator or alternator output. This is particularly important on older vehicles equipped with rather modest generators. The power output of your charging system should be at least 45 amps to support a four-light system and operate other electrical devices such as the heater motor, radio, air conditioning fan, and the like. This situation can be corrected, of course, by changing to a higher output alternator or generator, but this will also entail a change of voltage regulator and perhaps the battery as well.

Installation

The best position for mounting driving lights is on top of the vehicle, either on the cab roof (**Figure 12**), light bar (**Figure 13**), or on a roll bar (**Figure 14**). But not only will the lights light up the trail, they will also light up the vehicle hood and create glare. This can be easily remedied by painting the hood and fender tops with non-reflective paint, usually matte finish black or dark green.

Bumper-mounted lights represent a good compromise, particularly on vehicles with raised suspension. Care should be taken to mount them so they are protected by the bumper or a grille guard (**Figure 15**). The installation shown is functional (the beam centers are 45 in. above the road) and neat. Also, they are protected by the grille guard uprights.

Figure 16 illustrates an excellent four-light installation. Note that the two flood beams are angled so that they provide good side illumination, yet overlap to fill in any "holes." The in-

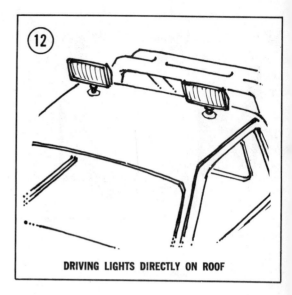

DRIVING LIGHTS DIRECTLY ON ROOF

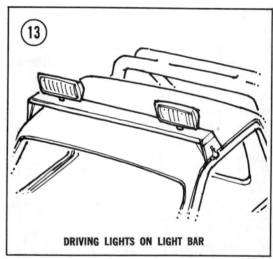

DRIVING LIGHTS ON LIGHT BAR

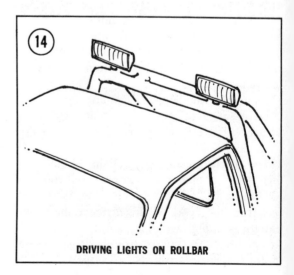

DRIVING LIGHTS ON ROLLBAR

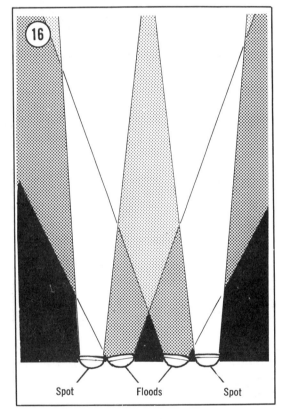

Spot   Floods   Spot

stallation shown in **Figure 17** represents a good four-light compromise in that the original headlights have been replaced with quartz-halogen units to fulfill the flood beam requirement.

CAUTION
Check local and state requirements or restrictions before installing quartz-halogen road lights. There are several on the market that are approved for use in most states. Non-approved units will not only earn you a citation for an equipment violation, but they are dangerous as well, in that they may blind oncoming traffic.

Off-road driving lights can be connected to the vehicle's fuse panel if there is an unused circuit. It is not a good idea to connect them to an existing circuit because their fuse requirements will no doubt be different from those of the components already using the circuit. The simplest electrical hookup is directly to the battery (**Figure 18**), using an inline fuse with the correct rating for the lighting system. A simple switch can be mounted easily for ready access. It's wise to check ordinances regarding installation and connection. California, for example, requires that the lights be covered (**Figure 19**) when the vehicle is operated on the highway, and the fuse must be removed from the fuse holder.

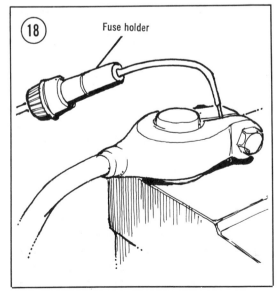

Fuse holder

12

SUSPENSION AND CHASSIS

For most applications, stock suspension — with the exception or original equipment shock absorbers — is adequate. In fact, for any use short of extensive travel over very rugged and rocky terrain, or racing, super-heavy-duty aftermarket suspension kits are unnecessarily expensive and provide a stiff ride that can become tiring and uncomfortable for long trips on conventional roads and highways.

Shock Absorbers

For light and moderate duty, stock shock absorbers should be replaced with any one of a number of good aftermarket units that are readily available from the suppliers recommended at the end of this chapter, or from auto supply stores. Most shock absorber manufacturers offer units tailored to off-road use. These include the more common brands such as Gabriel, Monroe, and Koni, as well as specialist companies such as Rough Country. No matter what your brand choice, the added cost of adjustable units is worth consideration; their softest settings provide a smooth and comfortable ride for street and highway use, and their firmer settings provide necessary increased damping for most off-road applications.

Dual-shock setups (**Figure 20**) are available for virtually all 4x4s and their use is recommended for extremely hard service. However, they shouldn't be considered as a remedy for soft suspension that frequently bottoms. While they will help to a degree, they cannot truly compensate for soft springs. In fact, they will be so overworked that they will wear out quickly. If bottoming is a problem, it can be cor-

rected only through the substitution of heavier springs.

Heavy-Duty Suspension

Many late-model 4x4s are equipped with factory-option heavy-duty suspension. If you purchased your vehicle new, you no doubt know if you have a "suspension package." However, if you bought the vehicle used, you may not know if the suspension is standard or heavy duty. To determine how it's equipped, check the vehicle identification plate; this plate contains coded information identifying production options, and your dealer can interpret the code for you.

Heavy-duty suspension components such as springs and shock absorbers are available through dealers but they are not cheap. A good alternative is a heavy-duty suspension kit from an aftermarket supplier. As with wheels and other aftermarket pieces, there is a broad range of quality available. Many so-called "kits" are packaged with no thought to matching spring rates with shock damping rates. Such bargain setups soon become very expensive when the supplied shock absorbers have to be replaced with suitable units.

As with most aftermarket products, the more expensive kits from long-time reputable manufacturers and suppliers such as Rough Country, Hickey, and Dick Cepek, Inc., prove to be the true bargains in the long run because their carefully matched spring and damping rates provide good handling performance, the parts are easily installed without a lot of modification, and the quality is such that they will provide a long service life.

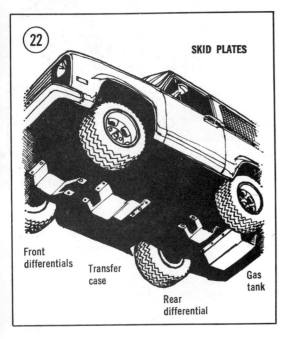

SKID PLATES

Front differentials

Transfer case

Gas tank

Rear differential

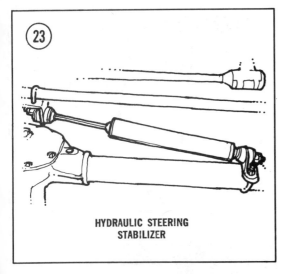

HYDRAULIC STEERING STABILIZER

Lift Kits

Lift kits, to raise the vehicle standing height and increase ground and wheel clearance, are available from several manufacturers and suppliers. Avoid those that offer extreme lift — four inches or better. Extreme lift raises the center of gravity of the vehicle excessively. This can lead to severe handling problems and increase rollover potential. A good rule is to raise the vehicle no more than is required for adequate tire clearance.

Axle Trusses

For severe use, and in instances where the vehicle is likely to become airborn on occasion, axle trusses are invaluable because they strengthen the axle housing and greatly reduce the possibilities of bending or breaking the outer tubes. For normal, light use, they are not necessary. A typical truss installation is shown in **Figure 21**.

Skid Plates

Skid plates for the differentials and the transfer case are essential for vehicles that are operated in rough, rocky terrain. Not only do they provide damage protection to expensive drive components, but they will allow the vehicle to slide over large obstacles.

If your off-roading dictates skid-plate "bulletproofing" for the drive train, consider also providing the same sort of protection for your fuel tank. **Figure 22** shows a typical skid plate installation.

Steering Stabilizers

For the driver who has had a thumb sprained by a steering wheel spoke, the need for a good steering stabilizer, or damper, need not be explained. Potholes and rocks can deflect a front wheel with such force that no amount of strong-arm technique can prevent the steering wheel from kicking back. Wide tires and wheels add to the problem with an increased mechanical advantage over the steering.

If your vehicle is not equipped with a stabilizer **(Figure 23)**, or if the stabilizer has been in service for many miles, a stabilizer kit or a replacement cylinder should be added. A

12

good kit is available through several suppliers and will generally cost less than $30. Replacement cylinders are usually less than $20.

ROLLOVER PROTECTION

Several years ago Federal law mandated rollover protection be included as standard equipment in any vehicle designed and sold primarily for off-road use that was not equipped with a fixed passenger compartment. Excluded were pickup trucks and the more recent sport models that have a fixed cab over the front seats. While some people may question having their personal safety regulated, the protection afforded by a good rollover structure is difficult to argue against.

It's important to note that the subject here is rollover protection — not flipover protection. Even the best commercially available rollbar or rollcage won't ensure that the occupants will walk away from a vehicle that has been involved in a high-speed, end-over-end crash. What they will do is offer reasonable protection during low-speed rollovers, such as those that occur during side-hilling on loose surfaces or when a bank or section of trail breaks away.

Ideally, a rollbar or cage should attach directly to the frame, but this is not always possible. It *should not* be attached only to unreinforced sheet metal. A well designed bar should have large mounting plates to distribute the load over a large area, and they should be located as close as possible to the corner of the cargo bed or a door jamb (**Figure 24**). A reinforcing plate mounted beneath the floor will prevent bolts from being pulled through the floor (**Figure 25**).

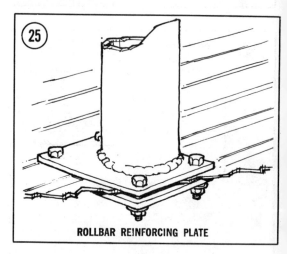
ROLLBAR REINFORCING PLATE

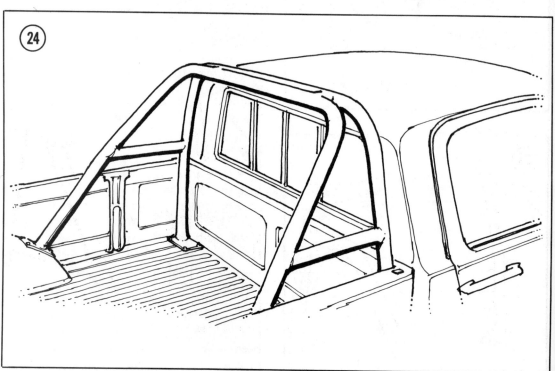

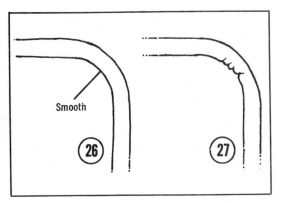

Smooth

26   27

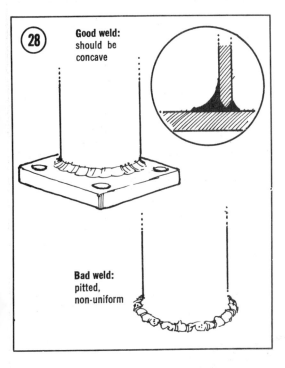

28

Good weld: should be concave

Bad weld: pitted, non-uniform

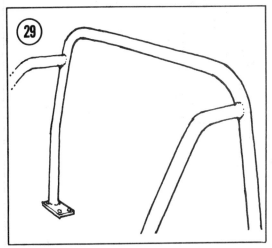

29

There are several other important points to look for when selecting a rollbar or cage. First, the tubing should have mandrel bends that are smooth along the inner diameter of the bend (**Figure 26**). Wrinkling along the inner diameter (**Figure 27**) is characteristic of a bend that was made without a mandrel. The folding will allow the bend to collapse in a rollover.

Second, check the tubing thickness. If the bar is 1¾-2 in. in diameter, wall thickness should be 0.125 in., and 3-inch bars should have a wall thickness of 0.095 in.

Third, inspect the welds. They should be uniform and clean. If they are rough, pitted, and vary in width, it's a sure bet that they were made by someone who knows little about welding (**Figure 28**).

Primary use of the vehicle should be taken into account when selecting a rollover structure. Good single- and double-tube bars work well for most situations where operating speeds are low and the surface is reasonably firm (**Figure 29**). If the vehicle is operated extensively in deep sand, and particularly if it does not have a rigid top, a sand bar (**Figure 30**) is an essential piece of insurance in that its plate will provide needed flotation. For rough, high-speed run-

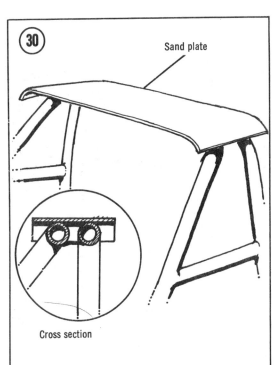

30

Sand plate

Cross section

12

ning, a full cage is a must **(Figure 31)**. A bolt-together socketed cage like the one shown in **Figure 32** is as strong as an all-welded unit and can be installed without removing the top.

For vehicles equipped with soft tops, or no top at all, the Grab-It, manufactured and sold by Dick Cepek, Inc., should be added **(Figure 33)**. Should a rollover occur, or at least be threatened, the first reaction of a passenger, and perhaps the driver as well, will be to grab for something to hang onto. And if that "something" is the rollbar itself, crushed or severed fingers are likely to be the result. The Grab-It can preclude such injuries by providing a safe handhold.

WINCHES

Many off-roaders consider a winch to be an expensive frill, and for most, it is. Few 4x4 enthusiasts get themselves into situations where a winch is the only quick way out. It's a seldom-if-ever-used device. But for the really adventurous back-country traveler a winch is an essential piece of equipment that could mean the difference between riding and walking.

There are two basic types of winches — mechanical and electrical. A mechanical winch is driven by the power takeoff — PTO — from the transfer case. Mechanical winches are at their best when extensive use of a winch is required, but they are expensive to install and they place a great load on the transfer case and transmission.

In today's market, the electrical winch has all but replaced the PTO type. Electric winches are relatively inexpensive and easy to install. They are simple to operate and can be used when the engine won't run or the grade is so steep that the carburetor floods and the oil pickup tube is out of the oil in the crankcase.

There are a number of good electrical winches available from several manufacturers, offering choices in installation type and location, pulling capacity, and price. **Figures 34 through 37** show typical winch types and installations. When installing a winch system, locate the switch relay as close to the battery as possible to minimize current loss.

The cost of an installation kit should be taken into consideration when making a selection; a kit can add as much as $150 to the price.

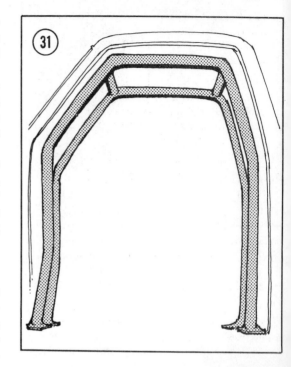

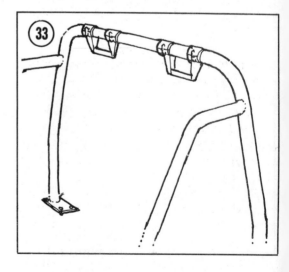

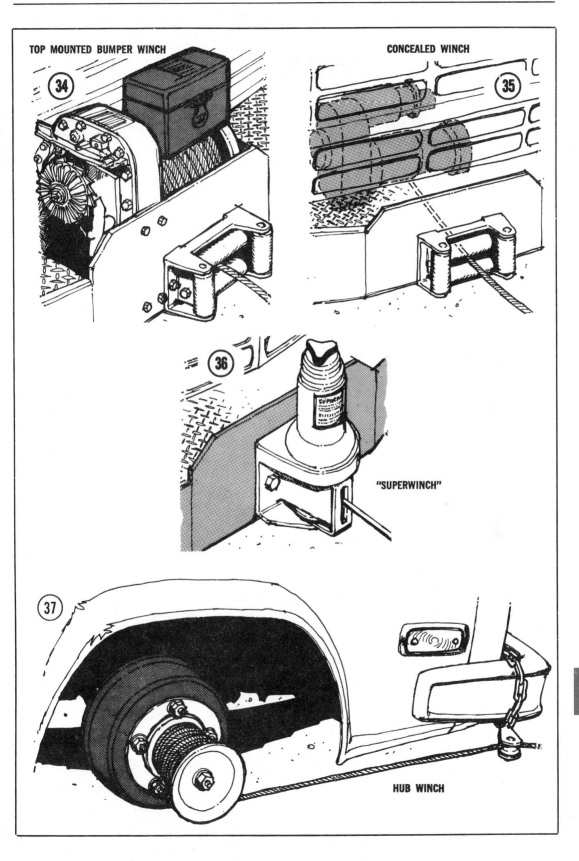

TOP MOUNTED BUMPER WINCH

CONCEALED WINCH

"SUPERWINCH"

HUB WINCH

12

Winch Operation

Don't wait until you need your winch to learn how it works. All of the manufacturers listed supply detailed operating information. Read and understand the instructions, then try out the winch with the vehicle on a level surface. Put the instructions safely away in the glove compartment so you can use them to refresh your memory when you need the winch to get your truck or someone else's unstuck.

Have respect for what the winch is capable of. Even the little Superwinch can pull 4,600 pounds up a 20 percent grade. Most of the larger units will lift 8,000 pounds — sufficient power to badly damage a frame or suspension on a severely stuck vehicle.

In many cases, a simple direct hookup will be sufficient (**Figure 38**). The capacity of the winch can be doubled with the use of a snatch block (**Figure 39**). Typical hookups are shown in **Figures 40 through 42**. For sand, you will probably have to provide your own anchor, such as another vehicle or a sand spike (**Figure 43**). A spare wheel and tire, buried in the sand and angled away from the vehicle, makes an excellent anchor (**Figure 44**). When you use a tree as an anchor, have some respect for the tree and protect the bark with padding to prevent the cable from cutting it.

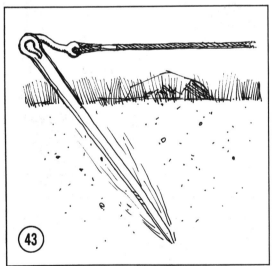

Keep people away from the cable when winching; a broken cable can inflict serious injury or damage on anyone or thing it strikes. Pay attention to the cable. If it starts to part, it will be apparent as fine outer strands begin to whisker (**Figure 45**). Stop winching at once! The situation won't improve and the cable is sure to break. Wrap jackets or canvas around the cable at several locations before winching (**Figure 46**). Should the cable break, they will prevent it from whipping about.

Finally, carry heavy work gloves in the vehicle to wear when handling the cable. They will preclude cut and scratched hands. And when you are done winching, wipe the cable clean as it is being rewound. Don't oil it; oil will attract sand and dirt.

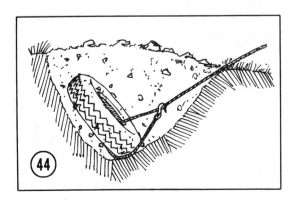

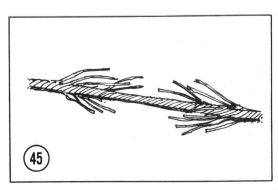

12

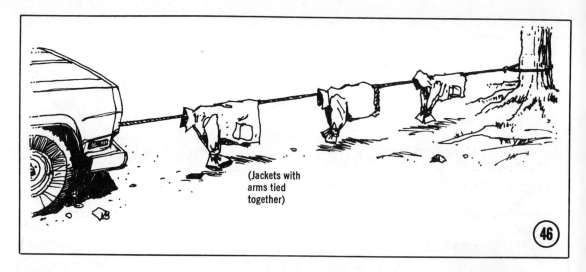

(Jackets with
arms tied
together)

46

TOOLS AND SAFETY EQUIPMENT

Ask a dozen off-roaders to give you a list of essential tools and equipment to take along for a trip into the boondocks and the lists will probably range from nothing more than a well-stocked beer cooler to enough equipment to wait out the Second Coming and sufficient tools to overhaul the truck, just to pass the time. Reason must prevail between the extremes of optimism and pessimism. If you were to prepare for every possible breakdown, injury, or disaster you would have little room for carrying passengers and just might exceed the GVW rating of your vehicle by several times over. But with repeated excursions into the wild country, certain difficulties are likely to occur, and the more likely ones can be handled with a rather modest inventory of tools and equipment.

The list that follows provides a good starting point:

1. *Tire Gauge* — This invaluable little device should be used frequently — not just during outings. Correct tire pressure is important during daily driving to ensure good ride and handling, as well as long tire life.

2. *First Aid Kit* — Even minor cuts and scrapes can become serious injuries if the wound isn't cleaned, disinfected, and protected immediately.

3. *Survival Kit* — A good kit, such as the SUR-VIVIT from Dick Cepek, Inc., could mean the difference between life and death. This one contains signal devices, compass, sawknife,

weather protection, and more.

4. *Water* — For man and machine. At least two 5-gallon containers are needed in dry regions.

5. *Gas and Oil* — Always top off your tanks and make sure you have a full 5-gallon can extra. A couple of quarts of motor oil take up little space — and there's no substitute for your engine's lifeblood.

6. *Hand Tools* — No need to prepare for an overhaul. Pliers, screwdrivers (both conventional and Phillips), a couple of crescent wrenches, some combination wrenches (from ⅜ to ¾ in.), a spark plug wrench, and a pocket knife.

7. *Tire Equipment* — High-lift jack, bead breakers, spare inner tube, tire boot, tire repair kit, valve core remover, and tire pump — particularly the spark plug type.

8. *Vehicle Spares* — Spare fan belt, radiator hoses, points, plugs, condenser and coil, fuses, radiator stop-leak, electrical tape, assorted screws, nuts and bolts, lug nuts, and baling wire.

9. *Fire Extinguisher* — Should be rated for gasoline and electrical fires.

10. *Digging Out Kit* — Shovel, axe, sand mats, towstrap.

11. *Bar of Soap* — Yes, you can use it to wash your hands. But you can also rub it over a leak in a gas tank or line and it will stop the leak until you have it permanently repaired.

Table 1   SOURCES

Company	Product/Service
Dick Cepek, Inc. 5309 Tweedy Blvd. South Gate, CA 90280	Wheels, tires and off-road accessories and camping equipment
Cleveland Off-Road Equipment 23792 Center Ridge Westlake, OH 44450	Off-road accessories and fiberglass bodies
Desert Dynamics 13720 E. Rosecrans Ave. Santa Fe Springs, CA 90670	Winches and off-road equipment
Dualmatic Manufacturing Co. 1241 N. Kimbark St. Longmont, CO 80501	Off-road accessories and equipment
Hickey Enterprises, Inc. 7100 Chapman Ave. Garden Grove, CA 92641	Off-road accessories and equipment, winches
Koenig Iron Works, Inc. Box 7726 Houston, TX 77007	Winches
Ramsey Winch Co. P.O. Box 15829 Tulsa, OK 74112	Winches
Recreational Vehicle Accessories 2111 South Leyden St. Denver, CO 80222	Off-road accessories and equipment
Rough Country, Inc. 1080 North Marshall Ave. El Cajon, CA 92020	Heavy-duty suspension kits, part-time transfer case conversions
Simpson Off-Road, Inc. 8456 E. Firestone Blvd Downey, CA 90241	Off-road accessories and equipment
Smittybilt 2124 North Lee Ave. El Monte, CA 91733	Rollbars, cages, and towbars
Warn Industries 19450 68th Ave. So. Kent, WA 98035	Winches, limited-slip differentials, locking hubs and hoists

12

SUPPLEMENT

1976 AND LATER SERVICE INFORMATION

This supplement presents detailed service information and specifications for 1976 and later Chevrolet/GMC 4x4 models. To save time and eliminate confusion, only procedures and specifications that differ from earlier models are included in this supplement. For instance, the engine oil capacity (Table 3, Chapter Four) is the same for 1976-1979 models as it is for 1975 and earlier models and is not therefore contained in this supplement; it is the same as shown in the main text.

Read the entire supplement carefully before beginning any work on 1976 or later models to familiarize yourself with important differences. It's a good idea to make notes in the main text so that frequently used information will be included with the procedure in which it is used.

TOWING

For 1976 models equipped with either conventional or full-time 4-wheel drive, and for 1977 and later models equipped with conventional 4-wheel drive, the transfer case and selector positions are the same as described in Chapter One, *Towing*. For 1977 models equipped with full-time 4-wheel drive, set the transfer case selector at NEUTRAL and the transmission selector at PARK.

HEI (HIGH-ENERGY IGNITION)

The only adjustments possible on the HEI are centrifugal and vacuum advance, both of which should be entrusted to a dealer or automotive ignition specialist. Suspected trouble should also be referred to a dealer or specialist; testing of the electronic module requires special tools and skills, and an otherwise good electronic circuit can be irreparably damaged by an incorrect test hookup.

MAINTENANCE AND LUBRICATION SCHEDULES

The maintenance and lubrication schedules for 1976 models are the same as for 1975 models. Refer to Chapter One, Table 3, and Chapter Four, Table 1.

The schedules for 1977 and later models are presented in **Tables 1-9** at the end of this supplement.

TUNE-UP

Tune-up intervals for 1976 and later models are 22,500 miles. The procedures are described in Chapter Five. Tune-up specifications for 1976-1981 models are presented in **Tables 10-14** at the end of this supplement. 1982 specifications are unavailable at this time. See engine emission control decal.

Electronic Module

If there is trouble in the electronic ignition module, the entire unit must be replaced. When installing a new module, the special silicone grease that is supplied with it must be applied to the module mounting surface. If it is not, the module will not cool correctly and will likely be damaged.

Spark Plug Leads

The spark plug wire boots seal tightly to the plugs and must be broken loose by turning them a half turn in either direction before pulling them off.

WARNING
Do not remove the spark plug leads with the engine running; the high voltage of the electronic ignition can jump a much greater distance than a conventional ignition and can cause severe shock.

Timing Light Connection

A timing light must be connected parallel to the ignition circuit, using an adapter connected to the No. 1 terminal on the distributor.

Tachometer Connection

A TACH connection is provided on the distributor (**Figure 1**). Connect the tachometer in accordance with the instrument manufacturer's instructions.

CAUTION
Do not ground the TACH terminal on the distributor. This could damage the HEI module.

ELECTRICAL SYSTEM

Fuse, circuit breaker, and lamp bulb specifications are the same as for 1975 models (Tables 3 and 4, Chapter Six). With the exceptions shown in **Tables 15 and 16** they are the same for 1977 models. Fuses, circuit breaker, and bulb data for 1978-1982 models are shown in **Tables 17 and 18**.

FRONT WHEEL BEARING ADJUSTMENT

The wheel bearing adjustment procedure for 1980-1982 models remains unchanged from previous years, but the final torque is 80 ft.-lb. (108 N•m) for 1980 vehicles and 160-205 ft.-lb. (217-310 N•m) for 1981-1982 vehicles.

EMISSION CONTROL SYSTEM

Some trucks use a Pulse Air Injection Reactor (PAIR) system (**Figure 2**) instead of an air pump. The PAIR system contains 4 one-way check valves. Engine operation creates a pulsating flow of positive and negative exhaust pressure. Negative pressure draws fresh air into the exhaust system through the PAIR valves. Positive pressure forces the pulse air valves to close. Since they operate in one direction only, exhaust gases cannot reverse their direction and flow through them. Use the following procedure to diagnose and check PAIR system operation.

PAIR System Diagnosis

1. Check the PAIR valves, connecting pipes, hoses and grommets for leaks or cracks.
2. Connect a hand vacuum pump to the grommet end of a PAIR valve. Draw a 17 in. Hg vacuum and note the leakdown rate. If the vacuum drops more than 6 in. Hg in 2 seconds, check the hose for leakage. If none is found, replace the valve.
3. Start the engine and run at idle. Listen for a hissing noise at each pulse air valve. If a hissing noise is heard, repeat Step 1.
4. PAIR valve failure will allow exhaust gases to enter the air cleaner, causing poor driveability. Check the valve-to-air cleaner hose for signs of deterioration. If found, remove the carburetor. Disassemble the carburetor, clean thoroughly and reassemble. Install the cleaned carburetor and a new valve-to-air cleaner hose.
5. Check the rocker cover plenum for signs of burned-off paint. Check plenum seals and replace grommets or rubber hoses as required.

13

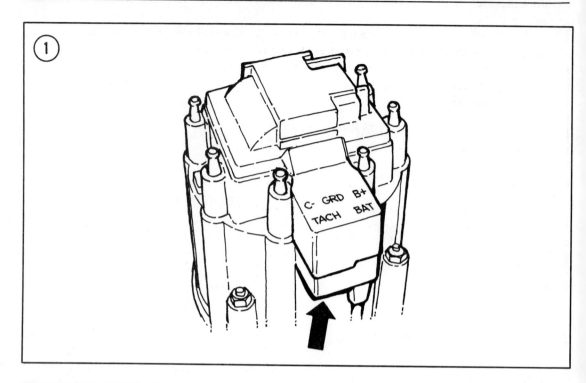

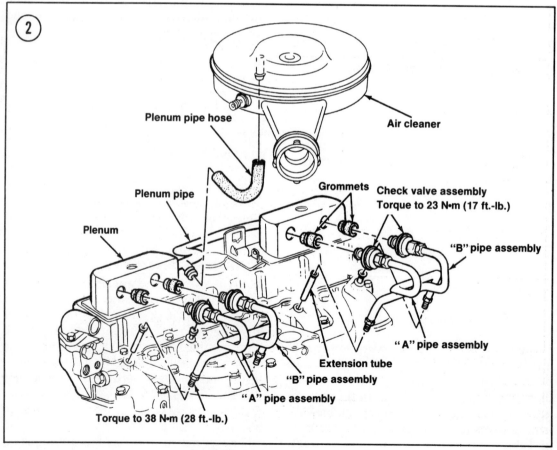

Plenum pipe hose

Air cleaner

Plenum pipe

Grommets

Check valve assembly
Torque to 23 N•m (17 ft.-lb.)

Plenum

"B" pipe assembly

"A" pipe assembly

Extension tube

"B" pipe assembly

"A" pipe assembly

Torque to 38 N•m (28 ft.-lb.)

Table 1   VEHICLE MAINTENANCE SCHEDULE — 1977
(SERIES 10 WITH V8 ENGINE AND LIGHT DUTY EMISSION SYSTEM)

When To Perform Services (Months or Miles, Whichever Occurs First)	Services
Lubrication and General Maintenance	
Every 12 months or 7,500 miles	Chassis lubrication Fluid levels check ① ② Engine oil change ② Oil filter change ②
Every 7,500 miles ④	Tire rotation
Every 7,500 miles	Rear axle lube change
Every 12 months	Air conditioning check
Every 12 months or 15,000 miles	Cooling system check ②
Every 30,000 miles	Wheel bearing repack Manual steering gear check Clutch cross shaft lubrication
Every 60,000 miles	Automatic transmission fluid and filter change ②
Safety Maintenance	
Every 12 months or 7,500 miles	Owner safety checks Tire, wheel, and disc brake check Exhaust system check ② Suspension and steering check Brake and power steering check
Every 12 months or 15,000 miles	Drive belt check ② Drum brake and parking brake check Throttle linkage check Underbody flush and check
Emission Control Maintenance	
At first 6 months or 7,500 miles — then at 18-month/22,500-mile intervals as indicated in log	Thermostat controlled air cleaner check Carburetor choke check Engine idle speed adjustment EFE system check Carburetor mounting torque Vacuum advance system, hoses check
Every 12 months or 15,000 miles	Fuel filter replacement PCV system check PCV valve and filter replacement
Every 22,500 miles	Spark plug wires check Idle speed-up solenoid check Spark plug replacement Engine timing adjustment and distributor check Carburetor vacuum break adjustment ①
Every 24 months or 30,000 miles	ECS system check and filter replacement Fuel cap, tank, and lines check
Every 30,000 miles	Air cleaner element replacement

① Also a safety service.   ② Also an emission control service.   ③ Applies to 305 cid engine only.
④ 15,000 miles for radial-ply tires.

13

Table 2   VEHICLE MAINTENANCE SCHEDULE — 1977
(SERIES 10 WITH L6 ENGINE AND LIGHT DUTY EMISSION SYSTEM)

When To Perform Services (Months or Miles, Whichever Occurs First)	Services
Lubrication and General Maintenance	
Every 12 months or 7,500 miles	Chassis lubrication Fluid levels check ① ② Engine oil change ② Oil filter change ②
Every 7,500 miles ③	Tire rotation
Every 7,500 miles	Rear axle lube change
Every 12 months	Air conditioning check
Every 12 months or 15,000 miles	Cooling system check ②
Every 30,000 miles	Wheel bearing repack Manual steering gear check Clutch cross shaft lubrication
Every 60,000 miles	Automatic transmission fluid and filter change ②
Safety Maintenance	
Every 12 months or 7,500 miles	Owner safety checks Tire, wheel, and disc brake check Exhaust system check ② Suspension and steering check Brake and power steering check
Every 12 months or 15,000 miles	Drive belt check ② Drum brake and parking brake check Throttle linkage check Underbody flush and check
Emission Control Maintenance	
Every 6 months or 7,500 miles, then 24 months or 30,000 miles then 12 months or 15,000 miles	Carburetor choke check
At first 6 months or 7,500 miles — then at 24-month/30,000-mile intervals as indicated in log	Thermostat controlled air cleaner check Engine idle speed adjustment EFE system check Carburetor mounting torque
Every 12 months or 15,000 miles	Vacuum advance system, hoses check Fuel filter replacement PCV system check PCV valve and filter replacement
Every 15,000 miles	Spark plug wires check
Every 30,000 miles	Idle stop solenoid check Spark plug replacement Engine timing adjustment and distributor check Air cleaner element replacement
Every 24 months or 30,000 miles	ECS system check and filter replacement Fuel cap, tank, and lines check

① Also a safety service.   ② Also an emission control service.   ③ 15,000 miles for radial-ply tries.

Table 3   VEHICLE MAINTENANCE SCHEDULE — 1977
(VEHICLES WITH HEAVY DUTY EMISSION SYSTEM)

When To Perform Services (Months or Miles, Whichever Occurs First)	Services
Every 4 months or 6,000 miles	Chassis lubrication Fluid levels ② Engine oil Air conditioning system
Every 6,000 miles	Tire rotation
At 1st oil change — then every 2nd	Engine oil filter ①
Every 12,000 miles	Rear axle
Every 12 months or 12,000 miles	Cooling system
Every 12,000 miles	Wheel bearings Automatic transmission
Every 36,000 miles	Manual steering gear
Every 4 months or 6,000 miles	Owner safety checks Tires and wheels Exhaust system Engine drive belts ① Suspension and steering Brakes and power steering
Every 6,000 miles	Disc brakes
Every 12 months or 12,000 miles	Drum brakes and parking brake Throttle linkage Underbody
At 1st 4 months or 6,000 miles — then at 12-month/12,000-mile intervals	Carburetor choke and hoses ③ Engine idle speed adjustment ③ Carburetor mounting ③
Every 12 months or 12,000 miles	Thermostatically controlled air cleaner ③ Manifold heat valve ③
Every 12,000 miles	Spark plugs ④ Engine timing adjustment and distributor check ④
Every 12 months or 12,000 miles	EGR system Carburetor fuel inlet filter ③ Engine idle mixture ③ Throttle return control ③ Idle stop solenoid PCV system
Every 24 months or 24,000 miles	ECS system Fuel cap, tank, and lines
Every 12,000 miles	Air cleaner element ④
Every 12 months or 12,000 miles	Spark plug and ignition coil wires ③

① Also an emission control service.

② Also a safety service

③ All except California 350 cid and 400 cid engines which receive this service at 24 months or 24,000 miles.

④ All except California 350 cid and 400 cid engines which receive this service at 24,000 miles.

13

Table 4   VEHICLE MAINTENANCE SCHEDULE — 1978–1979
(GASOLINE ENGINES WITH LIGHT DUTY EMISSION SYSTEMS)

When to Perform Services	Services
Lubrication and General Maintenance	
Every 12 months or 7,500 miles	Fluid levels check.[1] Clutch pedal free-play check. Engine oil change.[2] Oil filter change.[2] Chassis lubrication.[1] Tire rotation.
Every 4 months or 6,000 miles	Check oil level in transfer case. Check lube level in both axles. Lubricate propeller shaft slip joints. Lubricate constant-velocity joint on front propeller shaft.
Every 12 months or 15,000 miles	Check and test cooling system.[2]
Every 30,000 miles	Repack wheel bearings. Check manual steering gear seals. Lubricate clutch cross shaft.
Every 100,000 miles	Change automatic transmission fluid and filter.
Safety Maintenance	
Every 12 months or 7,500 miles	Perform owner safety checks. Check tires, wheels, and disc brakes. Check exhaust system.[2] Check suspension and steering. Check power brake and power steering hoses and connections.

Every 12 months or 15,000 miles	Check drive belts.[1]
	Check drum brakes and parking brake
	   adjustment.
	Check throttle linkage.
	Check bumpers for alignment and impact
	   protection.

Emission Control Maintenance	
At first 6 months or 7,500 miles, then every 18 months or 22,500 miles	Check thermostatically controlled switch on air cleaner. Check tightness of carburetor mounting. Check choke operation. Check EFE system. Check vacuum advance system and hoses. Check/adjust engine idle speed.
Every 12 months or 15,000 miles	Replace fuel filter. Check PCV valve, filter and hoses.
Every 22,500 miles	Check operation of engine idle stop solenoid. Check high-tension spark plug wires. Replace spark plugs. Check/adjust ignition timing. Check distributor. Check carburetor vacuum break.
Every 30,000 miles	Replace air cleaner element.
Every 24 months or 30,000 miles	Check ECS system and replace filter. Check fuel cap, tank, and lines.

1. Also a safety service.
2. Also an emission control service.

Table 5   VEHICLE MAINTENANCE SCHEDULE — 1978-1979
(GASOLINE ENGINES WITH HEAVY DUTY EMISSION SYSTEMS)

When to Perform Services	Services
Lubrication and General Maintenance	
Every 4 months or 6,000 miles	Check fluid levels.[1]
	Check clutch pedal free-play.
	Change engine oil.[2]
	Change oil filter.[2]
	Lubricate chassis.[1]
	Check oil level in transfer case.
	Check lube levels in both axles.
	Lubricate propeller shaft slip joints.
	Lubricate constant-velocity joint on front propeller shaft.
	Rotate tires.
Every 12,000 miles	Repack wheel bearings.
Every 12 months or 12,000 miles	Check and test cooling system.[2]
Every 24,000 miles	Change automatic transmission fluid and filter.
Every 36,000 miles	Check manual steering gear seals.
	Lubricate clutch cross shaft.
Safety Maintenance	
Every 4 months or 6,000 miles	Perform owner safety checks.
	Check tires, wheels, and disc brakes.
	Check exhaust system.[2]
	Check suspension and steering.
	Check power brake and power steering hoses and connections.
Every 12,000 miles	Check drive belts.[1]
Every 12 months or 12,000 miles	Check drum brakes and parking brake adjustment.
	Check throttle linkage.
	Check bumpers for alignment and impact protection.
(continued)	

13

Table 5   VEHICLE MAINTENANCE SCHEDULE — 1978–1979 (continued)
(GASOLINE ENGINES WITH HEAVY DUTY EMISSION SYSTEMS)

When to Perform Services	Services
Emission Control Maintenance	
At first 4 months or 6,000 miles, then every 12 months or 12,000 miles	Check/adjust engine idle speed. Check operation of engine idle stop solenoid.
Every 12,000 miles	Check spark plug wires. Replace spark plugs. Check/adjust ignition timing. Replace air cleaner element.
Every 12 months or 12,000 miles	Check thermostatically controlled switch on air cleaner. Check tightness of carburetor mounting. Replace fuel filter. Check PCV valve, filter, and hoses. Check manifold heat valve. Check throttle return control.
Every 24 months or 24,000 miles	Check choke operation. Check EFE system. Check vacuum advance system and hoses. Check ECS system and replace filter. Check fuel cap, tank, and lines. Adjust engine idle mixture (292-L6 engine only).

1. Also a safety service.
2. Also an emission control service.

Table 6   VEHICLE MAINTENANCE SCHEDULE—1980-1981
(GASOLINE ENGINES WITH LIGHT DUTY EMISSION SYSTEMS)

Lubrication and General Maintenance	
Every 12 months or 7,500 miles	Check fluid levels[1] Check clutch pedal free-play Change engine oil[2] Lubricate chassis[1] Check transfer case oil level Check lube levels in both axles Lubricate propeller shaft slip joints Lubricate constant-velocity joints on front propeller shaft Rotate tires
Every 12 months or 15,000 miles	Check and test cooling system[2] Change oil filter[2]
Every 30,000 miles	Repack wheel bearings Check manual steering gear seals Lubricate clutch cross shaft
Every 100,000 miles	Change automatic transmission fluid and filter
Safety Maintenance	
Every 12 months or 7,500 miles	Perform owner safety checks Check tires, wheels and disc brakes Check exhaust system[2] Check suspension and steering Check power brake and power steering hoses and connections
Every 12 months or 15,000 miles	Check drive belts[2] Check drum brake and parking brake adjustment Check throttle linkage Check bumpers for alignment and impact protection Check fuel cap, tank and lines[2]
Emission Control Maintenance Schedule I	
At first 6 months or 7,500 miles, then at 18 months or 22,500 miles	Check air cleaner Check carburetor choke Adjust engine idle speed Check EFE system Check tightness of carburetor mounting Check vacuum advance system and hoses
Every 15,000 miles	Replace fuel filter Check PCV valve, filter and hoses
Every 22,500 miles	Check spark plug wires Check idle stop solenoid and/or dashpot Replace spark plugs

(continued)

13

Table 6   VEHICLE MAINTENANCE SCHEDULE—1980-1981
(GASOLINE ENGINES WITH LIGHT DUTY EMISSION SYSTEMS) (continued)

Emission Control Maintenance Schedule II	
Every 15,000 miles	Check and adjust engine timing Check carburetor vacuum break operation
Every 30,000 miles	Replace air cleaner element Check ESC system and replace filter
At first 6 months or 7,500 miles, then every 24 months or 30,000 miles	Check air cleaner Check carburetor choke Adjust engine idle speed Check EFE system Check tightness of carburetor mounting Check vacuum advance system and hoses
Every 15,000 miles	Replace fuel filter Check PCV valve, filter and hoses Check spark plug wires
Every 30,000 miles	Check idle stop solenoid and/or dashpot Replace spark plugs Check and adjust engine timing Check vacuum break operation Replace air cleaner element Check ESC system and replace filter

1. Also a safety service.
2. Also an emission control service.

Table 7   VEHICLE MAINTENANCE SCHEDULE—1980-1981
(GASOLINE ENGINES WITH HEAVY-DUTY EMISSION SYSTEMS)

Lubrication and General Maintenance	
Every 4 months or 6,000 miles	Check fluid levels[1]
	Check clutch pedal free-play
	Change engine oil[2]
	Lubricate chassis[1]
	Check oil level in transfer case
	Check lube level in both axles
	Lubricate propeller shaft slip joints
	Lubricate constant-velocity joint on front propeller shaft
	Rotate tires
Every 12 months or 12,000 miles	Check and test cooling system[2]
Every 12,000 miles	Repack wheel bearings
	Change oil filter
Every 24,000 miles	Change automatic transmission fluid and filter
Every 36,000 miles	Check manual steering gear seals
	Lubricate clutch cross shaft

Safety Maintenance	
Every 4 months or 6,000 miles	Perform owner safety checks
	Check tires, wheels and disc brakes
	Check exhaust system[2]
	Check suspension and steering
	Check power brake and power steering hoses and connections
Every 12,000 miles	Check drive belts[2]
Every 12 months or 12,000 miles	Check drum brake and parking brake adjustment
	Check throttle linkage
	Check bumpers for alignment and impact protection
Every 24 months or 24,000 miles	Check fuel cap, tank and lines[2]

Emission Control Maintenance	
At first 4 months or 6,000 miles, then every 12 months or 12,000 miles	Check/adjust engine idle speed
	Check operation of idle stop solenoid
Every 12,000 miles	Check spark plug wires
	Replace spark plugs
	Check/adjust ignition timing
	Replace air cleaner element
Every 12 months or 12,000 miles	Check air cleaner operation
	Check tightness of carburetor mounting
	Replace fuel filter
	Check manifold heat valve
	Check throttle return control
	Check PCV valve, filter and hoses
Every 24 months or 24,000 miles	Check choke operation
	Check EFE system
	Check vacuum advance system and hoses
	Check ESC system and replace filter
	Adjust engine idle mixture (292-L6 engine only)

1. Also a safety service.
2. Also an emission control service.

13

Table 8   VEHICLE MAINTENANCE SCHEDULE—1982
(VEHICLES WITH LIGHT-DUTY EMISSION SYSTEM)

Lubrication and General Maintenance	
Every 4 months or 6,000 miles	Check transfer case fluid level
	Check front axle
	Lubricate propeller shaft slip joints
	Lubricate constant-velocity joint at front of propeller shaft
Every 12 months or 7,500 miles	Check fluid levels
	Lubricate chassis
	Change engine oil[1]
	Check clutch free-play
	Check suspension and steering
	Rotate tires
	Check disc brakes and brake lines
	Drain and refill rear axle
Every 12 months or 15,000 miles	Check drive belts[1]
	Change oil filter[1]
	Check throttle linkage
	Inspect fuel tank, cap and lines[1]
	Check drum and parking brake adjustment
	Check and test cooling system[1]
Every 24 months or 30,000 miles	Drain, flush and refill cooling system[1]
Every 30,000 miles	Check manual steering gear seals
	Repack wheel bearings

Emission Control Maintenance
49-State

At 6 months or 7,500 miles, then at 24 month or 30,000 miles	Check automatic choke operation
	Check tightness of carburetor mounting
	Check/adjust engine idle speed
	Check vacuum advance operation and hoses
At 7,500 miles, then every 30,000 miles	Check air cleaner operation
	Check EFE system operation
Every 15,000 miles	Check spark plug wires
	Replace fuel filter
	Check PCV valve, hoses and filter
Every 30,000 miles	Replace spark plugs
	Check/adjust ignition timing
	Check idle stop solenoid operation
	Check ECS system and replace filter
	Replace air cleaner and PCV filters
	Check EGR system operation

Emission Control Maintenance
California

At 6 months or 7,500 miles, then at 24 months or 30,000 miles	Check automatic choke operation
	Check tightness of carburetor mounting
	Check and adjust engine idle speed
At 7,500 miles, then every 30,000 miles	Check EFE system operation
Every 15,000 miles	Check PCV valve, filter and hoses
Every 30,000 miles	Check vacuum advance operation
	Check air cleaner operation
	Check spark plug wires
	Check and adjust ignition timing
	Check EGR system operation
	Replace air cleaner and PCV filters
	Replace PCV valve
	Replace oxygen sensor
	Check idle stop solenoid operation

1. Also an emission control service.

Table 9   VEHICLE MAINTENANCE SCHEDULE—1982
(GASOLINE ENGINES WITH HEAVY-DUTY EMISSION SYSTEM)

Lubrication and General Maintenance	
Every 4 months or 6,000 miles	Lubricate chassis Check fluid levels Change engine oil[1] Check clutch pedal free-play Check suspension and steering Check exhaust system[2] Rotate tires Check brake system and parking brake adjustment Check transfer case oil level Check front axle Lubricate propeller shaft slip joints Lubricate constant-velocity joint at front propeller shaft
Every 12,000 miles	Check drive belts[1] Repack wheel bearings Change oil filter[1] Drain and refill rear axle
Every 12 months or 12,000 miles	Check throttle linkage Check cooling system[1]
Every 24,000 miles	Change automatic transmission fluid and filter
Every 24 months or 24,000 miles	Check fuel tank, cap and lines[1]
Every 36,000 miles	Check manual steering gear seals
Emission Control Maintenance	
At first 4 months or 6,000 miles, then at 12 months or 12,000 miles	Check and adjust engine idle speed Check idle stop solenoid operation
Every 12,000 miles	Check spark plug wires Check and adjust ignition timing Replace air cleaner filter
Every 12 months or 12,000 miles	Check tightness of carburetor mounting Check air cleaner operation Check manifold heat valve Replace fuel filter Check PCV valve, filter and hoses
Every 24 months or 24,000 miles	Check ECS system and replace filter Check EFE system operation Check vacuum advance operation Check automatic choke operation Adjust idle mixture (292-L6 engine only)
Noise Emission Control Maintenance	
Every 12,000 miles	Check shields and underhood insulation Check air intake system
Every 12 months or 12,000 miles	Check engine cooling fan operation
Every 48 months or 48,000 miles	Check governor operation
NOTES 1. Also an emission control service. 2. Also a noise emission control service.	

13

Table 10   TUNE-UP SPECIFICATIONS—1976 MODELS

Engine	Emission Class	Timing	Spark Plug Type and Gap	Idle Speed
250 6 — All trans.	Heavy duty — Federal	6° BTDC	AC R46T (0.035 in.)	See engine decal
292 6 — All trans.	Heavy duty — Federal and Calif.	8° BTDC	AC R44T (0.035 in.)	See engine decal
350 V8 2bbl — Automatic trans.	Light duty — Federal	6° BTDC	AC R45TS (0.045 in.)	See engine decal
350 V8 2bbl — Manual trans.	Light duty — Federal	2° BTDC	AC R45TS (0.045 in.)	See engine decal
350 V8 4bbl — All trans.	Light duty — Calif.	6° BTDC	AC R45TS (0.045 in.)	See engine decal
350 V8 4bbl — All trans.	Light duty — Federal	8° BTDC	AC R45TS (0.045 in.)	See engine decal
350 V8 4bbl — All trans.	Heavy duty — Calif.	2° BTDC	AC R44TX (0.060 in.)	See engine decal
350 V8 4bbl — All trans.	Heavy duty — Federal	8° BTDC	AC R44TX (0.060 in.)	See engine decal
400 V8 4bbl — All Trans.	Heavy duty — Calif.	2° BTDC	AC R44TX (0.060 in.)	See engine decal
400 V8 4bbl — All trans.	Heavy duty — Federal	4° BTDC	AC R44TX (0.060 in.)	See engine decal

Table 11   TUNE-UP SPECIFICATIONS—1977 MODELS

Engine	Emission Class	Timing	Spark Plug Type and Gap	Idle Speed
292 6— All trans.	Federal and Calif.	8° BTDC	AC R44T (0.035 in.)	600 rpm See engine decal
305 V8 2bbl — All trans.	Federal only	6° BTDC	AC R44T (0.045 in.)	700 rpm See engine decal
350 V8 4bbl — All trans.	Federal only	8° BTDC	AC R44T (0.045 in.)	700 rpm See engine decal
350 V8 4 bbl — All trans.	Calif. only	2° BTDC	AC R44TX (0.060 in.)	700 rpm See engine decal
400 V8 4 bbl — All trans.	Federal only	4° BTDC	AC R44T (0.045 in.)	700 rpm See engine decal
400 V8 4bbl — All trans.	Calif. only	2° BTDC	AC R44T (0.045 in.)	700 rpm See engine decal

Table 12   TUNE-UP SPECIFICATIONS—1978-1979

Engine	Emission Class	Timing	Spark Plug Type and Gap	Idle Speed* Rpm
250-6	Federal	10° BTDC	AC R46TS (0.035 in.)	750 manual 600 automatic
292-6	Federal & Calif.	8° BTDC	AC R46TS (0.035 in.)	700 manual & automatic
305-V8	Federal	6° BTDC	AC R45TS (0.045 in.)	600 manual 500 automatic
350-V8	Federal & Calif. (heavy duty)	4° BTDC	AC R44T (0.045 in.)	700
350-V8	Federal & Calif. (light duty)	8° BTDC	AC R45TS (0.045 in.)	700 manual 500 automatic
400-V8	Federal & Calif. (heavy duty)	4° BTDC	AC R44T (0.045 in.)	700
400-V8	Federal & Calif. (light duty)	4° BTDC	AC R45TS (0.045 in.)	500

13

*See engine decal; specifications on decal supersede specifications shown in this table.
NOTE: The notation "heavy duty" refers to Series 30 vehicles. "Light duty" refers to Series 10 and 20 vehicles, including Blazer, Jimmy, and Suburbans.

Table 13   TUNE-UP SPECIFICATIONS (1980)

Engine	Usage	Transmission[1]	Timing (°BTDC)	Spark Plug Type and Gap	Idle Speed (rpm)
250-6	Federal	M	10	AC R46TS (0.035 in.)	750
292-6	Nationwide	M	8	AC R44T (0.035 in.)	700
305-V8	Federal	A	8[2]	AC R45TS (0.045 in.)	600
		A[3]	6	AC R45TS (0.045 in.)	600
350-V8	Nationwide	A	8	AC R45TS (0.045 in.)	500
350-V8	Federal	M	4	AC R44T (0.045 in.)	700
350-V8	Calif.	M	6	AC R44T (0.045 in.)	700
350-V8	Federal/ Calif.	M	8	AC R45TS (0.045 in.)	700
350-V8	Federal	A	4	AC R44T (0.045 in.)	700
350-V8	Calif.	A	6	AC R44T (0.045 in.)	700
400-V8	Federal	A	4	AC R44T (0.045 in.)	700
400-V8	Calif.	A	6	AC R44T (0.045 in.)	700

NOTES
1. M=Manual transmission; A=Automatic transmission.
2. Distributor No. 1103381.
3. Distributor No. 1103369.

Table 14   TUNE-UP SPECIFICATIONS (1981)

Engine	Usage/ Emission Code	Transmission[1]	Timing (°BTDC)	Spark Plug Type and Gap	Idle Speed (rpm)
250-6	Federal/ ACR, ACS	M	10	AC R45TS (0.035 in.)	750
250-6	Federal/ ACT, AUU, ACU	A	10	AC R46TS (0.035 in.)	650
292-6	Nationwide/ ADF, ADM, ADH	M	8	AC R44TS (0.035 in.)	700
305-V8	Federal/ AAN	A	6	AC R45TS (0.045 in.)	500
305-V8	Federal/ AAS	A	2	AC R45TS (0.045 in.)	500
350-V8	Federal/ AAT	M	8	AC R45TS (0.045 in.)	700
350-V8	Federal/ AAU	A	8	AC R45TS (0.045 in.)	500
350-V8	Calif./ AAZ, AAD	A	6	AC R45TS (0.045 in.)	550
350-V8	Calif./ AAD[2]	A	8	AC R45TS (0.045 in.)	550
350-V8	Federal/ ACJ	M	4	AC R44T (0.045 in.)	700
350-V8	Calif./ ACK	M	6	AC R44T (0.045 in.)	700
350-V8	Federal/ ACJ	A	4	AC R44T (0.045 in.)	700

NOTES
1. M=Manual transmission; A=Automatic transmission.
2. With distributor No. 1103339.

13

Table 15 FUSES AND CIRCUIT BREAKERS—1977

Applicability	Location	Amps
Idle stop solenoid, aux. battery, radio, time delay relay, emission control solenoid, transmission downshift	Fuse block	15
Fuel gauge, brake warning lamp, temperature warning lamp, oil pressure warning lamp	Fuse block	4

NOTE: Additional fuses and circuit breakers are listed in Table 3, Chapter Six.

Table 16 LAMP BULB DATA—1977

Used In	Quantity	Trade No.	Power
Dome lamp, cab	1	1004	15 cp
Heater or air conditioner	1	161	1 cp
Seat belt warning	1	168	3 cp
4WD indicator	1	168	3 cp

NOTE: Additional lamp bulb data is listed in Table 4, Chapter Six.

Table 17 FUSES AND CIRCUIT BREAKERS 1978-ON

Application	Location	Amps 1978/1979	Amps 1980/1982
Heater, front AC, generator warning	Fuse block	20	20
Idle stop solenoid, auxiliary battery, radio, time delay relay, emission control solenoid, transmission downshift	Fuse block	15	10
Cigarette lighter, clock, dome lamp, cargo lamp	Fuse block	20	20
Fuel gauge, brake warning lamp, temperature warning lamp, oil pressure warning lamp	Fuse block	4	5
Courtesy lamp, roof marker lamp, license plate lamp, parking lamp, side marker lamp, taillamp, clearance lamp	Fuse block	20	20
Directional signal indicator lamp, stop lamp, traffic hazard	Fuse block	15	20
Instrument cluster lamp, heater dial lamp, radio dial lamp, cruise control lamp, windshield wiper switch lamp	Fuse block	4	5
Windshield wiper/washer	Fuse block	25	25
Cruise control, rear window, auxiliary fuel tank, tachometer, backup lamp, directional signal indicator lamp, headlamp buzzer	Fuse block	15	20
Horn	Fuse block	20	20
Headlamp/parking lamp circuit	Light switch	15	15
Tailgate window motor	Firewall	30	30

Table 18   LAMP BULB DATA—1978-1982

	Quantity	Trade Number	Power
Dome lamp			
Cab	1	1004	15 cp
Suburban	1	211-2	12 cp
Oil pressure indicator	1	168	3 cp
Generator indicator	1	168	3 cp
Instrument cluster	5	168	3 cp
Headlamp beam indicator	1	168	3 cp
Tail/stop lamp	2	1157	3-32 cp
License plate	1	67	4 cp
Directional signal	2	1157 NA	2.2–24 cp
Headlamps*	2	6014	50–60W
Temperature indicator	1	168	3 cp
Directional signal indicator	2	168	3 cp
Clearance and markers	4	168	3 cp
Brake warning indicator	1	168	3 cp
Transmission control	1	1445	0.7 cp
Backup	2	1156	32 cp
Heater/AC	1	161	1 cp
Corner marker (platform)	7	67	4 cp
Cargo (cab)	1	1142	21 cp
Radio dial			
AM	1	1816	3 cp
AM/FM	1	216	1 cp
Cruise control	1	53	1 cp
Courtesy	1	1003	15 cp
Windshield wiper switch	1	161	1 cp
Clock	1	168	3 cp
Rear identification	10	1895	2 cp
Underhood	1	93	15 cp
Seat belt warning	1	168	3 cp
Cargo/dome	2	211-2	12 cp
Four-wheel drive indicator	1	168	3 cp

*Specifications and identification for sealed beam unit are given. Quartz-halogen equivalent
  identification number is preceded by "H"; e.g., "H6014."

13°

INDEX

14

14

NOTES

NOTES

NOTES